Foreign Affairs
and the Constitution
in the Age of Fighting Sail

Foreign Affairs
AND THE
Constitution
IN THE
Age of Fighting Sail

WILLIAM R. CASTO

University of South Carolina Press

© 2006 University of South Carolina

Published by the University of South Carolina Press
Columbia, South Carolina 29208

www.sc.edu/uscpress

Manufactured in the United States of America

15 14 13 12 11 10 09 08 07 06   10 9 8 7 6 5 4 3 2 1

Library of Congress Cataloging-in-Publication Data

Casto, William R., 1946–
  Foreign affairs and the Constitution in the age of fighting sail / William R. Casto.
     p. cm.
  Includes bibliographical references and index.
  ISBN-13: 978-1-57003-629-3 (cloth : alk. paper)
  ISBN-10: 1-57003-629-2 (cloth : alk. paper)
  1. United States—Foreign relations—Law and legislation—History. 2. Neutrality—United States—History. 3. United States—Foreign relations—1789–1797. 4. Shipping—United States—History. I. Title.
  KF4651.C375 2006
  342.73'0412—dc22
                                                                  2006010183

This book was printed on Glatfelter Natures, a recycled paper with 50 percent postconsumer waste content.

For Pamela and William,
my beloved wife and son

Contents

Preface ix
Acknowledgments xi
List of Abbreviations xiii

1 Introduction 1
2 Citizen Genet's Mission to the New World 5
3 The View from America 19
4 The French Maritime Campaign Begins 35
5 Presidential Power over Foreign Affairs 59
6 Neutrality in the Courts 83
7 Consulting the Supreme Court 103
8 A Naval Duel 122
9 The Fall 139
10 Lessons from the Founders 165

Table of Cases 193
Bibliography 195
Index 199

Preface

The title of this book is an homage to two authors who have influenced my love for and study of legal history. Although I did not learn to read until the fifth grade, I quickly acquired a voracious appetite for the written word. By the end of the ninth grade, I had read and reread all of C. S. Forrester's Hornblower series and come across his book on the War of 1812: *The Age of Fighting Sail*. I loved it and was intrigued by the idea that entertaining stories might be written about actual events that happened long ago. For the next ten years, I plowed through numerous histories, but my interests were quite antiquarian. While I was clerking for a federal judge after law school, I came across Louis Henkin's arcane book, *Foreign Affairs and the Constitution*. As with Forrester's book, I read it and loved it. Here was an author thoroughly grounded in the present who could weave the lessons and wisdom of our ancestors into a coherent vision of contemporary law and public policy. Professor Henkin's wonderful work has served as a model for my explorations of the founders' thoughts and actions.

I readily concede that this book, *Foreign Affairs and the Constitution in the Age of Fighting Sail,* has some antiquarian threads. I certainly never thought I would write the words "he sought to take the weather gage" in a book or article. I must say, however, that in addition to being intrinsically interesting, the details of the French maritime campaign of 1793 provide a factual background to the specific events that gave rise to the issues of constitutional law discussed in this book. These events document the real-life political problems that plagued George Washington's administration in 1793. They bring a sense of reality to the book and prevent it from becoming unduly dry and theoretical.

Acknowledgments

This book owes a debt to Louis Henkin's *Foreign Affairs and the Constitution* and his one-hour colloquium on Foreign Affairs and the Constitution, which I audited long ago at Columbia University. In particular, the final chapter is my attempt to make sense of this vital subject matter as it applies to the early twenty-first century.

Although I had some knowledge of the Neutrality Crisis of 1793 when I wrote my earlier book, *The Supreme Court in the Early Republic,* my special interest in the crisis began when the United States Capitol Historical Society asked me to talk about it as part of the society's 1996 conference titled "Neither Separate nor Equal: Congress and the Executive and Judicial Branches in the 1790s." The society was kind enough to publish my preliminary thoughts. I thank Kenneth Bowling and Donald Kennon for being willing to read more than they wanted to about *L'Embuscade.*

For my research in Europe, I was greatly assisted by a grant from the American Philosophical Society. I also thank Jerome Bayeaux for his assistance in working with the many French letters and documents that have added texture to my study. Jerome's brother, while performing his stint of mandatory French military service, found Citizen Bompard's personnel file at the Marine Archives in France.

My reconsideration of Pacificus and Helvidius benefited from comments on papers I presented at the 2001 annual meeting of the Society for the History of American Foreign Affairs and at a University of Tennessee College of Law Faculty Colloquium. My thoughts on advisory opinions benefited from comments on a paper I presented as the Inaugural Faculty Enrichment Lecture at the Ohio Northern University Pettit College of Law. I especially want to thank Scott Gerber at Ohio Northern. My thoughts on the judiciary benefited from comments on a paper I presented at a University of Tennessee College of Law Faculty Colloquium. My thoughts on the battle between *L'Embuscade* and the *Boston* benefited from comments on a paper I presented at the New York Military Affairs Symposium.

Finally, I would like to thank Paula McAfee. Like all the participants in the Neutrality Crisis, I write by hand with pen and ink. Paula spent countless hours transcribing my scrawl onto computer disk.

Abbreviations

The following list provides all repository symbols used in this book:

AECPE	Archives des Affaires Étrangeres, Correspondance Politique, Ministry of Foreign Affairs, Paris, France.
DLC	United States Library of Congress, Washington, D.C.
MB	Boston Public Library, Boston, Massachusetts
MNF	Forbes Library, North Hampton, Massachusetts
NHi	New-York Historical Society, New York, New York
NN	New York Public Library, New York, New York
PHi	Historical Society of Pennsylvania, Philadelphia, Pennsylvania
PRO:ADM	Public Record Office, Admiralty Records, Kew Gardens, Surrey, United Kingdom
PRO:FO	Public Record Office, Foreign Office Records, Kew Gardens, Surrey, United Kingdom
SHM	Service Historique de la Marine, Vincennes, France

CHAPTER 1 Introduction

In February 1793, Edmond Charles Genet and Jean-Baptiste François Bompard sailed from France on a mission to North America. The French had formed a revolutionary republic, beheaded Louis XVI, and gone to war against the most powerful kingdoms of Europe. Now Citizens Genet and Bompard were bringing the war to America. They became catalysts for the first major foreign affairs crisis under the Constitution and caused more trouble than any other visitors in American history. Bompard distinguished himself as one of the best frigate captains of the French revolutionary wars and the subsequent Napoleonic era. His exploits along the Eastern Seaboard became legendary and wrenched questions of American neutrality from the realm of theory to the arena of political crisis. Genet was not nearly as successful as Bompard, but he vigorously advanced the interests of France as he saw them. Before the year was out, a maritime war was raging along the Atlantic Coast, Alexander Hamilton had penned an essay that remains the single most powerful and comprehensive explanation ever written about presidential authority over foreign affairs, the federal courts had demonstrated their inability to provide timely legal advice during crises, and a challenge to a duel posted in a New York coffee house had led to a desperate battle at sea.

The Neutrality Crisis of 1793 forced the United States to grapple for the first time with many of the problems inherent in the Constitution's allocation of foreign affairs powers among the three branches of government. George Washington was president and Thomas Jefferson was secretary of state. The three authors of the Federalist Papers were also in government: John Jay was chief justice, James Madison was a member of Congress, and Alexander Hamilton was secretary of treasury. All five men, and others as well, strove to resolve many controversial issues implicated by the crisis. Their insights into the workings of the Constitution during a foreign affairs crisis are as valuable and instructive today as they were in 1793. Hamilton plays a leading role in this story—perhaps *the* leading role. In terms of enduring contributions to our understanding of the Constitution, he towers above all the other participants.

This book is not a complete history of the Neutrality Crisis. Rather, it concentrates upon resolution of the legal issues, especially the constitutional ones, generated by the French maritime campaign. There are a number of capable general treatments of the crisis,[1] but no one has attempted a constitutional study of it since the 1930s. I treat the war at sea in some detail because the naval operations provide the real-life context in which the constitutional problems arose. Although this book is a constitutional history of the crisis, two of its most prominent characters, Citizens Genet and Bompard, contributed virtually no ideas to the constitutional debate that raged in 1793. Genet and Bompard play such a notable role in the story because their vigorous and aggressive—in Genet's case, sometimes foolhardy—actions created most of the causes célèbres that forced the new nation to explore the meaning of its Constitution. The French maritime onslaught wrenched American neutrality from the realm of theory to the arena of political crisis. In 1793, the founders were not engaged in abstract theorizing. They had to work out the Constitution's meaning in the context of specific and highly controversial maritime incidents.

Although this is a constitutional history, it is a constitutional history without Supreme Court cases. Today, with a larder of more than two hundred years of Supreme Court adjudication, constitutional analysis and much constitutional history is dominated by the Court's opinions. But in 1793 there were no judicial opinions to guide Americans through the Constitution's avenues and alleys. The leading student of the Constitution's regulation of foreign affairs has noted that in matters of foreign relations, the "Supreme Court . . . intervenes only infrequently and its foreign affairs cases are few and haphazard."[2] And so it was in 1793.

Nevertheless, individual Supreme Court justices played significant advisory roles during the crisis. They wrote political essays in the form of grand jury charges, which they published in the nation's newspapers. Chief Justice Jay even lent his name to a public attack upon the French minister to the United States. But the Court, as a court, decided no cases during the crisis that specifically addressed the crisis. The justices' only significant collective action was a famous refusal to give President Washington formal legal advice. Similarly, the lower courts' only significant actions were to do nothing. They refused to decide cases challenging the legality of the French privateering campaign, and they Delphicly but clearly acquitted Americans prosecuted for helping the French.

1. The best treatment is Ammon, *Genet Mission*. In addition, Bowman, *Struggle for Neutrality;* DeConde, *Entangling Alliance;* and Elkins and McKitrick, *Age of Federalism* are good. Two much older studies, Hyneman, *First American Neutrality,* and Thomas, *American Neutrality in 1793,* are also useful.

2. Henkin, *Foreign Affairs and the Constitution,* 148.

Unlike a tree falling in a deserted forest, an issue of constitutional law decided in a judicial vacuum is readily heard and has a direct and palpable impact upon the development of constitutional law. Over the last two centuries, the judiciary and Congress usually have deferred to the president in the conduct of foreign affairs. This tradition began in 1793, when President Washington, with the advice of his cabinet, particularly Alexander Hamilton, took an expansive view of his constitutional power over foreign affairs. More than two hundred years later, Hamilton's advice provides an all but irrefutable constitutional analysis that justifies the president's broad authority and at the same time explains Congress's power to correct presidential error.

Although the story that emerges is fascinating on its own terms, it also teaches enduring lessons about our Constitution and the administration of foreign affairs. In this book's final chapter, those enduring lessons are used to illustrate the strengths and weaknesses of the federal government in the twenty-first century. In 1793, the federal courts played a relatively minor role in resolving the nation's foreign affairs problems, and so it is today. More than two hundred years ago, President Washington took an active role in establishing American foreign policy in a time of crisis, and Congress essentially acquiesced. Today's presidents continue to play the more active role in the foreign policy arena, and Congress continues to be relatively passive. Yet the founders understood that under the plan of the Constitution, Congress is empowered to correct presidential error.

A Note on Word Usage

Eighteenth- and twenty-first-century usages differ in some important regards. Americans of the founding generation drew a clear distinction between ambassadors and ministers. An ambassador was always given precedence because he was understood to have a close relationship with and the personal confidence of his king. Diplomats who lacked this special personal cachet were mere ministers. The distinction has lapsed into desuetude, and in any event, the eighteenth-century concept of an ambassador who has a special relationship with his king made little sense in republics such as the United States and France. During the Neutrality Crisis, George Hammond, the British minister to the United States, and Citizen Genet, the French minister, were not technically ambassadors, but in this book they occasionally will be referred to as ambassadors. Similarly, the phrases "international law" and "law of nations" are used interchangeably. In the eighteenth century, the law of nations included the modern idea of public international law that regulates relations among nations. The founders, however, also understood the phrase to encompass fields of private law, such as the law merchant, Admiralty law, and conflict of laws.[3]

3. For the distinction between ambassadors and ministers, see *A Digest of the International Law of the United States,* ed. Francis Wharton (Washington, D.C.: GPO, 1886), 1, sec. 88; and *Digest of International Law,* ed. Green Hackworth (Washington, D.C.: GPO, 1940), 4:394–95. For the difference between the law of nations in the eighteenth century and today's international law, see William Casto, "The Federal Courts' Protective Jurisdiction over Torts Committed in Violation of the Law of Nations," *Connecticut Law Review* 18 (1986): 505.

CHAPTER 2   Citizen Genet's Mission
               to the New World

> Genet is a "demagogue enragé."
> *Czarina Catherine II*
>
> What puny projects were those of Richelieu . . .
> compared with the worldwide risings, the gigantic
> revolutions, that we are called upon to achieve.
> *Jacques Pierre Brissot de Warville*

In February 1793, Citizens Genet and Bompard set sail from the port of Rochefort, France, on their mission to North America. The affairs of France were jumbled and confused. Louis XVI had just been executed, and the revolutionary government was fighting a momentarily successful war against most of the powerful kingdoms of Europe, including Great Britain. Genet and Bompard were determined to carry the war to North America.

Genet's father was Edme Jacques Genet, a capable bureaucrat in the French Foreign Ministry who specialized in British and American affairs. Young Edmond was a smart boy and a gifted linguist. He learned to read English, Swedish, German, Italian, Greek, and Latin. He also played the piano well and was a good singer. He was the family's only son and became the spoiled center of attention of his parents and four sisters. His father had extensive political connections through the Foreign Ministry, and Edmond's oldest sister was first *femme de chambre* to Queen Marie Antoinette. All benefits within the family's power were lavished on young Edmond.[1]

When Edmond was thirteen, the family helped him publish his translation of a book on Swedish history. In addition to engaging a tutor who assisted in the translation, the family arranged for the book's distribution throughout Europe. Edmond received much praise for his precocious tour de force, and the king of Sweden even honored him with a gold medal. The following year, he became a clerk in his father's office. In 1778, at the age of sixteen, he was commissioned a lieutenant of dragoons in the king's army, and his regiment was on orders to leave for America to fight alongside the rebelling colonists. The regiment remained in France, however, and young Lieutenant Genet returned to Paris. During the American Revolution,

---

1. Genet has no modern biographer, which leaves us with Meade Minnigerode's romantic and florid biography, *Genet*. Minnigerode is best for Genet's early and later life. The best overall biographical treatment is the sketch interspersed throughout Ammon's *Genet Mission*.

Edmond met most of the American diplomats in Paris as they worked closely with his father. In 1780, he took the Grand Tour of Europe and at the queen's request received temporary postings to French embassies in Berlin and Vienna. His father died the following year, and Genet returned to Paris to take his vacated position as chief of the Bureau of Interpretation.[2]

In 1787, the Bureau of Interpretation was eliminated, and Genet's sister convinced the queen to have him promoted to captain of dragoons and appointed secretary to the legation in St. Petersburg. Genet assumed his duties in 1788 and a year later became chargé d'affaires and head of the embassy when the ambassador departed on leave. In official correspondence, the ambassador wrote that he was impressed with young Genet: "His form, his bearing and conversation, corresponded perfectly with the eulogies that have been made of him." In private, the ambassador later remembered, "I found him witty, educated, speaking several languages and gifted with some agreeable talents, but he was very hotheaded." Genet's 1792 passport describes him as "five feet eight inches in height, hair and eyebrows auburn, forehead broad, eyes blue, nose aquiline, mouth small, chin round, face round."[3]

In the beginning, the Russians respectfully received Genet as the representative of an important nation, and Czarina Catherine even bestowed him with a silver medallion. But as the Revolution progressed back in France, things changed. The Revolution was anathema to Catherine, and her government's relations with the young chargé d'affaires deteriorated. At the same time, Genet enthusiastically embraced France's new constitutional monarchy. His conversations in Russia and letters back to the French Foreign Office emphasized the importance of the nation over the king and invoked the ideas of social contract and the elimination of class distinctions. By late 1791, he was a minor thorn in Catherine's side. She called him a "demagogue enragé," and he was under constant police surveillance. "My house is surrounded with spies; they follow me everywhere," Genet complained. As his isolation increased, he cleaved more and more to France's new revolutionary ideals. Finally, in the summer of 1792, the Russians ordered him out of the country.[4]

While Genet was in Russia, the Revolution back in France went through an interim phase of constitutional monarchy that effectively ended in 1792.

2. Ammon, *Genet Mission,* 2–5; Minnigerode, *Genet,* 8–83.

3. Ammon, *Genet Mission,* 5–6; Minnigerode, *Genet,* 82–91, 200 (quoting the ambassador and passport).

4. Ammon, *Genet Mission,* 5–9; Minnigerode, *Genet,* 82–118; William Blackwell, "Citizen Genet and the Revolution in Russia 1789–1792," *French Historical Studies* 3 (1963): 72–92.

Chaos and panic soon reigned. The country was at war with Austria and Prussia, and the French army broke and fled in one of its first encounters. In the summer of 1792, the Duke of Brunswick, who commanded the allied armies arrayed against the Revolution, proclaimed that he would end the anarchy in France and restore the king to his former authority. In response, the radical Paris commune took effective control of the capital and arrested the king. At the same time, the national Legislative Assembly decreed a national convention that would have plenary power to govern and would be elected by universal manhood suffrage. As the summer progressed, an allied victory over France seemed inevitable, and panic erupted when the Prussians bypassed the last fortress on the road to Paris. Mobs in the capital massacred well over a thousand people accused of being counterrevolutionaries.[5]

As the Prussian army slowly advanced on the capital, a levee of twenty thousand Parisian volunteers went to the assistance of the French army commanded by Charles-François Dumouriez. On September 20, the French and Prussians met at Valmy, less than a hundred miles west of Paris. In an almost miraculous victory, the French infantry held firm and an artillery cannonade repulsed the final Prussian charge. Dumouriez prevailed and stopped the Prussians. The Revolution was saved. The German poet Goethe, who was there, said, "Here and today a new epoch in the history of the world has begun."[6]

The day after Dumouriez saved the Revolution at Valmy, the new National Convention met and declared France to be a republic without a king. September also marked Genet's return to Paris from Russia. The revolutionaries immediately embraced him. Indeed, he had already become a minor celebrity. Word of his lonely fight in Russia for republican principles had circulated through revolutionary circles. He had made substantial monetary contributions in support of France's new government, including his gold medal from the king of Sweden and the silver medallion from Czarina Catherine. Jacques Pierre Brissot de Warville, who was for a brief time one of the most influential revolutionaries in France, described Genet in the Legislative Assembly as a true "democrat."[7]

Genet quickly gravitated toward the Girondin or Brissotin coalition, which maintained a tenuous working control of the National Convention. The Girondins were relatively moderate insofar as French domestic affairs

---

5. See Doyle, *Oxford History of the French Revolution,* 183–94.
6. See ibid., 192–93 (quoting Goethe).
7. See Ammon, *Genet Mission,* 17–19 (quoting Brissot); Blackwell, "Citizen Genet and the Revolution in Russia," 72–92.

were concerned but advocated an aggressive and radical foreign policy. They sought to spread the ideals of the French Revolution throughout Europe by force of arms. Brissot, their bombastic leader, proclaimed, "We cannot rest until all Europe is ablaze. What puny projects were those of Richelieu . . . compared with the worldwide risings, the gigantic revolutions, that we are called upon to achieve." Because the Girondins enthusiastically supported the war against Austria and Prussia, the initial military failures had briefly eroded their political power, but now they were riding high. The fact that General Dumouriez, who had saved the Revolution at Valmy, was a Girondin did not hurt.[8]

As the fall progressed, the Girondin policy of spreading the Revolution beyond France's traditional borders bore still more fruit. In November, the French army defeated the Austrians at Jemappes in northern France, and by the end of the year French revolutionary forces were on the advance everywhere. In the North, they overran the Austrian Netherlands and took Brussels. In the South, they struck Savoy, and in the West they drove across the Rhine. As the successes continued, the National Convention decreed "in the name of the French Nation, that it will accord fraternity and help to all peoples who wish to recover their liberty."[9]

Genet was an observer and became a minor participant in these heady successes. When the Girondins took over the Foreign Office, they found that experienced diplomats were in short supply. Aristocrats had always dominated the diplomatic corps, and with the Revolution, most experienced diplomats fled the country, were imprisoned, or were executed. The Girondins read Genet's dispatches from Russia and were impressed by his analyses, which were laden with republican ideals and phrases. Here was a trustworthy democrat with diplomatic experience. While Genet was making his way home from Russia, Pierre Henri Hélène Marie Lebrun, the new minister of foreign affairs, urged him to return as soon as possible: "Your known patriotism, and the distinguished talents that you have developed during your residence at Petersburg, are titles too precious not to require me to present you with new means of serving your country usefully."[10]

When Genet finally reached Paris, the Girondins quickly named him minister to the Hague, and the British Foreign Office believed that his

---

8. Ammon, *Genet Mission*, 20 (quoting Brissot); Doyle, *Oxford History of the French Revolution*, chap. 8.

9. See Doyle, *Oxford History of the French Revolution*, 197–99; Blanning, *Origins*, 135–38.

10. Ammon, *Genet Mission*, 17–18; Minnigerode, *Genet*, 119 (quoting Lebrun).

appointment was part of a plan "for bringing about a revolution in Holland [and] for the murder of the Stadtholder and his family." The likelihood of war with the Netherlands, however, delayed his taking the post. He then traveled briefly to Switzerland on a quasi-military mission with the rank of colonel and adjutant general. When he returned, he was designated the new minister to the United States. In 1793, the United States was an utterly insignificant military power that had no navy whatsoever and a pitifully small army. Just two years earlier, the army under the command of Gen. Arthur St. Clair had been crushed and ignominiously routed by the Wabash Indians. Nevertheless, America was a fellow republic and supported the ideals of the Revolution. Given Genet's gift for languages, especially his fluency in English, his trustworthiness, and his diplomatic experience, he seemed ideally suited for the new post.[11]

Genet, however, did not leave Paris immediately. The Girondins were committed to the Revolution and radical in their desire to foster revolution throughout Europe, but they had moderate views of how the Republic should govern within France's borders. They did not want to execute Louis XVI, and a few wished to exile him to America. Genet tentatively agreed to escort Louis across the Atlantic. More extreme revolutionaries, however, insisted on blood, and the final resolution of this dispute had ominous implications. The comparatively moderate Girondins, who were at the height of their political power, were unable to prevail. Even after the deposed king was tried and convicted, the Girondins did not acquiesce. The people were the ultimate source of sovereignty, and the Girondins argued in the National Convention that there should be "an appeal to the people" from the conviction. After the Convention rejected an appeal, Louis went to the guillotine on January 21. The very next day, Genet left Paris. He reached the port of Rochefort by the end of January, but his departure was delayed until February 20.[12]

Genet was to sail to America on the frigate *L'Embuscade,* and all of his belongings were on board by February 2, but one thing after another delayed his departure. Until recently the frigate had been laid up and was

11. Ammon, *Genet Mission,* 18–19; Edmond Genet to Thomas Jefferson, July 4, 1797, in Minnigerode, *Genet,* 413–25; James Bland Burgess to Lord Grenville, Nov. 4, 1792, in Grenville, *Fortescue,* 2:325–26; Leroy Eid, "American Indian Military Leadership: St. Clair's Military Disaster of 1791," *Journal of Military History* 57 (1993): 71–88.

12. See Ammon, *Genet Mission,* 29–31; Doyle, *Oxford History of the French Revolution,* 194–96; David Jordan, *The King's Trial: The Revolution vs. Louis XVI* (Berkeley and Los Angeles: University of California Press, 1979), chaps. 8 and 9.

not ready for a voyage across the Atlantic. By early February, she carried a six-month supply of food but virtually no armament. She was a large frigate, capable of mounting more than forty cannon, but when Genet arrived she had only four on board. Further, the crew's pay was in arrears and their morale was "very weak." This last issue was especially important because mutiny was rampant in the French navy. Just a year and a half earlier, *L'Embuscade*'s crew had famously mutinied on the frigate's maiden voyage to the West Indies. The crew had become dissatisfied with its mission to restore political order in the islands and required their captain to sail home to France. Upon the frigate's return, the government treated the mutiny as a political crime and granted the crew amnesty. After Genet arrived in Rochefort, the crew mutinied again, and Genet bragged to the Foreign Office that he had personally quelled the "little mutiny" with a long patriotic speech that ended with the crew cheering, "Long live the Nation, Long live the Republic."[13]

If anything, weather presented more serious problems than the crew's morale. Winter on Europe's Atlantic Coast is not a good time for sailing. Contrary winds made it difficult for *L'Embuscade* even to reach the port's roadstead, and shortly after she did, a serious storm devastated the port. The frigate "dragged her anchors, her launch, dinghies, rigging were damaged and one sailor died." On February 9, Genet hopefully reported, "Everybody is now working on fixing L'Embuscade and if we have fair wind we would be able to leave tomorrow." She finally departed a week and a half later.[14]

Still the stormy weather and adverse winds persisted. The ship's course was for Philadelphia, but she took two weeks to battle five hundred miles across the Bay of Biscay to Cape Finisterre in northern Spain. After this fortnight of pounding by winter gales and waves, the direct route to Philadelphia was abandoned. An American newspaper later reported that the frigate "was bound to Philadelphia but adverse winds obliged her to steer for [Charleston]." Now *L'Embuscade* sailed south toward the Azores to catch the trade winds that would take her more easily across the Atlantic. Genet probably experienced seasickness, but eventually most ocean travelers get their sea legs. In an obscure short story, Rudyard Kipling speculated

---

13. Edmond Genet to Minister of Marine, Feb. 2, 1793; Edmond Genet to Minister of Marine, Feb. 4, 1793; Edmond Genet to Minister of Foreign Affairs, Feb. 9, 1793, all in Genet Papers, DLC; Cormack, *Revolution and Political Conflict in the French Navy,* 111–12, 114; Edmond Genet to Minister of Foreign Affairs, Feb. 17, 1793, Genet Papers, DLC; Minnigerode, *Genet,* 159–60.

14. Edmond Genet to Minister of Marine, Feb. 4, 1793, and Edmond Genet to Minister of Foreign Affairs, Feb. 9, 1793, both in Genet Papers, DLC.

about *L'Embuscade*'s voyage across the Atlantic. With typical English disdain for the French, he assumed that "when Genet got rid of his land stomach and laid down the law after dinner, a rook's parliament was nothing compared to their cabin." Perhaps, but another of Kipling's speculations seems more likely. *L'Embuscade*'s captain was Jean-Baptiste François Bompard, and Kipling wrote that "day in and day out Bompard and Monsieur Genet talked."[15]

Except for Bompard's and Genet's shared enthusiasm for the Revolution, no two men could have been more dissimilar. Although both were bourgeois, Genet had led a pampered life of sophistication and luxury. He was fluent in many languages and spoke an elegant and sophisticated French. In contrast, Bompard was a relatively simple sailor. He wrote his reports in blunt, inelegant, and straightforward French. On a famous occasion when he accepted a challenge to a naval duel by an English captain, Bompard's response in French written in his own hand concluded with a blunt insult: "If you are not a braggart [*fanfaron*], do as I say." At the same time, a contemporary English translation published for propaganda purposes elegantly rephrased the insult to read, "If you are really the brave man that you pretend to be, pursue the above measures."[16]

Genet probably viewed Bompard as his inferior, and Bompard may have dismissed Genet as a posturing dilettante. Bompard had what Genet lacked—extensive experience in his craft. He had been to sea for twenty years, had extensive combat experience, and soon proved to be an indomitable combat leader. He was thirty-five in 1793 and had first gone to sea twenty years earlier as a fifteen-year-old volunteer on a two-year voyage to India. He knew the North and South Atlantic and the trade routes to India. He had year upon year of actual seagoing experience. After his voyage to India, Bompard served in the merchant marine for a few more years until the American Revolution. He almost immediately joined the French Navy and served as a volunteer until 1779, when he became a noncommissioned officer. During the war, he saw extensive combat experience and served with distinction with the French naval forces that assisted the rebelling colonies along the East Coast and operated in the West Indies. Despite his impressive experience in

---

15. Edmond Genet to Minister of Foreign Affairs, Apr. 16, 1793, Genet Papers, DLC; *United States Chronicle* (Providence, R.I.), May 2, 1793; "Brother Square-Toes," in *Rewards and Fairies,* by Rudyard Kipling (New York: Doubleday, 1910).

16. Compare J. B. F. Bompard to G. W. A. Courtnay, n.d., Bompard's Personnel File, SHM, with same letter, July 29, 1793, *Daily Advertiser* (New York), Aug. 1, 1793 (translation).

blue-water sailing and as a combat officer, he found promotion in Louis XVI's navy almost impossible.[17]

Bompard's problem was simple. He lacked influence. For most of the eighteenth century, sea officers of the French navy were divided into a class system with two seagoing officer corps. All commands of significant ships were reserved for members of the grand corps, which consisted of *officiers rouges,* who were exclusively of noble birth. They had a king's commission. In addition, there was a petit corps of warrant or auxiliary officers, who were drawn primarily from the merchant marine and the navy's noncommissioned officers. Most of the auxiliary officers were non-noble *officiers bleus.* The petit corps officers were allowed to stand watch but never to command an important ship. Although Bompard styled himself as de Bompard when he first transferred from the merchant marine to the navy, his father was in the French counterpart of the British East India Company, the Compagnie des Indes, and his pretension to nobility was dubious. Bompard was a member of the petit corps—an *officier bleu.*[18]

As an *officier bleu,* Bompard's chances of promotion were slim. In 1787, after fifteen years at sea, he was a pennyless, thirty-year-old auxiliary officer reduced to pleading for promotion to the lowest commissioned rank of vessel second lieutenant. Hopefully Genet did not brag to Bompard about receiving a king's commission when he was only sixteen. In any event, in 1787, Marshal de Castries, an army officer who recently had been appointed minister of marine, had instituted naval reforms designed to open the grand corps to non-nobles. With this encouragement, Bompard humbly petitioned de Castries for a commission. He reviewed his extensive service record and noted "the flattering service reviews from all his chiefs." He even invoked his mother, who had "exhausted her fortune." Although Marshal de Castries granted the petition, the promotion was not necessarily based upon merit. Bompard's petition has a brief note in the margin explaining that the commission was "recommended by Madame the Marquise de la Rivere and given by Madame the Marshal de Castries."[19]

17. This chapter's sketch of Bompard is based upon Casto, "Rights of Man."
18. Cormack, *Revolution and Political Conflict in the French Navy,* 35–41; Jenkins, *History of the French Navy,* 109, 147, 200. "Bompard, Jean-Baptiste François," in *Dictionaire de biographie français,* by M. Prevost and Roman d'Amat (Paris: Letouzey et Ane, 1954); *Les combattants français de la guerre americaine, 1778–1783* (Washington, D.C.: Imprimerie Nationale, 1905), 118 ("de Bompard").
19. Cormack, *Revolution and Political Conflict in the French Navy,* 43–45; Bompard to Marshal de Castries, n.d. (c. 1787), Bompard's Personnel File, SHM.

From 1787 to 1792, Bompard served five long years as a lowly second lieutenant, but the French Revolution changed everything. Suddenly there were no more *officiers rouges*. In 1789, noblemen began leaving the navy, and by 1792 almost all were gone. The Revolution turned the navy's officer corps upside down and swept away the stultifying system of promotion for *officers bleus*. Bompard enthusiastically embraced the ideals of the Revolution and detested the aristocrats who had left. In 1793, the French consul in New York, who was an aristocrat, penned in his private journal that "Bompard has only one way to judge the aristocracy: every person he hates is irrevocably an aristocrat." With the elimination of the navy's aristocratic class system, 1792 became a great year for Bompard. In January, the new navy promoted him vessel first lieutenant, and later that year he took the civic oath decreed by the National Assembly. Then, after only a year in grade as a full lieutenant, he leapt to the rank of captain and took command of *L'Embuscade*. He had been to sea for fifteen years before receiving a commission, but with the Revolution he needed only a year to become the captain of one of the navy's finest frigates.[20]

L'Embuscade was a magnificent platform ideally suited for independent action in distant waters. She was only three years old and was an early example of the tendency in the late eighteenth century to build ever larger frigates. She was two feet longer than the yet-to-be-built USS *Constitution* and four inches narrower. But *L'Embuscade* was undergunned. In later years the French enhanced the vessel's armament to forty cannon, but she mounted only thirty-six cannon on the voyage to America. The reason for her more modest armament in 1793 is unknown. Perhaps the navy yard in Rochefort had no more guns to spare. Genet suggests that the frigate's armament may have been reduced to enable her to carry more provisions on the mission.[21]

20. Cormack, *Revolution and Political Conflict in the French Navy,* chaps. 5–6; Summary of Bompard's Service, n.d., SHM; Jenkins, *History of the French Navy,* 204–6; Bompard's Civic Oath, Mar. 14, 1792, SHM; Hauterive, "Journal," entry of Nov. 3, 1793.
21. "État exact des Forces Navales de la République française qui se trouvent actuellement dans les États-Unis," July 15, 1793, AECPE, États-Unis 38:52. Compare David Lyon, *The Sailing Navy List* (London: Conway Maritime Press, 1993), 246 (L'Embuscade) with K. Jack Bauer and Stephen S. Roberts, *Register of Ships of the U.S. Navy* (New York: Greenwood Press, 1991), 8 (Constitution). Edmond Genet to Commander in Chief of the Navy, Feb. 4, 1793, Genet Papers, DLC.

Genet's Instructions

As *L'Embuscade* sailed across the Atlantic, Genet had ample time to think about his mission. His instructions from the revolutionary government were ambitious, broad ranging, and complex.[22] He was to negotiate a new treaty with the United States, obtain the early repayment of an enormous loan owed by the United States to France, secure United States support for a maritime war against British and Spanish merchant shipping, and mount military campaigns that would wrest the Florida and Louisiana territories from Spain and Canada from Great Britain. Some modern historians have condemned Genet's instructions as "grandiose," imbued with "unrealness" and "riddled with contradictions." Those who do not heap scorn on the instructions nevertheless concede that they were ambitious.[23]

In truth, the instructions were a mixture of pragmatism and idealism. To a significant degree, Genet's mission was a simple extrapolation of the Girondins' radical European foreign policy. Military successes such as Valmy and Jemappes did nothing but encourage Brissot's proclamation that "we cannot rest until all Europe is ablaze." France was to suffer a series of defeats in the spring and summer of 1794 that resulted in the execution of many of the Girondins, but no one foresaw these catastrophes when Genet's instructions were formulated. The Girondins saw only victories, and they envisioned setting European colonies in North America ablaze as well. At the same time, there was a fundamental pragmatism to Genet's mission. France was at war, and even revolutionaries with little foreign affairs experience could analytically deduce two basic principles: France's foreign policy should cause direct material harm to its enemies and bring direct material assistance to itself.[24]

The legal bedrock of Franco-American relations were two treaties dating from the American Revolution: the Treaty of Amity and Commerce and the Treaty of Alliance, both of which were negotiated in 1778. Because much had changed since then, Genet was instructed to propose a new treaty that would put the two countries in "intimate concert [and] promote the extension of the Empire of liberty." In particular, the French idealistically believed that the

---

22. The most valuable discussion of Genet's instructions is Ammon, *Genet Mission,* 22–29. Bowman, *Struggle for Neutrality,* 42–46, and Sheridan, "Recall of Edmond Charles Genet," 464–67, are also good.

23. Bowman, *Struggle for Neutrality,* 42, 50; Elkins and McKitrick, *Age of Federalism,* 333 ("contradictions"); Sheridan, "Recall of Edmond Charles Genet," 467.

24. Ammon, *Genet Mission,* 20 (quoting Brissot); Blanning, *Origins,* chap. 4; Doyle, *Oxford History of the French Revolution,* chap 9; Bowman, *Struggle for Neutrality,* 43.

new treaty would enable the two countries to "deliver our brothers in Louisiana from the tyrannical yoke of Spain, and perhaps add the glorious star of Canada to the American constellation." Brissot's proclamation of "worldwide risings [and] gigantic revolutions" are readily apparent in these schemes, and the miraculous military victories at Valmy and Jemappes lent credence to the instructions' viability. Brissot saw the Revolution as "a crusade for universal liberty," and others agreed. Lebrun, the Girondin foreign minister, anticipated that if the British government opposed France, there would be "inevitably an insurrection [in Britain], if not in a national, at least on a partial scale." Although the instructions are couched in idealistic and florid language, revolts in Spanish colonies and the annexation of Canada to the United States undoubtedly would have partially distracted Britain and Spain from their European war against France. In this sense, the goal of spreading the Revolution to Canada, Louisiana, and Florida had practical underpinnings.[25]

The Girondins understood that the negotiation of a new treaty might not be immediately feasible. In the meantime, Genet was to foster rebellion in Louisiana, Florida, and Canada without a new treaty. Although this charge was consistent with the Girondins' revolutionary ideals, nothing could be more pragmatic than sowing revolution in your enemies' possessions. On an equally practical level, Genet was instructed to seek substantial advance payments of French loans dating from the Revolutionary War with the proceeds to be used for purchasing food and other supplies for France.

The Girondins clearly assumed that the United States would favor France over Great Britain, and their assumption was quite reasonable. Twenty years earlier, when the American colonies rebelled against Great Britain, France had provided vital assistance. Even in the eighteenth century, major wars could not be fought without adequate financial resources. In 1788, an influential American explained, "Wars have now become rather wars of the purse, than of the sword." When the rebelling colonies needed funds, France opened its purse and loaned millions of livres to America. These massive loans were crucial for equipping the Continental army with proper arms, munitions, and logistical support. Now France wished the favor to be returned. Much of the debt (almost thirty million livres) was still outstanding in 1793 and was being slowly repaid in installments. The Girondin finance minister reasoned that France was now "occupied in defending her liberty and her independence, as the United States defended

25. Ammon, *Genet Mission,* 26 (quoting the instructions); Blanning, *Origins,* 111, 153 (quoting Brissot and Lebrun).

theirs when they borrowed the money." Therefore, Genet was instructed to seek a liquidation of the entire amount due.[26]

But ten years earlier France had been much more than an investment banker for the rebelling colonies. France did not restrict itself to a behind-the-scene financial role. French soldiers and sailors fought and died in America to secure independence from Britain. At one point, Genet was scheduled to go to America with his regiment, and Bompard had actually seen combat in support of the Revolution. A regular French army, including artillery train and cavalry, fought alongside George Washington's Continental army, and substantial French fleets offset Britain's overwhelming naval supremacy. The siege of Yorktown, the culminating victory of the Revolution, could not have been won without direct French military assistance. When Alexander Hamilton, then a young lieutenant colonel, led the bayonet assault on Redoubt No. 10, a French assault force simultaneously stormed Redoubt No. 9. Half of George Washington's besieging troops were French, most of the artillery siege train was French, and a naval victory by a French fleet prevented the Royal Navy from evacuating Yorktown.[27]

France truly lent vital assistance to the United States in its hour of need, and the French justifiably assumed that the United States would now return the favor. Genet sailed just ten years after the Revolutionary War had ended, and he sailed as the emissary of a Republic. Surely the United States would lend assistance in the new Republic's hour of need.

Those modern historians who have heaped scorn on Genet's instructions have given scant attention to the fact that he actually received two sets of instructions: the first to be made public and the second to be kept confidential. The public instructions are replete with florid language and grandiose plans. Although they were written in good faith and accurately reflected the Girondins' radical aspirations, they clearly were intended for public dissemination and thus were part of a public relations campaign. In flat contrast, the confidential supplement is starkly pragmatic.

Although the French justifiably expected enthusiastic support for their revolutionary cause, the confidential instructions foresaw that pro-British elements in the United States and American uncertainty about European

26. Oliver Ellsworth, speech of January 7, 1788, in *Documentary History of the Ratification of the Constitution,* ed. Merrill Jensen (Madison: State Historical Society of Wisconsin, 1978), 3:548–54; Bowman, *Struggle for Neutrality,* 45 (quoting the finance minister).

27. See Samuel Scott, *From Yorktown to Valmy* (Niwot: University Press of Colorado, 1998), chaps. 1–6; William Stinchcombe, *The American Revolution and the French Alliance* (Syracuse: Syracuse University Press, 1969).

affairs would likely delay the creation of a new treaty relationship. If the anticipated delay came to pass, Genet was to insist upon rigid enforcement of any treaty provisions that would directly support France's war efforts. The confidential supplement, however, made no mention of the treaties' most troubling provision. In Article 11 of the Treaty of Alliance, the United States guaranteed "from the present and forever . . . to his most Christian Majesty the present possessions of the Crown of France in America." Under this article, if Great Britain declared war on France and attacked French islands in the West Indies, the United States was obligated to go to war against Great Britain. The French, however, decided that they did not want America to enter the war because America was an insignificant military power. In official correspondence, Genet noted that the "Americans . . . will not be ungrateful [and] they will help us but they have no navy." Instead of military assistance, France wished the United States to remain neutral and support France by paying off the loan from the Revolutionary War, providing food, and facilitating a French maritime campaign against British shipping. Thus the National Convention approved an address to President Washington declaring that France did not expect the United States to enter the war.[28]

Although the French decided to waive the Treaty of Alliance's guarantee provision, Genet's confidential instructions insisted upon a firm application of other provisions that would help France's maritime war against its enemies. In particular, Articles 17, 21, and 22 of the Treaty of Amity and Commerce expressly guaranteed French ships and their prizes access to American ports and expressly barred the enemies of France from fitting out privateers in America and crewing them with Americans. In addition to these positive advantages, the French understood these articles to provide by negative implication a right to fit out French privateers in America and to crew them with Americans. Finally, the French government authorized Genet to commission privateers that would prey on British commerce and to grant officer's commissions to Americans who wished to attack the Spanish colony of Louisiana.

Genet probably did not discuss all of his instructions with Bompard, but the two men undoubtedly spent many hours talking about the coming maritime campaign against British shipping. Bompard was an immensely pragmatic sailor with extensive naval experience. As *L'Embuscade* sailed across

---

28. Treaty of Alliance, art. 11, in Miller, *Treaties and Other International Acts,* 2:39; Ammon, *Genet Mission,* 28; Edmond Genet to Minister of Marine, Feb. 2, 1793, Genet Papers, DLC.

the Atlantic, he almost certainly offered invaluable practical advice regarding the planned maritime campaign. In the event, the maritime campaign was a military success. But Bompard knew little of land-based military operations, and Genet's plans for Florida, Louisiana, and Canada never were to progress beyond grandiose projections. Based upon his naval experience, Bompard surely emphasized the importance of an immediate and vigorous attack upon British shipping at the very outset of war, when enemy ships might be caught unaware. The practical significance of this point became clear on the voyage over. In early April, a few hundred miles south of Bermuda, *L'Embuscade* spoke the *Four Brothers* bound from Nova Scotia to Barbados with a cargo of fish and lumber. The British ship could not know that war had been declared, and Bompard easily took her.[29]

Notwithstanding the successful capture of the *Four Brothers, L'Embuscade* was just one ship and could not be everywhere at once. During the Revolutionary War, Bompard had served for a time on French corsairs or privateers,[30] which were private armed vessels authorized to prey on enemy commerce. He understood the important contributions corsairs could make to the coming campaign. The fact that the maritime campaign against British commerce was to be the most successful aspect Genet's mission was not a coincidence. In his discussions with Genet, surely Bompard emphasized the need for commissioning a corsair fleet as quickly as possible, and Genet did just that as soon as he set foot on U.S. soil. These corsairs' onslaught, along with *L'Embuscade*'s vigorous depredations, caused immense political and constitutional problems for the Washington administration.

29. Bompard, "Record of Prize," n.d., Bompard's Personnel File, SHM; *Counter Case of Great Britain,* 612–13; *Charleston (S.C.) City Gazette,* Apr. 19, 1793; *Federal Gazette* (Philadelphia), Apr. 20, 1793.
30. Dictionary Notice, Bompard's Personnel File, SHM.

CHAPTER 3

The View from America

> The United States... should with sincerity and good faith adopt and pursue a conduct friendly and impartial towards the belligerent Powers.
> *Proclamation of Neutrality*
>
> I fear that a fair neutrality will prove a disagreeable pill to our friends, tho' necessary to keep us out of the calamities of a war.
> *Thomas Jefferson*

While Genet and Bompard were pondering and discussing their missions on the long voyage over from Europe, the United States remained ignorant of the outbreak of hostilities between France and Great Britain. Most knowledgeable Americans expected war among the European superpowers, but reliable reports took a long time to cross the Atlantic. The first transatlantic cable was many years in the future, so the news had to be travel by sail. France declared war on February 1, but word did not reach America until two months later, in early April.

Shortly before the news arrived, George Hammond, the British minister to the United States, wrote Lord Grenville, Britain's foreign secretary, a series of letters examining American attitudes on the very eve of the coming Neutrality Crisis. Hammond's prescient examination provides a good framework for understanding the issues and players that were to dominate the foreign policy debate in the United States over the next six months. He concentrated upon the executive branch and made no mention of either Congress or the courts. As the crisis unfolded, Congress was to be virtually irrelevant because it was not in session. Although the federal courts might have played a significant role, their contributions during the crisis were relatively modest.[1]

---

1. Hammond examined "*external*" relations" in George Hammond to Lord Grenville, Mar. 7, 1793, No. 6, PRO:FO 5/1, DLC (transcript); George Hammond to Lord Grenville, Mar. 7, 1793, No. 7, PRO:FO 5/1, DLC (transcript); George Hammond to Lord Grenville, Mar. 7, 1793, No. 8, PRO:FO 5/1, DLC (transcript); George Hammond to Lord Grenville, Mar. 7, 1793, No. 9, DLC; George Hammond to Lord Grenville, No. 11 ("Most Secret and Confidential"), PRO:FO 5/1, DLC (transcript); George Hammond to Lord Grenville, Apr. 2, 1793, No. 12, PRO:FO 5/1, DLC (transcript).

Ambassador Hammond wrote Lord Grenville in part to respond to a "most secret private and confidential" dispatch from the Foreign Office warning him that an American diplomat (probably William Carmichael) in Madrid had reportedly "received instructions to declare to that court that the United States think themselves obliged to support France in any aggression she might experience in the course of her troubles." The news from Madrid was especially disturbing, because, as the Foreign Office warned Hammond, "there is every possibility of our being engaged in a war with France before this letter can reach you." Hammond's response examines the likely extent of American support for the French cause in the event of war.[2]

Although the United States was an English-speaking country with strong cultural and commercial ties to Great Britain, the American Revolution, which had ended just ten years earlier, created powerful bonds between America and France. The Girondin assumption that most Americans remembered France's invaluable support to America's revolutionary cause and would want to return the favor was accurate. In January, Secretary of State Thomas Jefferson wrote William Short, the American minister in Holland, that "99 in an hundred of our citizens" support the French Revolution. A month later, Alexander Hamilton, who was hardly a friend of the Revolution, wrote Short that "the popular tide in this country is strong in favor of the last revolution in France." In addition to these natural bonds of good will, there were legal bonds between the two countries, specifically, the Treaties of Alliance and of Amity.[3]

Hammond began his analysis of American foreign policy by addressing the French treaties. At first glance the most troubling provision was the United States' obligation to "guarantee [French] possessions . . . in America." Hammond, who did not know that the French had already decided to waive their rights under the guarantee, conceded that an attack upon French possessions could "justly be considered as *casus foederis*," or cause to go to war. Nevertheless, he suggested that in practice the guarantee might not turn out to be that significant. First he noted that the guarantee "can indeed be only understood to apply to . . . possessions in the *West Indies*." An attack on France in Europe, therefore, would not implicate the United

---

2. James Bland Burges to George Hammond, Jan. 4, 1793 (in cipher), in *Instructions to the British Ministers to the United States, 1791–1812*, ed. Bernard Mayo (Washington: GPO, 1941), 33–34.
3. Thomas Jefferson to William Short, Jan. 3, 1793, *Papers of Thomas Jefferson*, 25:14; Alexander Hamilton to William Short, Feb. 5, 1793, *Papers of Alexander Hamilton*, 14:7. See Bowman, *Struggle for Neutrality*, 48–49.

States' guarantee. In addition, Hammond assured the Foreign Office that "persons of authority" had suggested to him that if the West Indies' islands were *"in a state of independence"* from the revolutionary government in France, the guarantee might not apply. In the event, Hammond's suggestion that the guarantee might be avoided came to pass.[4]

In addition to the guarantee, Hammond pointed to two other provisions of the treaties that granted the French "unquestionably considerable . . . advantages." Article 17 of the Treaty of Amity and Commerce allowed the French to bring their prizes into American ports and barred enemies of France from doing the same. Article 22 barred enemies of France from fitting out privateers in American ports. As the Neutrality Crisis developed through the spring and into the summer, the French constantly invoked these two provisions in defense of their actions. Indeed, Genet's confidential instructions specifically directed him to seek a rigorous enforcement of these two articles. When British owners sought to challenge the lawfulness of French captures, the French pointed to Article 17, which forbade "examination concerning the lawfulness of such prizes." Similarly, when the British challenged the outfitting of French privateers in American ports, the French insisted that Article 22, by negative implication, authorized fitting out French ships.[5]

A direct and explicit refutation of the Foreign Office's warning about anticipated American support of France would have been undiplomatic. Therefore, Hammond chose to write an implicit refutation of the rumors from Spain. He insisted that the three articles, which he discussed, were "the only stipulations which include anything like common principles of offence or defense." Nor were there any secret treaty obligations. Hammond knew this because Alexander Hamilton, who was secretary of treasury, and others in government had "repeatedly assured" him that there were no "secret engagements whatsoever."[6]

Although the treaties did not obligate the United States to support France, Hammond fully understood that the "French revolution is generally popular in this country." American enthusiasm for the Revolution inevitably would influence American policy, and Hammond accurately identified Secretary of State Jefferson as the leading American supporter of

---

4. George Hammond to Lord Grenville, Mar. 7, 1793, No. 6, PRO:FO 5/1, DLC (transcript).

5. Ibid.

6. George Hammond to Lord Grenville, Mar. 7, 1793, No. 6, PRO:FO 5/1, DLC (transcript).

the French cause. Hammond believed that Jefferson would be "blinded by his attachment to France, and his hatred of Great Britain," and would, therefore, "without hesitation commit the immediate interests of his country in any measure which might equally gratify his predilections [to favor France] and his resentments [against Britain]."[7]

If Jefferson was Britain's enemy, Hamilton was Britain's chief friend within the federal government. "Mr. Hamilton . . . has assured me," wrote Hammond, "that *he* shall exert his influence to defeat . . . any propositions . . . which . . . might ultimately render it necessary for this government to depart from the observance of as strict a neutrality as is compatible with its present [treaty] obligations." A few weeks later, still without certain knowledge of the outbreak of war, Hammond restated Hamilton's firm support for strict neutrality and added, "I learn that the President perfectly concurs in sentiment with Mr. Hamilton."[8]

Hammond's assessment of President Washington's attitude was accurate. The president's desire to remain neutral was essentially a matter of real politik. The same month that Hammond offered his assessment, Washington wrote in private to the American minister in Paris that America would be "unwise . . . in the extreme to involve ourselves in the contests of European Nations, where our weight could be but small; tho' the loss to ourselves would be certain." James Monroe, who ardently supported the French Revolution, agreed. He wrote Jefferson that going to war as an ally of France would be utter folly:

> We would neither aid her with men [i.e., military force] nor money. Of the former we have none, and of the latter our weak and improvident war with the Indians, together with other debts we have assumed will completely exhaust us. Our declaration [of war against France's enemies] would not be felt on the [European] continent.

The French minister in Philadelphia reported much the same thing: American "policy will always lean towards neutrality because it is the only position that can assure them advantage without exposing them to drawbacks."[9]

7. Ibid.
8. George Hammond to Lord Grenville, Mar. 7, 1793, No. 6, PRO:FO 5/1, DLC (transcript); George Hammond to Lord Grenville, Apr. 2, 1793, No. 11, PRO:FO 5/1, DLC (transcript).
9. George Washington to Gouverneur Morris, Mar. 25, 1793, in Fitzpatrick, *Writings of George Washington,* 32:402–3; James Monroe to Thomas Jefferson, May 28, 1793, *Papers of Thomas Jefferson,* 36–135; Jean Ternant to Minister of Foreign Affairs, Apr. 10, 1793, "Correspondence of the French Ministers," 192–93.

Although President Washington clearly wished the United States to remain neutral, he did not consider himself to be a friend of Britain and an enemy of the new French Republic. A few months before the Neutrality Crisis erupted, Washington learned that an American diplomat in Holland was severely criticizing the actions of the new French Republic, and he directed Jefferson to write the diplomat a letter of reprimand. At a personal level, the president was concerned about the safety of the Marquise de Lafayette and his family. In addition, as a matter of public policy, Washington considered France "the sheet anchor of this country and its friendship as a first object."[10]

Hammond had spoken several times with Hamilton on the anticipated arrival in the United States of France's new ambassador, Citizen Genet. Hamilton apparently told Hammond that the new ambassador would be accepted as the representative of a de facto government and that the French treaties would be considered as still binding. Hamilton assured the British minister, however, that "although these engagements could not be considered as null, yet that they would not be enforced to such an extent" as to cause "difficulties or disputes with other powers."[11]

Hamilton's discussions with Hammond paralleled a somewhat similar relationship with Maj. George Beckwith. A few years earlier, the British government had sent Beckwith on an informal and unaccredited mission to the United States to discuss Anglo-American relations. With the president's approval and Secretary of State Jefferson's general knowledge, Hamilton had a number of frank discussions with Beckwith in which Hamilton advocated policies contrary to those of Jefferson and provided Beckwith with confidential insights into the government's policies and attitudes. Some have condemned Hamilton's meetings with Beckwith as grossly improper, but this criticism is naïve. Hamilton acted with the president's knowledge and kept the president informed. If the president had wanted Jefferson to play a more significant role in these discussions, all he had to do was say so.[12]

10. Thomas Jefferson to William Short, Jan. 3, 1793 (in cypher, quoting Washington), *Papers of Thomas Jefferson,* 25:15. See Carroll and Ashworth, *George Washington,* 25–26.

11. George Hammond to Lord Grenville, Mar. 7, 1793, No. 6, PRO:FO 5/1, DLC (transcript).

12. Compare Julian P. Boyd, *Number 7: Alexander Hamilton's Secret Attempts to Control America Foreign Policy* (Princeton, N.J.: Princeton University Press, 1964) with Charles B. Ritcheson, *Aftermath of Revolution: British Policy toward the United States, 1783–1795* (Dallas: Southern Methodist University Press, 1969), 111–19. See also Bowman, *Struggle for Neutrality,* 25n44.

In his letters to the Foreign Office, Hammond discussed a second major issue in the relationship between France and the United States. During the Revolutionary War, the French government loaned the United States large sums of money to finance the war effort, and by 1793 the principal had been reduced to three million dollars. The French had proposed that the entire amount due be accelerated and paid off in the form of negotiable bonds payable by the United States. Upon the receipt of the bonds, the French would immediately sell them on the open market and apply the "proceeds to the purchase of American flour and wheat to be sent to France." In secret cabinet deliberations, the government decided to reject this proposal and continue paying installments on the loan "to the executive government of France, however it might be constituted, existing *de facto* at the periods at which they might be respectively due." Hammond saw the refusal to accelerate the debt as "decisive of [the government's] views relative of the actual position of France." If the government sought to help the French, "surely . . . it would have embraced this offer so highly beneficial to [France]."[13]

Ambassador Hammond's letters are particularly valuable for assessing the principal ways in which the United States could help France. No one, certainly not the French, anticipated that America would lend direct military assistance to the Revolution, but everyone knew that American ports provided a convenient base for mounting a maritime campaign against British commerce. In addition, American wheat would be of enormous aid if it could be safely transported across the Atlantic to French ports.

Hammond's reports also accurately predicted that within the government Hamilton would forcefully advocate a strict neutrality favorable to Britain and that Jefferson would be the principal proponent of policies favorable to France. The least trustworthy aspect of Hammond's assessment of American foreign policy is his analysis of Jefferson's motivations. Hammond frankly confessed, "I have very little intercourse with [Jefferson] except in cases of necessity." Hammond avoided Jefferson because "I cannot but consider him as the devoted instrument of a French faction." As the Neutrality Crisis played out, Jefferson clearly favored the French cause, but he was hardly, to use Hammond's words, "the devoted instrument of a French faction." Instead, Jefferson, as did Hamilton, consistently sought to create a policy that would favor American interests as he saw them.[14]

---

13. George Hammond to Lord Grenville, Mar. 7, 1793. Hammond learned of the secret cabinet deliberations from Alexander Hamilton. Hammond to Grenville, Mar. 7, 1793 (in cipher).

14. Ibid.

Hamilton's crowning achievement as secretary of the treasury was to place the United States on a strong financial footing. Coming out of the Revolution, the country was saddled with enormous debts. Hamilton proposed and Congress enacted comprehensive plans to repay the debt and give the government a sound credit rating. He initially was enthusiastic about the French Revolution and thought that it would lead to a constitutional monarchy, but when the Revolution began spinning into chaos, Hamilton changed his mind. In particular, he saw the war between France and Britain as a looming catastrophe. His carefully wrought and highly successful fiscal system depended upon trade with Britain. If America sided with France, he believed the fiscal system would collapse. Hamilton respected and admired the British political system, but his firm support of strict neutrality was not based simply upon a love of Great Britain. Rather, he wished to preserve the United States' fiscal stability and steer clear of the burgeoning chaos of the French Revolution.[15]

Like Hamilton and most other Americans, Jefferson was initially enthusiastic about the French Revolution, but his confidence in the triumph of republican principles in France, unlike his confidence in the Revolution itself, did not fade as quickly. He saw the French as continuing the Revolution that had begun in America, and he viewed Great Britain as America's natural enemy. Jefferson had an immense distrust of Hamilton because he believed that Hamilton wanted to bring the British system of privilege and money to the United States. He fully understood that American participation in the European war would be disastrous and therefore agreed the country had to remain neutral. Still, Jefferson saw the republican ideals of the French Revolution as the wave of the future and wished to support those ideals. Hamilton embraced the status quo in which Britain was the United States' predominant trading power, but Jefferson wanted to overturn that state of affairs and free America from British economic domination. A strong France under a republican government would be an ally in changing the status quo. Jefferson was an inveterate enemy of the British system and wished to free America from Britain's influence.[16]

War and the Proclamation of Neutrality

When firm news of the outbreak of war between France and Great Britain finally crossed the Atlantic, Jefferson and Hamilton dashed off letters to

15. See Gilbert Lycan, *Alexander Hamilton and American Foreign Policy* (Norman: University of Oklahoma Press, 1970), chap. 8. Robert Tucker and David Hendrickson, *Empire of Liberty* (New York: Oxford University Press, 1990), chap. 5.

16. See Tucker and Hendrickson, *Empire of Liberty,* chap. 5.

President Washington, who was at his estate in Mount Vernon. As Hammond had predicted to the Foreign Office, Washington immediately responded that he wanted "the Government of this Country to use every means in its power to prevent the citizens thereof from embroiling us with either of these powers, by endeavouring to maintain a strict neutrality." He left Mount Vernon the next day and arrived in Philadelphia five days later on April 18.[17]

While the president's carriage was creaking its way toward Philadelphia, he pondered the foreign affairs crisis that would soon engulf the nation. He believed from the outset that the United States should steer a course of neutrality between the warring European superpowers, and the members of his cabinet concurred. Nevertheless, neutrality was not a clear and precisely developed concept. As the Neutrality Crisis developed, many Americans, represented most prominently by Jefferson, sought to steer a course that would tacitly favor France. But others, represented most prominently by Hamilton, sought to direct the nation along a path more favorable to the British. This is not to say that Hamilton was simply pro-British and Jefferson was simply pro-French. Rather, each man reasonably saw the interests of the United States as best served by policies that would favor one side over the other.

Meanwhile, in Philadelphia, Hamilton engaged in a detailed and far-reaching consideration of the war's implications. Again and again his thoughts returned to the French treaties. He had told George Hammond that he and the president were determined to pursue a course of strict neutrality but that the treaties clearly gave France special rights in the event of war. He thus had warned Hammond that American policy would have to conform to or be "compatible with its present [treaty] obligations"[18] But after his earlier discussions with the British minister, a possible solution to the problem of the French treaties sprung into Hamilton's brilliant and supple mind. Why not simply declare the treaties suspended and sweep them from the table?

A week or two before firm news of the European war arrived, Hamilton organized his preliminary thoughts in an anonymous essay intended for a Philadelphia newspaper. His main concern was Article 11 in the Treaty of

---

17. Thomas Jefferson to George Washington, Apr. 7, 1793, and George Washington to Thomas Jefferson, Apr. 12, 1793, *Papers of Thomas Jefferson,* 25:518, 541; Alexander Hamilton to George Washington, Apr. 5, 1793, and George Washington to Alexander Hamilton, Apr. 12, 1793, *Papers of Alexander Hamilton,* 14:291–92, 314–15.

18. See note 9 above.

Alliance, which guaranteed French possessions in the West Indies, and he began the essay by pointing to a number of prudential considerations counseling against the article's vigorous enforcement. The guarantee was general and contained "no precise stipulations [that] point out special succours or special duties." In addition, if "all or nearly all the maritime powers shall be combined against France," the United States was simply too weak to give meaningful assistance. This very consideration led the French to waive their rights under Article 11.[19]

"But," continued Hamilton, "a still more serious question arises." Genet's confidential supplementary instructions had foreseen that uncertainty about European affairs might cause problems, and Hamilton's supple mind turned the element of uncertainty into a plausible legal argument. The United States' treaty obligations were to France, but who within France was authorized to demand compliance with the treaties? France was "in the midst of a *pending* and *disputed* revolution." Hamilton agreed that as a matter of "general principle" changes of government do not alter a country's treaty obligations, but he viewed this general principle as irrelevant to situations in which the government is actually in flux. The general principle applies only "to a *change* [in government], which has been finally *established* and *secured,* not to one which is *depending* and *in contest,* and which may never be consummated." Given the uncertain status of France's new government, Hamilton believed that the United States had discretion to suspend the French treaties.[20]

As Hamilton awaited the president's arrival, he mulled over his idea of suspending the treaties and realized that the reception of the new French minister was significant. He had previously told Hammond that the new minister would be received as the representative of France's de facto government, and now he was certain that Genet should not be received "*absolutely.*" A reception of Citizen Genet as the proper representative of France would in effect recognize the new French government and foreclose his suspension argument. The day after Hamilton sent word of the European war to the

---

19. For "*Gazette of the United States,*" see *Papers of Alexander Hamilton,* 14:267–68. Hamilton apparently did not send the essay to the *Gazette* (see 14:269n1). The precise date of the essay is unclear. Hamilton alludes to the execution of Louis XVI, which narrows its date to after mid-March, when the news of the execution reached America. See, for example, Thomas Jefferson to Joseph Fay, Mar. 18, 1793, *Papers of Thomas Jefferson,* 25:402. At the same time, Hamilton did not have certain news of the outbreak of war, which indicates that it was written before his April 5 letter to President Washington.

20. "*Gazette of the United States,*" in *Papers of Alexander Hamilton,* 14:267–68.

president, Hamilton wrote Chief Justice John Jay, who was home in New York, a letter outlining his suspension argument and his concerns about receiving the new French minister. Hamilton would dearly have loved to have a "personal discussion" with the chief justice but instead sought written advice.[21]

As soon as Hamilton posted his request for advice, his mind turned to the second major impediment to assuring a strict neutrality. He knew that most Americans loved the French Revolution and that many inevitably would take an active part in the war against Great Britain. Ideally, Congress should enact legislation forbidding active American support of the French, but Congress was not in session. The president, however, is always in session. Hamilton immediately dashed off a second letter to Chief Justice Jay, which he posted the same day. What did Jay think of a presidential proclamation declaring "neutrality" and "prohibiting our citizens from taking" part in the war?[22]

When Hamilton's letters arrived in New York two days later, the chief justice "was preparing to go out of town," but he immediately devoted his full attention to Hamilton's questions and fired off a response that same day. Jay tentatively agreed that France's new minister should not be received. In addition, the chief justice wrote a draft neutrality proclamation, which he enclosed in his letter to Hamilton. The chief justice's draft proclamation required all U.S. citizens to "abstain from acting hostilely against any of the belligerent powers" and directed those "in authority . . . to cause all offenders to be prosecuted and punished in an Exemplary manner."[23]

By the time the president reached Philadelphia on April 17, Hamilton had crafted a detailed analysis to support the suspension of the French treaties and assure a policy of strict neutrality that would favor Great Britain. Washington arrived on a Wednesday, and that same day Hamilton had a long meeting with Attorney General Edmund Randolph in which Hamilton carefully presented his detailed "chain of reasoning" regarding neutrality and the French treaties. Then Hamilton closeted himself with the president and presented his carefully rehearsed analysis. Hamilton was perhaps the most capable secretary of the treasury in American history, but he

---

21. Alexander Hamilton to John Jay, Apr. 9, 1793 (first letter), *Papers of Alexander Hamilton,* 14:297–99.

22. Alexander Hamilton to John Jay, Apr. 9, 1793 (second letter), *Papers of Alexander Hamilton,* 14:299–300.

23. John Jay to Alexander Hamilton, Apr. 11, 1793, *Papers of Alexander Hamilton,* 14:307–10.

was more than that to the president. He had served as a personal aide to Washington through much of the Revolutionary War. The two men were literally comrades in arms. Based on personal experience, the president respected, admired, and trusted Hamilton. The next day, Washington scheduled a Friday cabinet meeting, and to assist the deliberations, he sent each cabinet officer a detailed list of questions that established the meeting's agenda. Although the questions were in the president's handwriting, Randolph told Jefferson that "he recognized [the questions] the moment he saw them." They were "the skeletons" of Hamilton's "whole chain of reason."[24]

The first question on Washington's and Hamilton's agenda was whether the president should issue a neutrality proclamation. The next two questions dealt with the reception of the new French minister and whether he should be received absolutely or with qualification. Most of the remaining questions implicitly advanced the analyses that Hamilton had outlined in his unpublished newspaper essay and his letters to Chief Justice Jay. Questions four through six raised Hamilton's idea that the new French government was unstable and that the French treaties should be suspended "'till the Government of France shall be *established*." The next four questions advanced a new argument against Article 11's guarantee clause. Hamilton believed that the guarantee clause only applied when France had been attacked and was fighting a defensive war. Because France had started the conflict by declaring war on Britain, the guarantee clause was not operative. Finally, almost as an afterthought, the last question was whether it was "necessary or advisable" to convene Congress.[25]

When the cabinet met Friday morning, they immediately considered whether Washington should issue a proclamation of neutrality. Jefferson initially opposed the idea on legal and pragmatic grounds. Under the Constitution, only Congress has the power to declare war. Shortly before receiving firm news of the outbreak of war, Jefferson had written James Madison that only Congress could make a declaration of neutrality: "As the Executive cannot decide the question of war on the affirmative side, neither ought it to do so on the negative side." He reiterated this idea in the cabinet. Because "a declaration of neutrality was a declaration, there should be no war, . . . the Executive was not competent." Jefferson also believed that if a formal declaration were withheld, Britain and France "would bid for

---

24. George Washington to Cabinet, Apr. 18, 1793, and Jefferson's Notes on Washington's Questions, May 6, 1793, *Papers of Thomas Jefferson,* 25:568–70, 665–67.

25. George Washington to the Cabinet, Apr. 18, 1793, Enclosure, *Papers of Thomas Jefferson,* 25:568–70.

it, and we might reasonably ask as a price, the broadest privileges of neutral nations."[26]

Given the difficulties and immense delays inherent in transatlantic communication, Jefferson's notion of a kind of diplomatic auction was wildly impractical. His superficially plausible idea quickly collapsed under the weight of significant pragmatic considerations. In an attempt to put the best face on this minor defeat, Jefferson later said that his "objections to the impolicy of a premature declaration were answered by such arguments as timidity would readily suggest." The very real and pressing problem was that all along the seaboard Americans were preparing to show their support of France by plundering British commerce. As early as April 12, President Washington decided that the government needed to adopt "measures . . . without delay [because] I have understood that vessels are already designated as Privateers, and preparing accordingly." Each day of government silence on the issue of neutrality was an inducement to Americans who wished to sail against the British. Because meaningful concessions would have to come from London rather than the British minister to the United States, a proclamation based upon concessions would take months—probably almost a year. In the meantime, Americans from South Carolina to Maine would be going down to the sea in armed ships without guidance from the government. These were the type of patently powerful arguments that Jefferson dismissed as timid.[27]

Jefferson's opposition to a proclamation had little chance of success. Hamilton had already had extended private conferences with the attorney general and the president, and Secretary of War Knox always sided with Hamilton. Moreover, Chief Justice Jay, who was not present, had already endorsed Hamilton's proposal. Hamilton undoubtedly invoked the chief justice's opinion in support of the proclamation and probably had already shown the chief justice's draft proclamation to the president and attorney general. As for Jefferson's constitutional argument, Hamilton had a simple and powerful reply: "If the Legislature have a right to make war on the one hand—it is on the other the duty of the Executive to preserve Peace till war is declared."[28]

---

26. Thomas Jefferson to James Madison, June 29, 1793, and Thomas Jefferson to James Madison, Mar. 24, 1793, *Papers of Thomas Jefferson,* 26:346, 25:442.

27. Thomas Jefferson to James Madison, June 29, 1793, and George Washington to Thomas Jefferson, Apr. 12, 1793, *Papers of Thomas Jefferson,* 26:403, 541.

28. Pacificus No. 1, *Papers of Alexander Hamilton,* 15:40. Jefferson later told James Madison that this passage was a reiteration of Hamilton's argument on this point in

Then Attorney General Randolph put his oar in. He essentially agreed with Hamilton's argument. "When foreign nations engage in war," he said, "nothing can be more obvious and certain, than that it is '*the duty*' of the United States to pursue a peaceful line of conduct." He believed that the treaties with France complicated the issue, but he pointed out that not enough was known about French intentions. He accurately speculated that in all likelihood, the French government would wish the United States to remain neutral. Until more was known, a proclamation of neutrality would preserve the status quo of peace.[29]

By this time, everyone in the room could see that Jefferson's position was doomed. Jefferson himself began to worry that an obstinate opposition to the proclamation might "prejudice" his ability to defend the French treaties. By way of compromise, someone, probably Randolph, suggested that the proposed proclamation could be written merely to announce the United States' present disposition not to go to war and that the proclamation need not use the word "neutrality." Jefferson seized upon this compromise and acquiesced in the proclamation, and so the notes of the meeting reflect that it was "agreed by all that a Proclamation shall issue."[30]

The actual proclamation was written by the attorney general and formally issued on April 22. Although Randolph undoubtedly looked at Chief Justice Jay's draft, Randolph's proclamation was only about half as long. He left out three paragraphs on de facto governments and "the misfortunes... which the late King of France and others have suffered." He also left out a recommendation that the people and the press should avoid controversial public discussions. Randolph did follow Jay's fundamental ideas that the United States wished to remain at peace, that United States citizens should refrain from participating in the war, and that citizens who engaged in hostilities would be criminally prosecuted.[31]

---

the cabinet meeting. Thomas Jefferson to James Madison, June 29, 1793, *Papers of Thomas Jefferson*, 26:403.

29. *Dunlap's American Daily Advertiser* (Philadelphia), Apr. 29, 1793; Thomas Jefferson to James Madison, June 29, 1793, *Papers of Thomas Jefferson*, 26:401–4, referring to the *Dunlap's* article as being written by Randolph and as accurately summarizing Randolph's position at the cabinet meeting.

30. Thomas Jefferson to James Madison, June 23, 1793, *Papers of Thomas Jefferson*, 26:346; Cabinet Opinion, Apr. 19, 1793, *Papers of Thomas Jefferson* 25:570–71.

31. Compare Randolph's proclamation with Jay's draft, *Papers of Alexander Hamilton*, 14:308–10.

Although the Proclamation of Neutrality did not use the word "neutrality," it declared that the disposition of the United States was "with sincerity and good faith to adopt and pursue a conduct friendly and impartial towards the belligerent Powers." It also warned American citizens against "committing, aiding, or abetting hostilities against any of the said powers." Finally, the proclamation instructed prosecutors "to cause prosecutions to be instituted against all persons, who shall . . . violate the law of nations, with respect to the Powers at war." The proclamation substituted the word "impartial" for "neutral," but President Washington referred to it as a neutrality proclamation and so it has been considered ever since.[32]

The next items on Washington's agenda were questions involving the reception of the new French minister. At the initial cabinet meeting on April 19, Hamilton used this seemingly technical issue to launch a direct assault upon the entire Franco-American relationship. He immediately "took up the whole subject" in what amounted to a comprehensive attack upon the treaties. He carefully laid out his suspension analysis but did not stop there. Based upon further research in international law, he expanded his own analysis to a new and breathtaking claim that the United States could lawfully declare the treaties "for ever null." As soon as Hamilton finished, Secretary Knox immediately endorsed Hamilton's idea but candidly admitted that he "knew nothing about it." Jefferson was appalled. In his private notes, he dismissed Knox as a "fool" and confined his remarks to the merits of Hamilton's arguments. Although Jefferson was willing to compromise on the neutrality proclamation, he refused to budge on the treaties: "I was clear the treaties remained valid." When Attorney General Randolph agreed with Jefferson, the vote was two to two.[33]

Hamilton tenaciously clung to his position and insisted that his nullification argument was supported by no less than Emerich Vattel, one of the most respected writers on international law. In the face of Hamilton's citation of respected authority, Randolph changed his vote to undecided, and Washington postponed the question. At the attorney general's suggestion, everyone agreed to submit written opinions on the issue, and the meeting adjourned. Meanwhile, someone leaked Hamilton's opposition to recognizing the new French ambassador to the press. A pro-French writer condemned the idea

---

32. Neutrality Proclamation, Apr. 22, 1793, *American State Papers,* 140; Thomas, *American Neutrality in 1793,* 46–47.

33. Notes on Washington's Questions, May 6, 1793, *Papers of Thomas Jefferson,* 25:665–67; Opinion on the Treaties with France, Apr. 28, 1793 (summarizing Hamilton's arguments at the April 19 meeting), *Papers of Thomas Jefferson,* 25:608.

and implicitly attributed it to Hamilton. According to a pro-French newspaper in Philadelphia, this "disgraceful [idea] could only have originated with some *rotten-hearted* fellow that would sell his country to Britain for a 'funding system.'"[34]

As the cabinet members worked on their opinions, Vattel turned out to be at best a slender reed incapable of supporting the weighty claim that the French treaties could be declared void. Hamilton had discovered a single unelaborated passage in which Vattel stated,

> But if this change [from a kingdom to a republic] renders the alliance useless, dangerous or disagreeable to [the other country], it is free to renounce it [i.e., the alliance]. For it may say with truth, that it would not have allied itself with this nation, if it had been under the present form of its government.

The *Times* of London liked this argument, but Thomas Jefferson made short work of it. In private and perhaps to President Washington, he dismissed the passage as "an ill-understood scrap." With palpable disdain, he sneered to James Monroe that "H. is panick struck if we refuse our breach to every kick which G. Brit may chance to give it." James Madison rejected Hamilton's argument as "contemptible for the meanness and folly of it." In a written opinion, Jefferson carefully established that other respected writers were in flat disagreement and that the passage was even inconsistent with most of Vattel's own work. Finally, Jefferson completely destroyed Hamilton's claims by briefly accepting the "ill-understood scrap" for the purpose of argument. Even assuming that a "disagreeable" change of government might justify renouncing a treaty, "who is the American who can say with truth that he would not have allied himself to France if she had been a republic? Or that a Republic of any form would be as *disagreeable* as her [France's] antient despotism?" This irrefutable argument was repeated in public and private by others. Although Secretary of War Knox joined with Hamilton, as he always did, the attorney general agreed with Jefferson, and the president decided the issue against Hamilton. In so doing, Washington assured Jefferson "he had never had a doubt about the validity of the treaty: but since a question had been suggested he thought it ought to be considered."[35]

---

34. Notes on Washington's Questions, May 6, 1793, *Papers of Thomas Jefferson,* 25:665–67; *National Gazette,* Apr. 27, 1793. See also Marcellus, *Boston Gazette,* June 10, 1793 (linking Hamilton's arguments to the "funding system").

35. *Times* (London), Aug. 22, 1793; Thomas Jefferson to James Madison, Apr. 28, 1793; Thomas Jefferson to James Monroe, May 5, 1793; and James Madison to

Once the administration decided that a neutrality proclamation should be issued and that the French treaties should remain in effect, the cabinet paid scant attention to the remaining issues presented by Hamilton's carefully crafted agenda. Newspapers reported that an early session of Congress would be called, but the cabinet unanimously decided to the contrary. There is no record of the reasons for this decision. As for Hamilton's other questions, the press of events quickly turned the government's attention from grand theoretical issues such as neutrality and the validity of the French treaties to a welter of important practical issues created by the onset of the French maritime campaign.[36]

Thomas Jefferson, May 8, 1793, all in *Papers of Thomas Jefferson,* 25:619, 661, 689; Thomas Jefferson, Opinion on the Treaties with France, Apr. 28, 1793, *Papers of Thomas Jefferson,* 25:614–17 (citing Grotius, Puffendorf, Wolf, and Vattel); Jean Badollet to Albert Gallatin, June 6, 1793, quoted in Casto, "Pacificus and Helvidius Reconsidered," 615; "The Rights of Man," *New York Journal,* Aug. 10, 1793; "Secretarius," *National Gazette,* Aug. 10, 1793; editorial note on Jefferson's Opinion, *Papers of Thomas Jefferson,* 25:597–602; Notes on Washington's Questions on Neutrality and the Alliance with France, May 6, 1793, *Papers of Thomas Jefferson,* 25:666.

36. *Federal Gazette,* Apr. 22, 1793; Notes on Washington's Questions, May 6, 1793, *Papers of Thomas Jefferson,* 25:666.

CHAPTER 4

The French Maritime Campaign Begins

> We are armed for the defense of the rights of man.
> *Flown from* L'Embuscade's *mizzenmast*
>
> It is incontestible that the treaty of commerce (Art. XXII), expressly authorizes our arming in the ports of the United States.
> *Edmond Genet*

While Jefferson and Hamilton were in Philadelphia preparing for President Washington's arrival, *L'Embuscade* finally reached American waters. She appeared outside Charleston Harbor in the morning of April 8 but had to wait because larger ships could not cross the bar at low tide. In the afternoon, the frigate sailed into port and fired a broadside salute in Genet's honor. Genet was quite pleased. "A huge crowd," he reported, "was waiting for me on the bank curious and eager to know if the war was declared." The French consul, Michel Mangourit, was in the crowd and immediately took the new minister to visit Governor William Moultrie and other state officials.[1]

Citizen Genet became the toast of the town, except among those inclined to support Britain. He hit it off well with Governor Moultrie and quickly "established a very truthful relationship" with him. Other French diplomats had proudly insisted that government officials come to them, but Genet rejected "the old regime's" haughty notions of hierarchy. He believed that "the true friends of liberty saw in my attitude the desire I have to establish the fraternity that must rule between us and their fellow citizens." The port's leading citizens threw numerous parties for Genet and the officers of *L'Embuscade*. On the very evening of their arrival, Commodore Gillon feted everyone "in an elegant and hospitable style." Given this enthusiastic reception, there seemed to be little need for Genet to exercise discretion in vigorously and publicly pursuing his mission. Nor did it help that Consul Mangourit, the first French representative Genet encountered in America, was himself a rash and intemperate revolutionary.[2]

1. *South Carolina Gazette,* Apr. 16, 1793; *Federal Gazette,* Apr. 20, 1793; *Soult v. Africaine,* 22 F. Cas. 805, (D.S.C. 1804), No. 13,179 (discussing the bar); Edmond Genet to Minister of Foreign Affairs, Apr. 16, 1793, "Correspondence of the French Ministers," 211–13.

2. Edmond Genet to Minister of Foreign Affairs, Apr. 16, 1793, "Correspondence of the French Ministers," 211–13; *Federal Gazette,* Apr. 20, 1793 (Gillon); Ralph

The *Morning Star* and *Four Brothers*

Although Bompard and his officers may have drunk much wine at Commodore Gillon's house, they were up bright and early the next morning. As soon as tide and wind permitted, *L'Embuscade*'s crew weighed anchor, set sail, crossed the bar, and stood out to sea. Bompard's purpose was to catch enemy ships coming and going. Charleston was a major commercial port, and when Bompard arrived, there were about "14 British Vessels [in port] ready to sail for the West Indies and Britain." While the French frigate patrolled beyond the bar, the British ships could not sail. At the same time, Bompard could expect to take Charleston-bound ships whose masters did not know that war had been declared. Each day, *L'Embuscade* would pass the bar and cruise outside the harbor. In effect, Bompard was blockading Charleston. As news of *L'Embuscade*'s presence spread, fear and uncertainty bottled up thirty more British ships in Savannah, Georgia, and Wilmington, Delaware.[3]

The first day on patrol proved the merit of Bompard's tactics and demonstrated the value of hovering beyond the bar. He spied the brigantine *Morning Star* bearing fourteen puncheons (about fourteen hundred gallons) of rum for a merchant house in Charleston and snapped her up. A Philadelphia newspaper described the capture as happening "as she was entering [Charleston] harbour," and an angry reader immediately complained that international law forbade the taking of prizes in neutral territory, which the reader defined as extending the distance of a cannon shot out to sea. Any failure of the United States to protect its neutral territory had grave implications for American sovereignty: "If we permit our rights to be violated we should soon be held cheap, and treated accordingly." In Charleston, however, ships outside the bar were more than three miles from the coast, so Bompard's cruising station assured that American sovereignty would not be violated. He could take incoming ships before they could reach the three-mile limit. If enemy shipping had the temerity to sail from Charleston, Bompard had only to wait until they crossed the bar before taking them.[4]

Izard to unknown, Apr. 17, 1793 (dinner at Izard's house), MB; Robert Palmer, "A Revolutionary Republican: M. A. B. Mangourit," *William and Mary Quarterly,* 3rd ser., 9 (1952): 483–96.

3. John Ewing to James Blank, Apr. 20, 1793, PRO:FO 5/3, Domestic Letters; George Miller to Lord Grenville, May 6, 1793, PRO:FO 5/2, Consular Correspondence; *National Gazette,* Apr. 24, 1793.

4. *Federal Gazette,* Apr. 20, 1793 ("entering our harbor"); *Counter Case of Great Britain,* 612–13; *Pennsylvania Journal* (Philadelphia), May 8, 1793 (rum); *Soult v. L'Africaine.*

As the week progressed, Bompard added the *Success* of Bremen, "laden with dry goods, iron, etc.," and the *Wilhelm* of Hamburg to his catch. In addition, the *Four Brothers,* which he had captured off Bermuda on the voyage over, finally made port. The people of Charleston could not help but be impressed with *L'Embuscade*'s onslaught against enemy shipping.[5]

These captures gratified the men of *L'Embuscade.* In addition to inflicting harm on the enemy, Bompard and his crew relished the prize money they would receive. The *Success* and the *Wilhelm,* however, were disappointments. France was at war with most of Europe but not with the independent, imperial cities of the Hanseatic League, which included Bremen and Hamburg. Because the Hanseatic League was neutral, Citizen Genet ordered the German ships released. There would be no prize money from these two captures.[6]

To add insult to injury, Genet took a condescending attitude to the ignorant sailors who did not understand the finer points of diplomacy. He snidely quipped that the sailors "had difficulties distinguishing an imperial city from a city belonging to the emperor." Yet he assured the minister of foreign affairs back in France that the crew, "who are very brave, very patriotic, and full of confidence in my sentiments accepted my decision." Perhaps the crew believed that Genet's heart was in the right place, but the loss of two prizes was a hard blow.[7]

Fortunately, the prizes *Four Brothers* and *Morning Star* remained, and their disposal illustrates some of the commercial realities of eighteenth-century prize law. The ships, themselves, had little value to the French crew. There was no possibility that the French sailors would take actual title to the prizes and embark upon a commercial voyage. The crew probably would have been pleased to take personal possession of the *Morning Star*'s cargo of Jamaican rum, but there were prudential reasons for not allocating the cargo in kind among the sailors. As a practical matter, the prizes and their cargoes had to be converted to cash. They had to be sold.

Although pragmatic considerations dictated selling the prizes, prospective buyers might have qualms about the sellers' legal title to the property. The French possessed the *Four Brothers* and the *Morning Star,* but their possession

5. *Federal Gazette,* Apr. 20, 24, 30, 1793. The *Four Brothers* is erroneously called the *Four Sisters* in the *Boston Gazette,* May 13, 1793, and *Sally* in the *United States Chronicle,* May 2, 1793.

6. *Federal Gazette,* Apr. 30, 1793; Edmond Genet to French Minister of Foreign Affairs, Apr. 16, 1793, "Correspondence of the French Ministers," 211–13.

7. Edmond Genet to French Minister of Foreign Affairs, Apr. 16, 1793, "Correspondence of the French Ministers," 211–13.

came from an exercise of raw military power. Moreover, the capture of a particular prize might be illegal, which would render a subsequent purchaser's ownership dubious. For example, the taking of the Hanseatic ships was improper because France was not at war with the Hanseatic League. If these neutral ships had been sold instead of returned to their owners, the sale would have been unlawful. To resolve the legality of particular captures, the European maritime nations had evolved systems of prize courts to review the legality of particular captures and issue judicial decrees of condemnation. As a result, the property could be sold based upon a judicial decree of condemnation rather than the seller's mere possession.

These judicial decrees played a crucial role in assuring prospective buyers that they would indeed become the lawful owners of the captured ship and cargo. A few years later, Britain's leading Admiralty judge, Sir William Scott—later Lord Stowell—explained that mere possession by a captor is insufficient to confer lawful title. It is not "thought fit, in civilized society, that property of this sort should be converted without the sentence of a competent Court." By 1793, the practice of condemnation by a prize court had become deeply ingrained. The mere sailing of a prize into port was not enough to validate a subsequent sale because "no man buys under that title; he requires a sentence of condemnation, as the foundation of the title of the seller." Of course, Sir William was a judge describing the applicable legal rules as he knew them. In contrast, markets have never been great respecters of mere legal rules. A buyer in the market might very well seek a heavily discounted price in lieu of a valid sentence of condemnation. The seller, however, would much prefer to sell at the higher price warranted by legitimate condemnation.[8]

The requirement of a judicial condemnation presented problems for the French. Traditionally, a captor sailed a prize to the nearest port controlled by his country and commenced judicial proceedings there. Tradition, therefore, would have dispatched French prizes across the Atlantic to France or to a French port in the Caribbean, but the voyage would be perilous. Along the way there was a good chance that the prize would be retaken by the British. After all, Britain was the world's predominant naval power and usually maintained effective control of the Caribbean and Atlantic sea lanes. Even if the prize made it to a distant French port, the condemnation, sale,

---

8. *The Henrick and Maria,* 165 Eng. Rep. 529 (Adm. 1799); Henry Bourguignon, *Sir William Scott, Lord Stowell, Judge of the High Court of Admiralty, 1798–1828* (London: Cambridge University Press, 1987).

and proceeds of the sale would be far away and beyond the captor's immediate control.

Rather than subject prizes to the perils of a long voyage and possible recapture, the French came up with a quick and dirty solution. Each major port in the United States had a French consul, and these consuls could establish prize courts in America. In Charleston, the captures of the *Morning Star* and the *Four Brothers* were submitted to Consul Mangourit, and he quickly condemned them as lawful prizes. *L'Embuscade* took the *Morning Star* on April 9, and Mangourit formally condemned her just six days later on April 15. He apparently condemned the *Four Brothers* that same day. The ships and their cargoes were immediately advertised for a public sale to commence on April 22 "precisely at eleven o'clock, on Mey's wharf to the highest bidder. Conditions—cash." The inventory, including the rum, could be viewed, and hopefully sampled, at the establishment of Abraham Sasportas, a local merchant who served as the prize agent.[9]

Sasportas promptly sold both vessels on April 22, but the price was a bit low. The *Four Brothers,* including the rum, was valued at £2,000 but sold for only £380. Similarly, the estimated value of the *Morning Star* was £800, but she sold for only £212. These are fairly steep discounts even for a distress sale. Perhaps the "cash only" terms discouraged bidders. Both vessels were purchased by the firm of Penman and Company, a local British merchant and the ships' original owner. As a New England newspaper described the sale, Penman "ransomed" its vessels.[10]

The summary justice meted out by Citizen Mangourit in his Consular Court boded well for the maritime campaign against France's enemies. Up and down the Eastern Seaboard, prizes could be taken, sailed into the nearest American port, condemned by the French consul, and sold—all within a matter of days. The British consul in Baltimore tersely described the entire process as "capture often illegal, unlawful condemnation, and precipitate sale." A newspaper reported that "English prizes carried into Charleston, are suffered to be sold without any other previous ceremony than an advertisement." But there was a fly in the ointment. The initial two sales brought in about six hundred pounds, which was a substantial amount of money, but the sales netted only about 20 percent of the prizes' estimated value. Perhaps prospective buyers were reluctant to bid because they had doubts about the

---

9. *Charleston (S.C.) City Gazette,* Apr. 19, 1793; *Pennsylvania Journal,* May 8, 1793; *Boston Gazette,* May 13, 1793.

10. *Counter Case of Great Britain,* 612–13; George Miller to Lord Grenville, May 6, 1793, PRO:FO 5/2, Consular Correspondence; *Boston Gazette,* May 13, 1793.

validity of Citizen Mangourit's decrees. If the Consular Courts were illegal, their decrees would not prevent a British court from returning the captured vessels to their original owners if the vessels were later sailed into a British port.[11]

The *Grange*

News of *L'Embuscade*'s arrival spread up the Eastern Seaboard as fast as sail would permit, and captains of British ships in American ports were presented with an exquisite dilemma. They could remain safely anchored in neutral ports, or they could set sail immediately on their planned voyages. Staying in port would guarantee their safety, but maritime commerce is about profit, and a ship swinging at anchor turns no profit. On the other hand, a departure chanced an encounter with Citizen Bompard and his crew. The decision whether to sail was complicated by the fact that *L'Embuscade* could not be everywhere at once and probably could be avoided.

In Philadelphia, Capt. Edward Hutchinson of the *Grange* went with the odds and set sail on April 18 bound for Liverpool. The next day, he was at Chester and picked up three passengers, Joshua Sutcliff and Mr. and Mrs. George Dillwyn. As the *Grange* gradually continued down the Delaware River, she became wind bound at Reedy Island. While waiting for the wind to shift, the pilot of an inbound ship brought distressing news: "A French twenty gun Ship was on the coast . . . intending for Philadelphia." Captain Hutchinson agonized over this news, and the river pilot who was guiding the *Grange* thought that "the information seemed to deter the Captain for some time from endeavoring to get out to sea." Hutchinson resolutely decided to compromise. He dropped on down the river and out into Delaware Bay, where he anchored at a sand bank a number of miles from Cape Henlopen.[12]

On the morning of April 25, six days after leaving Philadelphia, the *Grange* was at anchor waiting for "a fair wind to carry [her] clear of the Coast." Instead of a fair wind, Captain Hutchinson encountered the unnerving sight of a large man of war standing up the broad mouth of the bay. He could not help but think that the strange ship was French, and perhaps he

---

11. Edward Thornton to James Bland Burges, Nov. 3, 1793, James Bland Burges Papers, Bodleian Library, Oxford University; *Federal Gazette,* July 10, 1793. For British cases rejecting the validity of consular decrees, see *The Flad Oyen,* 165 Eng. Rep. 124 (Adm. 1799); *The Perseverance,* 165 Eng. Rep. 302 (Adm. 1799); *The Henrick and Maria.*

12. My recounting of the *Grange*'s capture is drawn primarily from Affidavits of Gilbert McCraiken, Joshua Sutcliff, and George Dillwyn, May 2, 1793, Genet Papers, DLC, summarized in *Papers of Thomas Jefferson,* 25:638–39.

thought of flight. But the man of war was under full sail, and her speed was enhanced by a flood tide coming in from the sea. Before Hutchinson could decide what to do, he saw that the stranger was a frigate nearly twice the size of the reported twenty-gun Frenchman. Moreover, the strange sail was flying British colors. With relief, the crew of the *Grange* ran up their own British colors.[13]

Captain Hutchinson's relief was short lived because the frigate was *L'Embuscade,* and as she approached, Bompard struck his false colors and hoisted the flag of the new French Republic. The previous evening Bompard had taken the brigantine *Little Sarah,* laden with flour and Indian cornmeal. Now a second prize was in the offing. When *L'Embuscade* was within cannon range, the French fired a warning shot and snapped up the *Grange.* The British crew transferred to *L'Embuscade,* and the two prizes were sent into Philadelphia. Rather than accompany the prizes, Bompard patrolled the mouth of Delaware Bay for a day or two, but the word was out, and no more prizes were to be had.[14]

The arrival of the *Grange* and the *Little Sarah* in Philadelphia was a sensation. As soon as they came into harbor, word sped through town and virtually everyone who could rushed to the wharves. Thomas Jefferson gleefully reported, "Upon [the prizes] coming into sight thousands and thousands of the *yeomanry* of the city crowded and covered the wharfs." Jefferson had never seen such a large crowd at the waterfront, and as the prizes got closer, the "British colours were seen *reversed,* and the French flying above them." The crowd spontaneously "burst into peals of exultation."[15]

The procession of the prizes was just a prologue to *L'Embuscade*'s arrival a few days later. As the frigate glided into Philadelphia Harbor, almost every vessel in port flew its colors to honor the ship's arrival. Although Bompard was above all else a man of action, he understood that his ship represented the Revolution's spirit and martial prowess. He ordered a fifteen-gun salute, and cannon at Market Street Wharf responded in kind. When *L'Embuscade* gracefully emerged from the smoke, everyone saw that she was decorated from stem to stern with red caps of liberty. As the frigate dropped anchor,

---

13. Affidavit of Gilbert McCraiken, May 2, 1793, Genet Papers, DLC.
14. George Hammond to Officer Commanding His Majesty's Ships at Halifax, Apr. 27, 1793, PRO, DLC (transcript); Memorial from Benjamin Holland and Peter Mackie, May 24, 1793, *Papers of Thomas Jefferson,* 16:106.
15. Thomas Jefferson to James Monroe, May 5, 1793; Thomas Jefferson to Thomas Mason Randolph Jr., May 6, 1793; and Thomas Jefferson to John Wayles Eppes, May 12, 1793, all in *Papers of Thomas Jefferson,* 25:660–62, 668–69, 26:7–8.

people could read the inscribed flags she was flying. From the foremast came the warning, "Enemies of equality, reform or tremble," from the mainmast, "Freemen, we are your friends and brothers," and from the mizzenmast, "We are armed for the defense of the rights of man."[16]

In addition to these stirring slogans, Bompard literally turned his ship into a stage. On public occasions, he and his crew delighted in serenading spectators with fervent renditions of the new revolutionary song, the "Marseillaise." Years later, Charles Biddle recalled *L'Embuscade*'s serenade in Philadelphia. The "yards were manned, and every person on board joined with utmost enthusiasm." Biddle insisted that "there never was a more animating song."[17]

In Philadelphia and other ports, Bompard welcomed visitors to his ship. Jefferson visited the frigate on May 28 and tipped the French boatmen two dollars. Visitors saw in Citizen Bompard the epitome of Liberty, Equality, and Fraternity. He was a true republican who dressed simply in a sailor's jacket without badges of rank. Instead of the aristocratic cocked hat, he wore the red stocking cap of liberty. He was not elegant in manners. He spoke simply and directly. After entertaining visitors with dinners and numerous toasts, he would have the frigate's boatswain give an "artless and energetic [speech] replete with feeling." Americans were bowled over by Bompard, who came "armed for the defense of the rights of man."[18]

In Philadelphia, Bompard and his crew hosted a dinner on board *L'Embuscade* for the city's leading citizens, including Governor Mifflin and Secretary of War Knox. After dinner, "several hymns sacred to Liberty were sung." Then the toasts began:

> 1. The American and French republics—May they be forever united! (a salute of twenty-one guns.) . . .
> 3. The Rights of Man—may they become universal law!

Governor Mifflin was an enthusiastic supporter of the French Revolution and a heavy drinker. After the numerous toasts, he spontaneously volunteered the final one. He raised his glass and said, "The Frigate *L'Ambuscade*."[19]

---

16. *National Gazette,* May 4, 1793.

17. Charles Biddle, *Autobiography of Charles Biddle* (Philadelphia: E. Claxton, 1883), 253. Posthumously published.

18. *Jefferson's Memorandum Books,* ed. James Bear and Lucia Stanton (Princeton, N.J.: Princeton University Press, 1997), 2:895; *Federal Gazette,* Aug. 9, 1793; *Carlisle (Pa.) Gazette,* June 5, 1793.

19. *Federal Gazette,* May 30, 1793; John Alexander, "Thomas Mifflin," *American National Biography* (New York: Oxford University Press, 1999), 15:440–41.

L'Embuscade's rampage up the Eastern Seaboard was a stunning public relations victory. Less than a month after Bompard's arrival in Charleston, an English merchant some fifteen hundred miles to the north in Nova Scotia confided to his diary that *L'Embuscade* had already "taken upwards of 20 sail of English Vessels." Others reported that Bompard "had captured or destroyed upwards of 60 British vessels." But one frigate, no matter how capably and aggressively sailed, cannot cover the vast stretch of sea from Charleston to Boston. The 1793 campaign against British shipping in North America was successful. An incomplete tabulation by British consuls suggests the extent of the depredations. That summer and fall the French took at least sixty-two British vessels valued at about two hundred thousand pounds. In addition, the French took many prizes from other nations, such as Spain. But only seven of the British vessels were taken by French frigates, six by *L'Embuscade* and one by *Concorde,* which arrived a few months later. The remaining fifty-five British prizes were taken by privateers.[20]

Privateering

The practice of privateering has long since faded from our national consciousness and lapsed into desuetude, but in 1793 it was an integral part of maritime warfare. A major objective of war at sea has always been the capture, destruction, and disruption of the enemy's commercial shipping. During the sailing era, a country at war could substantially augment its regular navy by authorizing merchant sailors to prey upon the enemy's shipping. These private commerce raiders were called "privateers" in English-speaking countries and "corsairs" in France.[21]

The practice of privateering required adventurers to refit small merchant vessels by mounting a few cannon. The resulting commerce raider might be weak but would have sufficient strength to attack and capture unarmed merchantmen. The owner of a privateer also would have to hire an abnormally large complement of sailors. The crew of a two-masted schooner operating in a commercial mode would seldom exceed six men, but the same ship converted to a privateer usually would carry a crew of forty or fifty.[22]

---

20. Casto, "Rights of Man," 266; *Counter Case of Great Britain,* 609–21.

21. See generally Donald Macintyre, *The Privateers* (London: Paul Elek, 1975); Carl J. Kulsrud, *Maritime Neutrality in 1780* (Boston: Little Brown, 1936), 37–60. For an account of French privateering in European waters, see Patrick Crowhurst, *The French War on Trade: Privateering 1793–1815* (Hants, U.K.: Scolar Press, 1989).

22. See Harold Hahn, *The Colonial Schooner, 1763–1775* (Annapolis, Md.: Naval Institute Press, 1981), 76.

These extra hands made the schooner easier to sail and were especially useful for boarding and overwhelming another ship. They could also be used to man sweeps when becalmed. In addition, after capturing an enemy ship, members of the privateer's crew would have to be transferred to the captured ship to serve as a prize crew. The leader of the prize crew was the prize master and was responsible for sailing the captured ship into a port where it could be sold. A privateer's oversized crew made it possible to dispatch a number of prizes into port without seriously affecting the privateer's ability to continue cruising.

Privateering enabled countries to maintain relatively modest navies during peacetime, but with the onset of war, a host of commerce raiders could be created with the stroke of a pen. In exchange for a privateering commission, merchant adventurers would assume the capital costs of obtaining and refitting a suitable vessel and the operating expenses of crewing and running the vessel. These costs and expenses were not defrayed from the national treasury. Instead privateers recouped their investments from the sale of prizes.

There were three prerequisites to a successful privateering campaign. Adventurers had to refit suitable merchant vessels for war and significantly augment their crews, and the government had to provide an effective system of prize courts. The importance of the first two requirements are virtually self-evident, but the vital need for prize courts is not as obvious to twenty-first-century minds. Prize courts played an important role in respect of captures by regular navy units such as *L'Embuscade,* but they were essential to the effective use of privateers. During the Revolutionary War, James Wilson and a group of Philadelphia merchants petitioned for the creation of effective American prize courts because "in the privateering trade in particular, the very life of which consists in the adventurers receiving the rewards of their success and bravery as soon as the cruise is over, the least delay is uncommonly destructive." A prize court's timely decree of condemnation made it easier for corsairs to sell prizes and reap the rewards of success.[23]

In addition to facilitating sales, prize courts also served an important regulatory function. The simple fact was that privateers were not entirely trustworthy. Unlike regular navy units, they were not subject to military discipline, and they had to recoup all of their capital costs and operating expenses from the sale of prizes. To use an Enlightenment idea, privateers

---

23. *Essays in the Constitutional History of the United States in the Formative Period, 1775–1789,* ed. J. Jameson (Boston: Houghton Mifflin, 1889), 25–26 (quoting the petition).

were rational wealth maximizers. Their profit motive rendered them inherently unreliable for the accomplishment of particular missions.[24] Morever, if left unchecked, their thirst for wealth could lead to appalling abuse. In theory, if not in practice, prize courts provided a disinterested judicial review of potentially abusive misconduct.

Eighteenth-century Europeans were familiar with the problem of uncontrolled greed leading to abusive misconduct at sea. They called it piracy, and privateers looked a lot like pirates. Both privateers and pirates roamed the seas attacking merchant vessels for private gain. Indeed, many of the most famous pirates of the eighteenth century began their careers as privateers with formal government commissions. When Captain Kidd sailed the Indian Ocean, he had a privateer's commission. Eventually, however, he was held to have exceeded his commission, and he was hanged as a pirate. Similarly, Blackbeard was at one time a British privateer.[25]

By the 1790s, there were few illusions about the nobility of the privateering trade. Justice William Paterson of the U.S. Supreme Court bluntly recognized that "it is a sort of licensed depredation. . . . Activated by a predatory spirit, how often do privateers perpetuate outrages, that shock the moral sense, and disgrace the human character." Another federal judge explained that privateers are "activated by a spirit of lucre, which not only incites to plunder the base and lawless freebooter, but tarnishes even heroism, by seducing into unjustifiable actions the bravest men." Even Alexander Hauterive, the French consul in New York during the Neutrality Crisis, had a disdain for the practice. A few years later, he wrote that privateering is a "monument of ignorance and barbarity [that] should disappear from the legislation of these enlightened times."[26]

The First Wave of Corsairs

Almost as soon as Genet set foot in Charleston, word swept through the port that privateer commissions were available for those who wished to pillage

---

24. See C. S. Forester, *The Age of Fighting Sail* (Garden City, N.Y.: Doubleday, 1956), 92–96.

25. See Robert Ritchie, *Captain Kidd and the War against the Pirates* (Cambridge: Harvard University Press, 1986); Lindley Butler, *Pirates, Privateers, and Rebel Raiders on the Carolina Coast* (Chapel Hill: University of North Carolina Press, 2000), chap. 2.

26. Unpublished opinion of Justice Paterson, prepared for *Del Gol v. Arnold,* 3 U.S. (3 Dall.) 333 (1796), quoted in Casto, "Origins of Federal Admiralty Jurisdiction," 124; *Findlay v. The William,* 9 F. Cas. 57, 59 (D. Pa. 1793) (No. 4790); Alexander Hauterive, *State of the French Republic at the End of the Year VIII* (Dublin: J. Stockdale, 1801) (translated by Lewis Goldsmith).

British commerce for profit. Genet later told Jefferson that he "was surrounded suddenly by Frenchmen full of zeal for their country, . . . that they would fit out their own vessels, provide everything, man them, and only ask a commission from him." Genet broached the matter with Governor Moultrie, who assured him that "he knew no law to the contrary." Governor Moultrie's assumption that fitting out privateers was permissible was not unusual. Other state officials in other ports, as well as newspaper articles, reached the same conclusion. The mayor of Norfolk, Virginia, wrote his governor, "It appears by the Treaties with Holland & France, that both have power to arm vessels in our ports, & sell prizes." In South Carolina, nevertheless, Governor Moultrie discreetly "begged that whatever was to be done, might be done without consulting him, that he must know nothing of it &c." With this tacit official support, Genet quickly commissioned four privateers with suitable revolutionary names: *Citoyen Genet, Sans Culottes, Republican,* and *Anti-George*. The *Citoyen Genet* was originally to be named the *Patriote Genet,* but in an unusual act of discretion, Genet changed *Patriote* to *Citizen*. The *Citoyen Genet* and the *Sans Culottes* were to be the most successful of this first wave of corsairs.[27]

The *Citoyen Genet* and *Sans Culottes* were schooners of the type frequently used as pilot vessels along the coast and were ideal for privateering in American waters. They were small vessels between thirty-five and sixty feet long and lightly armed, but they were fast and seaworthy. A British captain who was in Charleston described the *Citoyen Genet* as a "small fast sailing schooner" with a crew of between forty and fifty men. In a little over a week, Charleston shipwrights refitted her to carry between four and six small cannon, and the new corsair was ready to sail.[28]

---

27. Jefferson, Memorandum of Conversations with Edmond Charles Genet, July 26, 1793, *Papers of Thomas Jefferson,* 26:572; Thomas Newton to the Governor of Virginia, Apr. 29, 1793, *Calendar of Virginia State Papers,* ed. Sherwin McRae (Richmond: Public Printing Office, 1886), 358; "Americanus," *Federal Gazette,* May 31, 1793; *Columbia Herald* (Charleston, S.C.), Aug. 6, 1793; *Boston Gazette,* July 29, 1793; "Salem," *Salem Gazette,* Aug. 13, 1793; Edmond Genet to Minister of Foreign Affairs, Apr. 16, 1793, "Correspondence of the French Ministers," 211–13; Melvin Jackson, "The Consular Privateers: An Account of French Privateering in American Waters, April to August, 1793," *American Neptune* 22 (1962): 81; Ammon, *Genet Mission,* 44.

28. Jackson, "Consular Privateers," 83; George Miller to Lord Grenville, May 6, 1793, PRO:FO 5/2, Consular Correspondence; John Ewing to James Blank, Apr. 20, 1793, PRO:FO 5/3, Domestic Letters.

Most of the work in fitting out a corsair involved the enhancement of the ship's armament. When the French converted a schooner a few months later in Baltimore, they had to procure the cannon and build the gun carriages with the attendant iron work. In addition, a schooner might have "a small gunnel of six inches above the deck and open railing of about two feet and a half from the deck." This flimsy railing could not bear the tackle of a gun carriage, so the railing had to be "planked up and closed with inch-plank, and port-holes cut therein." Finally, "ring bolts and other iron-work for [the gun] carriages" had to be installed. Further, merchantmen with their small crews did not use sweeps, but corsairs did. Thus "a considerable number of sweeps . . . for the purpose of rowing the schooner" had to be purchased and "iron cranes for the sweeps" had to be installed. While this work progressed, gun powder, cannon balls, bullets, and "144 canisters which were filled with pieces of old iron" had to be purchased.[29]

As the work on reconfiguring the *Citoyen Genet* moved forward, the owners went about finding a crew of forty or fifty men. They quickly hired Peter Johannene, a Frenchman, and he immediately received a commission. The port of Charleston, however, did not have enough Frenchmen to man four privateers. Therefore, Captain Johannene had to hire a number of Americans to fill out his crew. The French opened recruiting offices on the waterfront flying the French flag, and American sailors lined up to join the war against British commerce. Among them were Gideon Henfield, an experienced captain from Salem, Massachusetts, and John Singleterry from South Carolina. At least one American, Capt. Jacob Whittemore from Boston, joined *L'Embuscade* as a lieutenant. Rumors abounded that British merchants were offering rewards to any pilot who would run the French frigate aground, so Bompard hired Whittemore for his general knowledge of American waters. The British Consul protested these recruitment activities, and Governor Moultrie ordered the French flag struck from the recruiting office. Nevertheless, the process of crewing and fitting out the corsairs continued.[30]

The *Citoyen Genet* was ready to sail on April 18 and departed that same day in search of British ships. Her sailing must have been a relief to Bompard,

---

29. Depositions of Warren Nicoll, Benjamin Baker, John McClarity, Benjamin King, and Michael Ballard, Sept. 15, Oct. 21, 1793, *Counter Case of Great Britain*, 550–52.

30. *National Gazette,* May 8, 1793; *Federal Gazette,* Apr. 24, 1793; Stephen Drayton to Michel Mangourit, June 9, 1783, Mangourit Papers, MB; George Miller to Lord Grenville, May 6, 1793, PRO:FO 5/2, Consular Correspondence.

who had kept *L'Embuscade* in Charleston. His patrol outside the bar was unsuccessful after the first day or two because news of the war and of *L'Embuscade*'s presence spread fast. The "British Merchants of Charleston" actually hired a large pilot boat to carry the news up the coast. Bompard left the day before the *Citoyen Genet* sailed with the sure knowledge that the new threat of the corsairs would keep the British merchantmen in Charleston bottled up. A few days after the *Citoyen Genet* sailed, the *Sans Culottes* followed. As the two corsairs independently sailed north, they captured at least twelve vessels and sent them into American ports for condemnation. The British consul in Norfolk soon reported that "British trade is much annoy'd here by Small Privateers," and he instructed the "many British vessels now in the Road" at Norfolk to delay their departure "in hopes that Some British Frigates will arrive soon."[31]

One of the most significant of the corsairs' prizes was the *William,* which the *Citoyen Genet* took on May 3. The *William,* forty-two days out of Bremen and bound for Maryland, was approaching the capes of Delaware under a fair wind when her crew spotted a schooner standing out from the capes. The *William*'s master mistook the strange sail for a revenue cutter and did not alter course. At about the same time, the wind abated, and the approaching schooner, which was the *Citoyen Genet,* put out sweeps and bore down upon the hapless British ship. The prospect of a rich prize lent enthusiasm to the crew as they bent to their long oars. Perhaps the *William*'s master became uneasy, but he was momentarily reassured when he saw that the "revenue cutter" was flying "American Colours." As the corsair drew near, her crew ran up the "French Colours," fired a gun, and hailed the hapless British ship. In a shouted conversation between the two vessels, Captain Johannene verified that the *William* was British and then took her. He immediately dispatched his new capture into Philadelphia under a prize crew commanded by Gideon Henfield and including John Singleterry.[32]

The *William* was a moderately rich prize. Appraisers valued the hull and equipment at thirty-two hundred dollars. The cargo was "Eighty Nine pieces of Oznaburg & Ticklinburg," which were huge bolts of coarse linen,

---

31. John Hamilton to Lord Grenville, May 1793, and John Hamilton to Lord Grenville, May 12, 1793, both in PRO:FO 5/2, Consular Correspondence; Anonymous Advice, n.d., Mangourit Papers, MB.

32. My account of the taking of the *William* is drawn from the statements of her master and her mate. Affidavit of James Legget, June 7, 1793, and Affidavit of John Whiteside, June 7, 1793, *Findlay v. The William,* Case Files, National Archives Regional Archive, Philadelphia.

valued at $1,460. The French consul in Philadelphia quickly ruled that she was a lawful prize and issued a decree of condemnation so that the vessel could be sold.[33]

Diplomatic Protests and Remedies

As the initial fruits of France's maritime campaign came sailing into American ports, the crisis quickly progressed from general theoretical questions about the nature of neutrality to very specific and practical issues directly related to France's ability to stage a maritime campaign from American ports. To complicate matters further, passions ran high in favor of France. Edward Livingston wrote his brother, the governor of New York, "The unexpected arrival of the Ambuscade seems to have at once revived the dormant spirit of seventy-six." Many years later, Chief Justice John Marshall recalled that the outbreak of war

> restored full vivacity to a flame, which a peace of ten years had not been able to extinguish. A great majority of the American people deemed it criminal to remain unconcerned spectators of a conflict between their ancient enemy and republican France.

Newspapers thundered, "The cause of France is the cause of man, and neutrality is desertion."[34]

Notwithstanding the public's support for France, President Washington and Secretary Hamilton steadfastly remained committed to a strict neutrality. Even if they had wanted to adopt a policy of benign neglect toward the French depredations, the British ambassador forcefully insisted that the government grapple with the legality of France's onslaught. In a series of memorials, Hammond vigorously protested the illegality of French activities within American territorial waters, the illegality of fitting out corsairs in American ports, the illegality of the Consular Courts, and the illegality of Americans serving on corsairs. He was not stating hypothetical questions. Hammond's protests could not be ignored. His memorials were based on

---

33. Appraisal, June 11, 1793, *Findlay v. The William,* Case Files, National Archives Regional Archive, Philadelphia; Osnaburg and Ticklinburgh, *Oxford English Dictionary,* compact ed., 1971, s.v. "osnaburg" and "ticklenburgs"; Phineas Bond to Lord Grenville, June 8, 1793, PRO:FO 5/2, Consular Correspondence.

34. Edward Livingston to Robert Livingston, May 15, 1793, Robert Livingston Papers, NHi; John Marshall, *The Life of George Washington,* rev. 2nd ed. (Philadelphia: J. Crissy, 1832), 8; *National Gazette,* May 15, 1793; *Boston Gazette,* Apr. 29, 1793 ("The Cause of France Is the Cause of Universal Liberty").

actual incidents involving significant amounts of property, and everyone knew that the incidents were just the beginning of the French campaign.

The day after the *Grange* sailed into Philadelphia, Hammond protested that *L'Embuscade* had taken the vessel within United States territory and that the capture thus violated international law. He "respectfully" requested the executive branch of the federal government to procure her "immediate restoration," and Jefferson quickly referred the matter to Attorney General Randolph. The *Grange* presented an interesting question of international law. Although the ship clearly was within Delaware Bay when taken, the French argued that the capture was not in United States territory. The rule of thumb under international law was that a country's territory extended only as far as a cannon could reach, which was generally taken to be one sea league or three nautical miles. The bay has a very broad mouth, and the prize was anchored within the bay but twelve miles from land. Because Delaware Bay has such a broad mouth, the French argued that the capture was not in American territorial waters. The French position was quickly published in the press, but Attorney General Randolph decided the matter to the contrary in a long and carefully written opinion. Following a cabinet meeting, Jefferson directed Genet to have the *Grange* restored, and Genet immediately complied. This loss of yet a third prize at Genet's request must have rankled Bompard and his crew.[35]

Although the government managed to resolve the dispute over the *Grange* fairly easily, other incidents proved to be virtually intractable. In particular, the corsair *Citoyen Genet* and her capture of the *William* resulted in an omnibus challenge to French privateering. The *William*'s arrival in Philadelphia with Gideon Henfield as prize master caused a diplomatic stir. She was taken on May 3, and just five days later the British minister, George Hammond, filed two formal protests with the executive branch. When word of the *Citoyen Genet*'s activities reached England, the London commercial establishment viewed "the fitting out of the privateer Genet" as evidence that the United States would be "joining the French." Hammond protested that the *Citoyon Genet*'s operations were breaches of neutrality and

35. Memorial from George Hammond, May 2, 1793, and Thomas Jefferson to Edmund Randolph, May 2, 1793, *Papers of Thomas Jefferson*, 25:637–40, 641; Jean Ternant to Minister of Foreign Affairs, May 1, 1793, "Correspondence of the French Ministers," 196–97; Rapport du Consul général [de La Forest], c. May 9, 1793, *Papers of Thomas Jefferson*, 25:703–5; Edmund Randolph's Opinion on the Grange, May 14, 1793, *Papers of Thomas Jefferson*, 26:31–36; Carroll and Ashworth, *George Washington*, 66–67; Thomas Jefferson on Jean Baptiste Tenant, May 15, 1793, *Papers of Thomas Jefferson*, 26:42–44; *National Gazette*, May 4, 1793 (synopsis of French argument).

that the creation of French Consular Courts were not authorized by international law.[36]

Citizen Genet had landed in Charleston a month earlier but was not yet in Philadelphia. Instead of accompanying *L'Embuscade* on Bompard's rampage up the coast, he elected to travel north by land. His reasons are unknown. Perhaps he had suffered unduly from seasickness on his voyage across the North Atlantic. He later stated that he went by land because he was "tired of the sea." Before setting out on his overland journey, Genet told the French Foreign Ministry that he was going by land in order to stop at Mount Vernon to visit President Washington. Although Jean-Baptiste de Ternant, France's lame duck minister, was in Philadelphia when Hammond lodged his memorials with Jefferson, the cabinet decided to reply to Hammond's memorials without formally providing a copy of the complaints to Ternant. In any event, Ternant was strongly inclined to take no positions until Genet, "who was best informed of the opinions of our government," arrived.[37]

In a series of meetings held within a week of the *William*'s arrival, the cabinet worked out a policy regarding most of the principal issues raised by the French maritime campaign. These initial decisions generally favored British interests over the French, and they evidently were unanimous. A few weeks earlier Jefferson had told James Madison, "I fear that a fair neutrality will prove a disagreeable pill to our friends, tho' necessary to keep us out of the calamities of a war." These initial decisions were truly bitter pills, and there is no evidence that Jefferson opposed them. He understood the need for neutrality.[38]

In letters to the British and French ministers, which had been approved by the president, Jefferson condemned the Consular Courts in the strongest possible language. They were not warranted under either international law or United States domestic law, and thus a decree of condemnation from one of the Consular Courts "is a mere nullity, can be respected in no Court,

---

36. Memorial from George Hammond, May 8, 1793, and second memorial, *Papers of Thomas Jefferson*, 25:685, 686; Letter from London, *Columbian Gazetteer* (New York), Aug. 26, 1793.

37. Edmond Genet to Thomas Jefferson, July 4, 1797, in Minnigerode, *Genet*, 413–27 (app.); Edmond Genet to Minister of Foreign Affairs, Apr. 16, 1793, "Correspondence of the French Ministers," 213; Thomas Jefferson to Jean Baptiste Ternant, May 15, 1793, *Papers of Thomas Jefferson*, 26:42; Jean Baptiste Ternant to Minister of Foreign Affairs, May 10, 1793, "Correspondence of the French Ministers," 197–99.

38. Thomas Jefferson to James Madison, Apr. 28, 1793, *Papers of Thomas Jefferson*, 25:619.

make no part in the title to the vessel, nor give to the purchaser any . . . security." Jefferson bluntly told the British minister that assuming the Consular Courts actually were issuing decrees, their operations are "an act of disrespect towards the United States." More circumspectly, he told the French that the establishment of Consular Courts "could not be deemed an act of indifference," but the government was "disposed to view it, in this instance, as an error of judgement." A writer in Rhode Island quipped that if France could establish courts on American soil, the French may "next undertake to establish Primary Assemblies amongst us."[39]

Turning to the charge that Americans were serving in the French corsairs, Jefferson clearly stated that the government "condemns in the highest degree the conduct of any of its citizens, who may personally engage in committing hostilities at sea against any of the nations, parties to the present war." The government would "exert all means with which the laws and constitution have around them to discover such as offend herein and bring them to condign punishment."[40]

Jefferson continued by emphatically stating that the "practice of commissioning equipping and manning vessels, in our ports to cruise on any of the belligerent parties, is equally and entirely disapproved." Jefferson's reasoning on this important issue was that it is wrong for a neutral country "(where not constrained by treaties) to permit one party in the present war to do what cannot be permitted to the other." Because Article 22 of the Treaty of Amity and Commerce barred Great Britain from fitting out privateers, the United States should refuse to permit the French to do so. Jefferson believed that the treaty was simply silent as to French corsairs and therefore left "us free to refuse." As a matter of policy, a "refusal [was] necessary to preserve a fair and secure neutrality." Jefferson promised Hammond that the government would "take effectual measures to prevent" any more French corsairs from being fitted out in American ports.[41]

The cabinet, however, sharply disagreed about Hammond's request that prizes taken by the Charleston corsairs be restored to their original owners. In the president's absence, the cabinet split two to two, with Hamilton and

---

39. Thomas Jefferson to George Hammond, May 15, 1793, and Thomas Jefferson to Jean Baptiste Ternant, May 15, 1793, *Papers of Thomas Jefferson,* 26:38–40, 42–44; *United States Chronicle,* May 23, 1793.

40. Thomas Jefferson to George Hammond, May 15, 1793, *Papers of Thomas Jefferson,* 26:39.

41. Ibid.; Jefferson's Opinion on the Restoration of Prizes, May 16, 1793, *Papers of Thomas Jefferson,* 26:50–51.

Knox urging restitution and Jefferson and Randolph opposing. Jefferson believed that although the fitting out of the Charleston corsairs was unlawful, it was done without guidance or approval from the executive and could not realistically have been prevented. He thus thought an apology to Great Britain would be enough. The president agreed with Jefferson and Randolph.[42]

Meanwhile, Genet was traveling northward in a triumphal and deceptively inspiring procession. His reception in Camden, South Carolina, is representative. The Camden Troop of Horse met him outside of town and escorted him into town to a residence traditionally reserved for honored guests. A local official delivered a formal address proclaiming, "Your nation has a just claim for our gratitude, for the services rendered us in the hour of our distress, whilst we contended against tyranny and oppression." Afterward, there was "a sumptuous dinner" at which the "Marseillaise and songs of both nations were sung standing." Then there were the usual toasts, beginning with "The Republic of France—May her success induce mankind to be free." As Genet continued his northward journey, he encountered the same enthusiastic reception in town after town. Everything confirmed his preconceived understanding that the United States would enthusiastically support France in its republican struggle against European royalty. Although Genet learned of the Proclamation of Neutrality while journeying northward, he initially dismissed it as a "fabrication" and later during the journey decided that it "had no further object than to decide that the United States would not take any active part in the war."[43]

Genet's reception in Philadelphia was a fitting culmination of his triumphant procession from Charleston. The day after he arrived, a committee of thirty prominent Philadelphians walking three abreast led "a vast concourse" of over one thousand people to Genet's lodgings and presented a formal address to him that was published the next day. The committee assured Genet that the Franco-American alliance was cemented with blood and founded on a "similarity of sentiment and principle." This strong union

---

42. Jefferson's Opinion on the Restoration of Prizes, May 16, 1793, *Papers of Thomas Jefferson,* 26:50–51; Hamilton's Opinion, May 15, 1793, *Papers of Alexander Hamilton,* 14:451–60. See Dumas Malone, *Jefferson and the Ordeal of Liberty* (Boston: Little, Brown, 1962), 100.

43. Thomas Kirkland and Robert Kennedy, *Historic Camden* (Columbia, S.C.: State Company, 1905), 315–18; *Charleston (S.C.) City Gazette,* May 4, 1793; Ammon, *Genet Mission,* 52–53; Edmond Genet, "Report on the Arming of Privateers," n.d., Edmond Genet Papers, DLC.

between the two countries would "resist the most violent efforts of those whose interest it might be to disturb it." Later, the "streets . . . resounded with congratulations and applause."[44]

A series of parties throughout the capital followed, and on the first Saturday night after Genet's arrival, a grand reception and dinner took place at Oellers Hotel. Over a hundred people attended at four dollars a plate. The main table "was decorated with the tree and cap of liberty, and the French and American flags." Bompard and some of his crew were there, and Genet sang a song "suited to the *navy* of France." There were at least fifteen toasts, beginning with "Liberty and equality," continuing with the "Union and perpetual fraternity between the free people of France and of the United States," and ending with "May all heads be soon under one cap, that of liberty." After this last toast, someone grabbed the cap of liberty and put it on Genet's head. As the saying goes, wine flowed and mirth abounded.[45]

At the end of the dinner, the tree and cap of liberty were presented to a delegation from *L'Embuscade* led by Bompard, who "promised to defend them till death." Then the guests formed a procession to escort Genet back to his lodgings. The procession strolled through the streets of Philadelphia "amidst the acclamations of a large concourse of citizens, whose repeated huzzas were answered by shouts of *God save the United States*."[46]

Genet's official reception contrasted sharply with his popular reception. The same week he arrived in Philadelphia, Jefferson informed the French Embassy of the administration's determination that the French Consular Courts, and the fitting out of corsairs, and the recruitment of Americans were unlawful. On the afternoon of the extravaganza at Oellers, Genet presented his credentials to President Washington. The meeting was formal; indeed, months later Genet complained that his reception was "cold."[47]

Jefferson undoubtedly reassured Genet that Washington's natural style was stiff and formal, but Genet could not ignore the substance of the administration's emerging neutrality policy. The following week, Genet formally requested the acceleration and repayment of the United States' debt to

---

44. Ammon, *Genet Mission,* 54–56; Thomas Jefferson to James Madison, May 19, 1793, *Papers of Thomas Jefferson,* 26:61; *Federal Gazette,* May 18, 21, 1793.

45. Ammon, *Genet Mission,* 57–58; *Federal Gazette,* May 22, 1793; *National Gazette,* May 25, 1793.

46. *Federal Gazette,* May 22, 1793; *National Gazette,* May 25, 1793.

47. Ammon, *Genet Mission,* 59 (quoting Genet); Carroll and Ashworth, *George Washington,* 73–75.

France, and after extensive deliberations within the administration, Jefferson denied the request.[48]

Although some modern historians have thought that Genet vigorously challenged the Washington administration's neutrality policy from the outset, Genet's initial communications were polite and even tentative. After informal discussions with Jefferson and with Jefferson's encouragement, Genet responded to the government's initial position on the British minister's complaints. Regarding the Consular Courts, he indicated that their decrees were related to France's treaty rights under Article 17 to bring prizes into American ports. If Consul Mangourit in Charleston acted improperly, Genet promised to "take care, sir, that this error be avoided for the future." Genet went on to explain that Governor Moultrie had tacitly assented to fitting out corsairs. Nor should there be any problem with enlisting American citizens in the corsairs' crews. When men such as Gideon Henfield enlisted, the president's neutrality proclamation had not been published. They "knew only the treaties and the laws of the United States, no article of which imposes on them the painful injunctions of abandoning us [France] in the midst of the dangers which surround us." In any event, by enlisting with French corsairs, Americans "renounced the immediate protection of their country" and became French citizens. Although Genet indicated to Jefferson that he would acquiesce in the president's final decisions on these issues, he assumed that the president's final decision would favor France. Finally, Genet accepted Attorney General Randolph's "learned conclusions" regarding the taking of the *Grange*. Although the prize had "considerable value," he agreed to return her to the British "to convince the American Government of our deference and of our friendship."[49]

The government's relations with Genet quickly deteriorated. When Genet learned that two Americans actually had been arrested for serving on a French corsair, he became, to use his word, "indignant." He dashed off a quick, emotionally charged note. Americans serving on French corsairs were "defending ... the common and glorious cause of liberty." Genet could

---

48. Edmond Genet to Thomas Jefferson, May 22, 1793, and Thomas Jefferson to Edmond Genet, June 11, 1793, *Papers of Thomas Jefferson,* 26:82–87, 252; see editorial note, *Papers of Thomas Jefferson,* 26:174–76.

49. Edmond Genet to Thomas Jefferson, May 27, 1793, *Papers of Thomas Jefferson,* 26:124–27. Memorandum of Conversations with Edmond Charles Genet, July 26, 1793, *Papers of Thomas Jefferson,* 26:571–73 (Jefferson's recollection of earlier conversations).

not believe that this could be a crime—a "crime which my mind cannot conceive, and which my pen almost refuses to state."[50]

Perhaps Genet believed that President Washington would shift the government's policy to a course more favorable to France, but that was not to be. On June 5, Jefferson formally replied to Genet's arguments. He assured Genet that Washington "had . . . taken the case into further consideration, and after mature consultation and deliberation" decided that fitting out French corsairs in American ports was indeed contrary to American neutrality. As a remedy for the breach of neutrality, the United States insisted that all corsairs that had been unlawfully fitted out "should depart from the ports of the United States."[51]

By this time, Genet probably had some informal intimations that his request for the repayment of the debt would be rejected. This likely rejection coupled with the reiteration of the administration's position on the corsairs were major blows to the French cause. The accelerated repayment of the debt and the maritime campaign were key parts of his mission. Genet was distressed, and he began his reply by frankly stating that he had read Jefferson's letter "with pain." Without elaborating, he replied that the existing treaties gave France a right to fit out and man corsairs in American ports. Genet knew that most Americans wished to support France, and he could not understand why President Washington did not. These apparent inconsistencies led Genet to make the startling argument that the president was violating the Constitution. "As long as the States, assembled in Congress, shall not have determined that [the treaty obligations] should not be performed," he wrote, "no one has a right to shackle our operations, and to annul their effect." The idea of a foreign diplomat instructing a government on the proper operation of the government's own internal laws is unusual and officious.[52]

Genet's final words were particularly disturbing. In France, the Girondins were committed to an extreme ideal of popular sovereignty. Unlike Congress and the president, the National Convention was elected on the basis of universal manhood suffrage. The Girondins were somewhat inclined to submit truly important issues like the execution of Louis XVI to

50. Genet, "Report on the Arming of Privateers"; Edmond Genet to Thomas Jefferson, June 1, 1793, *Papers of Thomas Jefferson,* 26:158.

51. Thomas Jefferson to Edmond Genet, June 5, 1793, *Papers of Thomas Jefferson,* 26:195–96. For the drafting history of this letter, see 196n.

52. Edmond Genet to Thomas Jefferson, June 8, 1793, *Papers of Thomas Jefferson,* 26:231–33.

a direct appeal to the people. Genet could not understand why President Washington seemed to be acting contrary to the obvious wishes of the American people. As a supplement to his constitutional argument, he invoked "the people of America." The treaties between France and the United States were public engagements between "two peoples," he declared, and a presidential decision to hinder rather than assist France was "certainly not the intention of the people of America." After instructing the Washington administration on its proper role as a representative of the people, Genet angrily concluded by charging that the federal government's conduct amounted to "the cowardly abandonment of their friends in the moment when danger menaces them."[53]

When the Washington administration persisted in steering a "cowardly" course contrary to the will of the people, Genet wrote, if anything, a more intemperate protest toward the end of June. He began with the brusque sentence "Discussions are short, when matters are taken upon their true principles." Rather than "lower ourselves to the level of ancient politics by diplomatic subtleties," he wished for a "frank . . . plain and sincere" relationship. "It is incontestible," he insisted, "that the treaty of commerce (art. XXII), expressly authorizes our arming in the ports of the United States." Instead of frankly recognizing France's incontestable right, the administration resorted to "extremely ingenious [arguments] to justify or excuse infractions committed on positive treaties."[54]

By this time, Genet was developing a personal dislike for Washington. In a draft despatch to the Foreign Ministry in Paris, he disdainfully called him the "old Nestor" and then scratched out this insult. Instead, he reported that "old Washington, who is very different from the man whose name is engraved in history, does not forgive me my successes." In a letter to Jefferson, he attacked the Proclamation of Neutrality as nothing more than "the private or public opinion of the President." Again Genet attempted to instruct the government on internal American law. He pressed the constitutional argument that Congress, not the president, was the proper branch of government to determine American policy toward France. Again he insisted, "It is not thus that the American People wish we should be treated." The next month he bitterly complained to Paris that "seeing myself upheld

---

53. Ibid.
54. Edmond Genet to Thomas Jefferson, June 22, 1793, *Papers of Thomas Jefferson*, 26:339–41. For an able elaboration of France's right under the treaty to fit out corsairs, see "Salem," *Salem Gazette*, Aug. 13, 1793.

by the American people I thought that a government sprung from it would show itself worthy of its trust by obeying its supreme voice."[55]

Within the cabinet, Hamilton and Knox were appalled and yet undoubtedly delighted by Genet's intemperance. They wrote President Washington that Genet's latest letter was "the most offensive paper, perhaps, that ever was offered by a foreign Minister to a friendly power." Jefferson was simply appalled. He confided to James Monroe, "I am doing everything in my power to moderate the impetuosity of [Genet's] movements." Genet's frequent references to the wishes of the "American People" were particularly worrisome. Jefferson was trying his best "to destroy the dangerous opinion, which has been excited in him, that the people of the U.S. will disavow the acts of their government, and that he has an appeal from the Executive to Congress and from both to the people." Within a month, however, Jefferson concluded that his efforts to moderate Genet's impetuosity were hopeless.[56]

55. Edmond Genet to Minister of Foreign Affairs, June 19, 1793, "French Minister's Correspondence," 216–18; Minnigerode, *Genet,* 203 (translation); Edmond Genet to Thomas Jefferson, June 22, 1793, *Papers of Thomas Jefferson,* 26:339–41; Edmond Genet to Minister of Foreign Affairs, July 30, 1793, "Correspondence of the French Ministers," 228–31; Minnigerode, *Genet,* 272 (translation).

56. Reasons for the Opinion of the Secretary of the Treasury and the Secretary at War Respecting the Brigantine Little Sarah, July 8, 1793, *Papers of Alexander Hamilton,* 15:75; Thomas Jefferson to James Monroe, June 28, 1793, *Papers of Thomas Jefferson,* 26:393.

CHAPTER 5

Presidential Power over Foreign Affairs

> The executive Power shall be vested in a President.
> *U.S. Const., art. 2, sec. 1*
>
> The Executive . . . may establish an antecedent state of things.
> *Alexander Hamilton*

While Genet was attacking the Proclamation of Neutrality as a cowardly and even unconstitutional abandonment of France, similar charges appeared in the press. "An Old Soldier" went so far as to suggest that George Washington had adopted a *"royal demeanor,"* and Washington became furious. In a private conversation with Jefferson, the president "was evidently sore and warm" and told Jefferson that "he despised all their attacks on him personally" and on the government in general. Other attacks soon followed. Jefferson confided to James Madison that Washington was "extremely affected by the attacks made and kept up on him in the public papers. I think he feels those things more than any person I ever yet met."[1]

The most virulent attacks were a series of open letters to the "President of the United States" written under the pseudonym Veritas. We do not know Veritas's identity. Washington was already "sore and warm" over the public attacks on him and his administration, and Jefferson speculated that Veritas was one of Hamilton's minions, playing on the president's anger and turning him against the French. Genet foolishly believed that Jefferson wrote the essays.[2]

The first Veritas letter charged that the Proclamation of Neutrality "has the appearance of double dealing [and] savours of monarchical mystery and court intrigue." In subsequent letters, Veritas insisted that "court satellites may have deceived" the president. These satellites, which all knowledgeable

---

1. Notes on a Conversation with George Washington, May 23, 1793, *Papers of Thomas Jefferson,* 26:102 (discussing "An Old Soldier," *National Gazette,* May 22, 1793). Thomas Jefferson to James Madison, June 9, 1793, *Papers of Thomas Jefferson,* 26:241; "To the President of the United States," *National Gazette,* May 15, 1793; "An American," *National Gazette,* June 12, 1793; "It is at all times the privilege," *National Gazette,* Aug. 7, 1793 (reprinted from a New York newspaper).

2. "Veritas," *National Gazette,* June 1, 5, 8, 12, 1793; Ammon, *Genet Mission,* 78.

readers would have understood as a reference to Alexander Hamilton, were "interested and designing men." Veritas also repeated Genet's constitutional argument and asked the president "whether you consider yourself vested with legal powers to annul solemn treaties by proclamation." He urged that Congress "be speedily convened [to] let all branches of the government unite their councils and their efforts for the promotion of the public good."[3]

Essayists quickly leapt to the president's defense. "A Friend of Peace" dashed off a long, meandering, and unorganized defense. "Verior Hac Veritate" more pithily condemned Veritas as "mean, weak, malicious, and false, in fact." A few weeks later, Hamilton himself entered the lists with a series of seven essays. He probably thought that he could do a better job defending the president's policy of neutrality, and he certainly resented the suggestion that he was a "court satellite." In addition, he certainly wanted to put before the public his complete and detailed analysis of the issue. And finally, a vigorous defense of the Proclamation of Neutrality would score points with the president. Although he wrote under the pseudonym Pacificus, which means "peacemaker," his authorship was widely known and even alluded to in newspapers.[4]

All but one of the Pacificus essays addressed the legal effect of the French treaties and the prudence of the president's policies and therefore are of little or no lasting significance today. In contrast, the wisdom of his Pacificus No. 1 is as valuable two centuries later as it was the day it was written. In diplomatic correspondence, the French minister was challenging the president's constitutional authority to issue the Proclamation of Neutrality, and newspapers were trumpeting the same charge of unconstitutionality. In his first essay, Hamilton carefully explained the basis for the president's constitutional authority.[5]

Pacificus No. 1 specifically addressed the objection by Veritas and others that the Proclamation of Neutrality was made without lawful authority. Hamilton explained that the proclamation was made simply to announce to the countries at war that the United States "is in the condition of a Nation

---

3. *National Gazette,* June 1, 5, 8, 12, 1793.

4. "A Friend of Peace," *Federal Gazette,* June 11, 1793; Pacificus Nos. 1, 2, 3, 4, 5, 6, and 7, June 29–July 27, 1793, *Papers of Alexander Hamilton,* 15:33–43, 55–63, 65–69, 82–86, 90–95, 100–106, 130–35; "A Democrat," *National Gazette,* Aug. 14, 1793; "Verior Hac Veritate," *Federal Gazette,* June 15, 1793; "A Freeman," *Federal Gazette,* July 2, 1793; *New York Journal,* July 31, 1793 ("Pacificus H_m_l_t_n").

5. Pacificus No. 1; Daniel Lang, *Foreign Policy in the Early Republic* (Baton Rouge: Louisiana State University Press, 1985), 99–109 (discussing Hamilton's non-constitutional arguments).

at Peace with the belligerent parties, and under no obligations of Treaty, to become an *associate in the war* with either of them." At the same time, the proclamation informed American citizens of the United States' status as a neutral country and warned them not to violate the nation's duties of neutrality. "This, and no more," wrote Hamilton, "is conceived to be the true import of a Proclamation of Neutrality."[6]

Hamilton agreed that Article 11 of the Treaty of Alliance required the United States to go to war under certain circumstances, but he believed that as a matter of what today we call "international law," the war in Europe did not trigger the treaty's guarantee clause. The proclamation, in other words, "is virtually a manifestation of the sense of the Government that the U States are, *under the circumstances of the case, not bound* to execute the clause of Guarantee." He presented his argument in more detail in later essays. In Pacificus No. 2, for example, he noted that by the treaty's express terms, the Franco-American alliance was "defensive" but that France's hostilities with Great Britain were offensive because they were commenced by France's declaration of war. Thus the guarantee was not applicable because the treaty's "stipulated assistance is to be given to the ally, when engaged in a *defensive* not when engaged in an *offensive* war." Other sophisticated observers, such as John Adams and William Vans Murray, came up with the same defensive/offensive dichotomy.[7]

Hamilton's analysis of the president's constitutional authority is methodical and comprehensive. He began by implicitly denying that the states could issue proclamations of neutrality. Under the Constitution, the states lack authority over foreign affairs. Instead, "the affairs of this country with foreign nations is confided to the Government of the U States." Thus the inquiry must be which branch of the federal government is the "proper one to make a declaration of Neutrality." Hamilton obviously thought the executive was the proper branch, and he initially supported this proposition by a logical process of elimination.[8]

Hamilton argued that neither the legislative nor the judicial branch was empowered to make a declaration of neutrality and that the power therefore

---

6. Pacificus No. 1, 15:34.
7. Ibid. 15:36; Pacificus Nos. 2 and 3 (discussing Guarantee Clause), *Papers of Alexander Hamilton,* 15:55–63, 65–69; John Adams to Tench Coxe, Apr. 25, 1793; William Vans Murray to Tench Coxe, Apr. 29, 1793; and William Vans Murray to Tench Coxe, May 2, 1793, all in Tench Coxe Papers, PHi. See also "A Friend of Peace," *Federal Gazette,* June 11, 1793.
8. Pacificus No. 1, 15:36–37.

must as a matter of logic reside in the executive. He noted the obvious fact that the judicial power is limited to the adjudication of "litigated cases" and plainly did not extend to making a declaration of neutrality. As for the legislative department, Congress "is not the *organ* of intercourse between the United States and foreign Nations." Nor does its power extend to "*making* [or] *interpreting* Treaties." It is thus "not naturally that Organ of Government which is to pronounce the existing condition of the Nation, with regard to foreign Powers."[9]

While Hamilton's restrictive reading of the judicial power is almost self-evidently correct, his cursory analysis of congressional power is not persuasive and amounts almost to a sleight of hand. The problem is that the Constitution explicitly vests Congress with extensive foreign affairs powers. Congress is to "provide for the common Defense and general Welfare of the United States . . . ; To regulate Commerce with foreign Nations . . . ; To define and punish . . . Offenses against the Law of Nations; . . . [and] To declare War." In addition, Congress has a general supplemental authority under the Constitution's "necessary and proper" clause. Just two years earlier, Hamilton himself had famously construed this clause as broadly as possible. These provisions obviously comprehend extensive foreign relations powers including the power to make a declaration of neutrality. Indeed, since the time of the Neutrality Crisis, Congress generally has been the branch that has declared the nation's neutrality.[10]

Fortunately for Hamilton, lack of congressional authority was not a sine qua non for his analysis. One of his key insights was that Congress and the president have concurrent powers over many aspects of foreign relations. Under the theory of concurrent powers, lack of congressional power was not necessary, but proof of presidential authority was essential.

Hamilton began his analysis of presidential authority by stating that as a general proposition a proclamation of neutrality falls naturally within the purview of the executive department. Anticipating a famous 1800 speech by John Marshall, Hamilton noted that the executive is "the *organ* of intercourse between the Nation and foreign Nations." Moreover, the executive must interpret and enforce laws, including treaties. Finally, the president as commander-in-chief "is charged with the command and application of Public Force." These conclusory assertions were presented to introduce, not

9. Ibid., 37–38.
10. U.S. Constitution, art. 1, sec. 8; Opinion on the Constitutionality of an Act to Establish a Bank, 1791, *Papers of Alexander Hamilton,* 8:97; see Casto, "Pacificus and Helvidius Reconsidered," 618–19.

complete, his analysis. In particular, Hamilton's and Marshall's understanding that the president is the "organ of intercourse" with foreign nations should not be stretched too far. There is a substantial difference between being the sole organ for simply communicating with other nations and being the sole organ for actually making public policy. Neither Hamilton nor Marshall believed that the president had unilateral authority to override congressional decisions regarding foreign policy, war, or neutrality. Indeed, Hamilton expressly stated that the Proclamation of Neutrality could be overridden by Congress.[11]

Like all good lawyers, Hamilton began his detailed analysis with the precise words of the document he was construing. Needless to say, he found confirmation of his natural reading of the president's authority in the words of the Constitution. The crucial language is the opening sentence of Article II: "The executive Power shall be vested in a President of the United States of America." Thus Hamilton rejected the notion that these words are not a significant grant of power. To the contrary, he read the article's opening sentence as the Constitution's fundamental grant of presidential power. Hamilton explained that a general grant was necessary due to "the difficulty of a complete and perfect specification of all the cases of Executive authority."[12]

As a matter of textual analysis, the most significant objection to Hamilton's emphasis upon the "executive Power" clause is the embarrassing fact that the second and third sections of Article II contain lists of specific presidential powers and duties. If the "executive Power" clause is a general grant of authority, these specific provisions seem redundant. A century and a half later, Justice Jackson noted that if the "executive Power" clause is a general grant of authority, "it is difficult to see why the forefathers bothered to add several specific items, including some trifling ones." Hamilton anticipated this kind of objection and pointed out that Article I contains a roughly parallel grant of legislative powers, which includes a list of specific powers. The express language of Article I, however, vests Congress only with the "Legislative powers *herein* granted." In contrast, the "executive Power" clause in Article II is a flat grant of executive power that is not expressly limited to the specific "powers *herein* granted."[13]

11. Pacificus No. 1, 15:38; John Marshall's speech of March 7, 1800, in *Papers of John Marshall,* ed. Charles T. Cullen and L. Tobias (Chapel Hill: University of North Carolina Press, 1984), 4:82; see Casto, "Pacificus and Helvidius Reconsidered," 619n21; Powell, "Founders and the President's Authority," 1511–28.

12. Pacificus No. 1, 15:38–39.

13. Ibid., 39; *The Steel Seizure Case,* 343 U.S. 579, 640–41 (1952) (Jackson, J., concurring).

In other words, the Constitution's more specific grants of executive power are indeed redundant, or as Hamilton more elegantly explained, the enumeration of specific executive powers and duties "ought rather therefore to be considered as intended by way of greater caution, to specify and regulate the principal articles implied in the definition of Executive Power; leaving the rest to flow from the general grant of that power." The general grant itself should be "interpreted in conformity to other parts of the Constitution and to the principles of free government." By "other parts of the Constitution," Hamilton had in mind "the *exceptions* and *qualifications* which are expressed in the instrument." He specifically mentioned the treaty power and war powers, which America's inherited western European tradition classified as royal or executive powers.[14]

In addition to this textual analysis, Hamilton pointed to a significant legislative precedent that supported his expansive view of the Constitution's general grant of executive power. In a three-sentence paragraph, he alluded to the 1789 debate in Congress over the president's constitutional authority to remove cabinet officers. Although the Constitution specifically tells us that the president appoints officers with the advice and consent of the Senate, it does not expressly tell us who may remove them. In the decision of 1789, some congressmen, most notably James Madison, argued that the "executive Power" clause gave the president the power to remove officers, and Congress passed legislation providing or recognizing a presidential removal power. Relying upon this legislative decision, Hamilton noted that his analysis of the clause is a "mode of construing the Constitution [that] has indeed been recognized by Congress in formal acts, upon full consideration and debate."[15]

Having established the president's general executive authority, Hamilton turned to the problem of Congress's war powers. At first glance, a declaration of neutrality seems the very opposite of a declaration of war and therefore does not implicate war powers. But Hamilton accepted that the legislative power to declare war "includes the right of judging whether the Nation be under obligations to make War *or not.*" This expansive reading of the legislative power to declare war obviously would embrace a declaration of neutrality. In addressing the idea of judging whether the nation should make war or not, Hamilton was not indulging in theoretical speculation. The guarantee clause in the Treaty of Alliance potentially obligated the

14. Pacificus No. 1, 15:39; *Steel Seizure Case,* 640–41.
15. Ibid., 40; Fisher, *Constitutional Conflicts,* 50–54, 54–58 (discussing the "decision of 1789"); Casto, "Pacificus and Helvidius Reconsidered," 620n25.

United States to go to war. Hamilton, however, was arguing that in the absence of a congressional resolution of the issue, the president was empowered to judge for himself the nation's obligations.[16]

Hamilton advanced another argument that can be supported by reference the words of the Constitution. He clearly believed that only Congress could declare war, and he understood this power to include authority to judge whether the nation should make war or not. The power to make war is explicit, but the power to decide not to go to war is implicit. Hamilton believed that the implicit congressional power to reject war did not exclude the president from preliminarily deciding that the nation was not obligated by treaty to go to war and consequently to take executive action to preserve peace:

> If the Legislature have a right to make war on the one hand—it is on the other the duty of the Executive to preserve Peace till war is declared; and in fulfilling that duty, it must necessarily possess a right of judging what is the nature of the obligations which the treaties of the Country impose on the Government; and when in pursuance of this right it has concluded that there is nothing in them inconsistent with a *state* of neutrality, it becomes both its province and its duty to enforce the laws incident to that state of the Nation.

In short, there was nothing wrong with the president taking unilateral steps to preserve the status quo of peace.[17]

Hamilton believed that the executive power clause, standing alone, gave the president authority to make this determination, but he bolstered his analysis by noting that the Constitution expressly obligates the president to take care that federal laws, including treaties, are "faithfully executed." As part of this obligation, the president inevitably must interpret the laws to determine their meaning. Even Jefferson agreed with this self-evident point. For example, the Treaty of Amity and Commerce gave France a number of privileges, and Hamilton reasoned that

> the necessary consequences of this is, that the Executive must judge what are the proper bounds of those privileges—what rights are given to other nations by our treaties with them—what rights the law of Nature and Nations gives and our treaties permit, in respect to those Nations with whom we have no treaties.

---

16. Pacificus No. 1, 15:40.
17. Ibid.

Hamilton envisioned a broad authority that extended to determining all "the reciprocal rights and obligations of the United States & of all & each of the powers at War." He understood that the Proclamation of Neutrality could be justified solely on the president's duty to see that the laws are "faithfully executed," and he briefly noted this alternative analysis at the end of Pacificus No. 1.[18]

Hamilton's decision to deemphasize his alternative argument exemplifies his superior talents as an attorney/adviser. Everyone who has advised clients, especially clients in government, on significant matters has encountered situations in which a proposed course of action may be justified by two different analyses. Of course, the belt-and-suspenders approach is the only way to go in this situation, but there is a tendency to avoid personal responsibility by placing equal emphasis on each analysis. The result may be unfocused, perhaps even confusing, advice that has an aura of indecision. Hamilton fought this tendency and clearly emphasized the executive power clause. Being a gifted attorney/adviser, he knew that his "client," the president and future presidents, would encounter future questions of authority in which the treaty interpretation approach would not be available. With an eye to unforeseeable future questions, Hamilton chose to emphasize the executive power clause because it was the more "broad and comprehensive ground."[19]

Finally, although unnecessary to his constitutional analysis, Hamilton insisted on reiterating his argument that the change of government in France had suspended the French treaties. When he had made the argument in cabinet, Washington, Jefferson, and Randolph handed him his head. Still smarting from his defeat, Hamilton could not resist parading his rejected idea before the public. It was "Once more unto the breach." Hamilton again insisted that the change of government suspended the treaties and that the president had the power to revive the treaties or not by acknowledging the new French government or not. But Harfleur was not to be carried. Hamilton's pet theory of suspension was a forlorn hope that had already been repulsed by the president and has never gained footing in the United States as a legitimate principle of international law.[20]

18. U.S. Constitution, art. 2, sec. 3; Jefferson's Memorandum, July 10, 1793, *Papers of Thomas Jefferson,* 26:465; Pacificus No. 1, 15:41–43; *Accord,* "A Friend of Peace," *Federal Gazette,* June 11, 1793.

19. Pacificus No. 1, 15:43.

20. Ibid., 41–42; American Law Institute Restatement (third) of the Foreign Relations Law of the United States, sec. 208 (1987); *Digest of International Law,* ed. Marjorie Whiteman (Washington, D.C.: GPO, 1963), 2:771–78; *Digest of International Law,* ed. Green Hackworth (Washington, D.C.: GPO, 1943), 5:512.

Helvidius Responds

As soon as Pacificus No. 1 appeared, Thomas Jefferson angrily attacked the essay in a letter to James Madison. Jefferson did not seriously object to the proclamation itself. He had agreed to it in cabinet and told Madison that the proper basis for it had been explained in an earlier essay, which Jefferson presumed was written by Attorney General Randolph. According to Randolph, when foreign nations engage in war, it is the duty of the United States "to pursue a peaceful line of conduct; unless some treaty [required otherwise]." Randolph then noted that the Treaty of Alliance, "as things stood at the time of" the proclamation, could not be construed as requiring the United States to go to war. Presumably he was referring to the fact that Britain had yet to attack any of the French possessions in the West Indies. Moreover, communications from the French government indicated that the United States was not "expected [by the French] to participate in the war." Jefferson did not object to this weak, "milk and water-view" of the proclamation, but he emphatically disagreed with some "heresies" embedded in Hamilton's elaborate essay.[21]

In the letter to Madison, Jefferson pointed to three specific "heresies." The first two related to the status of the Treaty of Alliance. Jefferson objected to the specific claim that "we are *not bound to execute the guarantee,*" and he opposed the more general claim that "until the new [French] government is acknowledged the treaties &c. are of course suspended." The third heresy was the idea that the executive was competent "to declare neutrality (that being understood to respect the future)." Jefferson did not believe that a president could unilaterally bind the country to a continuing course of neutrality that would extend into the "future." He thought that these battles had been fought and won in the cabinet, and he was incensed that Hamilton was trying to read his heresies into the president's proclamation. In a cabinet meeting five months later, Jefferson reiterated these same objections to Hamilton's position.[22]

Jefferson broadly hinted that Madison should refute Hamilton's arguments: "But is it not a miserable thing that the three heresies . . . should pass . . . unanswered?" When Madison did not take the hint, Jefferson made his

---

21. Thomas Jefferson to James Madison, June 29, 1793, *Papers of Thomas Jefferson,* 26:403–4; "When Foreign Nations Engage in War," *Dunlap's American Daily Advertiser,* Apr. 29, 1793.

22. Thomas Jefferson to James Madison, June 29, 1793, *Papers of Thomas Jefferson,* 26:401–4; Jefferson's Notes of Cabinet Meetings, Nov. 8, 18, 1793, *Papers of Thomas Jefferson,* 27:399–401.

wishes utterly clear. In a subsequent letter, he urged, "For god's sake, my dear Sir, take up your pen, select the most striking heresies, and cut him to pieces in the face of the public."[23]

Madison, who was at his rural estate of Montpelier, was reluctant to assume the task. He bemoaned that he was in "the hottest weather of the hottest year remembered," and he worried that he did not have access to an adequate library of international law materials. Moreover, he did not have a clear understanding of what compromises had been reached "behind the curtain" in the cabinet or how far the president was "actually committed" to all of Hamilton's ideas. Ever the practical politician, Madison was also worried that his lack of detailed insider knowledge might lead him to make "vulnerable assertions or suppositions which might give occasion to triumphant replies." Nevertheless, he could not refuse Jefferson's direct request.[24]

Even after Madison took pen in hand, his reluctance to enter the fray did not abate. He frankly confided to Jefferson, "I can truly say I find it the most grating [task] I ever experienced." Although Hamilton's essay was straightforward and easily understood, Madison decided to write a technical and complex reply. He believed that "none but intelligent readers will enter into such a controversy, and to their minds [my reply] ought principally be accommodated." He chose to publish his thoughts under the pseudonym Helvidius (a Roman senator who had vigorously challenged the aggrandizement of imperial power).[25]

After a preliminary ad hominem attack upon Pacificus, whom Madison knew to be Alexander Hamilton, Madison explained the specific objectives of the Helvidius essays. His purpose obviously was to address the three very specific heresies that had infuriated Jefferson. Madison restated the heresies by describing them as "the extraordinary doctrine that the powers of making war and treaties, are in their nature executive; and therefore comprehended in the [Constitution's] general grant of executive power, where not

---

23. Thomas Jefferson to James Madison, June 29, 1793, and Thomas Jefferson to James Madison, July 7, 1793, *Papers of Thomas Jefferson,* 26:401–4, 443–44.

24. James Madison to Thomas Jefferson, July 22, 1793; James Madison to Thomas Jefferson, July 30, 1793; and James Madison to Thomas Jefferson, Aug. 20, 1793, all in *Papers of James Madison,* 15:46–47, 48–49, 62. See Irving Brant, *James Madison: Father of the Constitution, 1787–1800* (New York: Bobbs-Merrill, 1950), 377–79.

25. James Madison to Thomas Jefferson, July 30, 1793, and James Madison to Thomas Jefferson, July 22, 1793, both in *Papers of James Madison,* 15:48–49, 46–47. For Helvidius Priscus, see Jakub Pigon, "Helvidius Priscus, Eprius Marcellus, and indicium senatus: Observations on Tacitus, 'Histories' 4.7–8," *Classical Quarterly* 42 (1992): 235.

specially and strictly excepted out of the grant." A refutation of the "extraordinary doctrine" that the president had unilateral constitutional authority to make treaties would address Jefferson's concerns that Hamilton sought to establish the president's right to effect a unilateral suspension or alteration of the French treaties. Similarly, refuting the claim of unilateral presidential authority to make war would address Jefferson's objection to the notion that the president was competent to make a declaration of neutrality that would preclude the nation from going to war. In the first four Helvidius essays, Madison addressed the general question of presidential power to make war and treaties, and in the final essay he turned to the guarantee clause. In other words, he did not write Helvidius as a general discourse upon the scope of the president's executive power. Rather, his goals were relatively narrow. Insofar as the Constitution was concerned, his sole purpose was to address the president's power to make war and to make treaties. He explicitly stated his narrow objective in Helvidius No. 1 and restated this narrow objective in each of the subsequent essays.[26]

The disconnect between Helvidius and Pacificus is self-evident. The two essayists never joined issue. Hamilton did not dispute Madison's assertion that the president lacks constitutional authority to make war. To the contrary, he stated and restated in Pacificus and on other occasions that only Congress is constitutionally empowered to "transfer the nation from a state of Peace to a state of War." Similarly, Hamilton never contended that the president had unilateral power to remove the guarantee clause from the Treaty of Alliance. Instead, he argued that under settled principles of international law, the United States is *"under the circumstances of the case, not bound"* by the guarantee clause. Hamilton's position was based upon a plausible interpretation of the treaty's legal import rather than unilateral presidential power to ignore or rewrite the guarantee clause. Similarly, neither Madison nor Jefferson ever disputed Hamilton's assertion in Pacificus that the executive power clause was a significant general grant of authority. In 1790, Jefferson and apparently Madison actually advised President Washington that the clause was a grant of significant authority. Indeed, there is general agreement that Jefferson's and Madison's words and actions on other occasions indicate that they agreed with Hamilton's broad theory of executive power.[27]

26. Helvidius Nos. 1, 2, 3, 4, and 5, *Papers of James Madison,* 15:66–67, 72–73, 80, 95, 106, 113; Casto, "Helvidius and Pacificus," 624–25nn35–36.

27. Pacificus No. 1, 15:40–42; Jefferson's Notes of Cabinet Meetings, Nov. 8, 18, 1793, *Papers of Thomas Jefferson,* 27:399–401; Alexander Hamilton to James McHenry, May 17, 1798, *Papers of Alexander Hamilton,* 21:461–62; "The Examination

One of the several self-evident points that Hamilton made in Pacificus was the simple fact that the phrase "executive Power" was not cut from whole cloth at the Constitutional Convention. The phrase had a well-known (albeit amorphous) meaning. In Europe, the executive power was wielded by kings, and in the field of foreign affairs, that power was broad. Madison urged that the western European understanding be rejected because it was not really focused on the concept of separation of powers and Europeans had "their eyes too much on monarchical governments, where all powers are confounded in the sovereignty of the prince." If Madison is making the prudential point that a republic should avoid the undiscriminating adoption of a concept inevitably imbued with monarchial values, his point is well taken. In contrast, Madison could not possibly have meant that the Americans who framed and ratified the Constitution understood the phrase "executive Power" as a concept unrelated to their common European heritage. Madison's rejection of the European understanding of the concept of executive power must be read in context. He was speaking specifically about executive power to make treaties and wage war. Given the Constitution's express provisions that deprive the president of unilateral authority over these two specific matters, Madison's analysis makes eminent sense. That does not mean, however, that Madison rejected the European understanding in respect of the administration of foreign affairs that does not involve declaring war or making treaties.[28]

Madison's exclusive concern with wars and treaties is particularly evident when he turned to Hamilton's discussion of Congress's 1789 decision on the removal of executive officers. Hamilton used the earlier congressional decision that the president had this constitutional authority as legislative precedent for Hamilton's construction of the executive power clause, and Madison could hardly disagree. In those earlier congressional debates,

---

No. 1," Dec. 18, 1801, *Papers of Alexander Hamilton,* 25:455–56; Thomas Jefferson, Opinion on the Powers of the Senate, Apr. 24, 1790, *Papers of Thomas Jefferson,* 16:378–80, discussed in Prakash and Ramsey, "Executive Power over Foreign Affairs," 305–7. For Madison and Jefferson, see Corwin, *President,* 17, 207–12; Henkin, *Foreign Affairs and the Constitution,* 338n13; Abraham Sofaer, *War, Foreign Affairs and Constitutional Power: The Origins* (Cambridge, Mass.: Ballinger, 1976), 231, 296, 303.

28. Helvidius No. 1, 15:68–72. For the founders' shared understanding of the concept of executive powers, see John C. Yoo, "The Continuation of Polities by Other Means: The Original Understanding of War Powers," *California Law Review* 84 (1996): 196–217; Prakash and Ramsey, "Executive Power over Foreign Affairs," 265–95.

Madison publicly argued that the clause gives the president a power to remove executive officers and that the power may not be limited by Congress. Thus he agreed in Helvidius that "the power of removal . . . appears to have been adjudged to the President." Given Hamilton's and Madison's agreement that the executive power clause vests the president with unenumerated powers, the notion occasionally advanced that "the Framers" did not intend the clause as a grant of substantive authority must be reassessed.[29]

Instead of renouncing the position he had espoused four years earlier, Madison chose the lawyerly tactic of distinguishing the congressional precedent. He tacitly admitted that the executive power clause was a significant grant of authority but denied that the clause gave the president unilateral power to make treaties and wars. Given the clauses in the Constitution that explicitly address war and treaties, Madison's distinction makes sense and is similar to his treatment of the European understanding of executive power. Yet his analysis of the removal precedent, which Hamilton had cited, indicates that he actually agreed with Hamilton's fundamental point that the executive power clause vests the president with significant constitutional authority.

Madison next turned to a functional analysis of the powers to declare war and make treaties. "A treaty," he wrote, "is not an execution of laws: it does not pre-suppose the existence of laws." Instead, a treaty is itself a law. To say, therefore, that "the power of making treaties which are confessedly laws, belongs naturally to the department which is to execute laws, is to say, that the executive department naturally includes a legislative power." Madison found confirmation of his natural analysis in the words of the Constitution. He noted that treaties are "emphatically declared by the Constitution to be 'the supreme law of the law'" and that the power of making treaties is expressly "vested jointly in the President and in the Senate." From these provisions, he concluded that the executive power clause could not reasonably be read to vest the president with unilateral treaty-making powers.[30]

Madison concluded the first Helvidius essay by quoting Hamilton's Federalist No. 75. As a preliminary matter, he explained that the Federalist was a valuable tool in construing the Constitution because it was "made at a time

---

29. Helvidius No. 1, 15:72; Madison's speeches of June 7 and 16, 1789, *Documentary History of the First Federal Congress of the United States of America: Debates in the House of Representatives,* ed. Charles Bangs Bickford, Kenneth R. Bowling, and Helen E. Veit (Baltimore: Johns Hopkins University Press, 1992), 11:845–47, 895–97, 921–23. For the erroneous notion about the founders, see Koh, *National Security Constitution,* 76, 264n35 (citing others).

30. Helvidius No. 1, 15:69–71.

when no application to *persons* or *measures* could bias: The opinion given was not transiently mentioned, but formally and critically elucidated: It related to a point in the constitution which must consequently have been viewed as of importance in the public mind." Although Madison relished quoting Hamilton against Hamilton, the passage from Federalist No. 75 did little more than establish that the power of making treaties was a hybrid combination of executive and legislative functions. Moreover, the passage was not pertinent to Hamilton's analysis because Hamilton did not write Pacificus No. 1 to establish a unilateral presidential power to alter the Treaty of Alliance. Hamilton consistently took the position that the treaty itself, when properly construed in accordance with legitimate principles of international law, did not obligate the United States to take action in support of France.[31]

Turning to war powers, Madison wrote a brilliant explanation of the constitutional decision to strip the power to declare war from the executive and vest it in the legislative. Although Europeans and the British viewed the power as executive, Madison insisted that it was really legislative, and he backed up his assertion with a wonderfully lucid explanation. A declaration of war is inherently legislative because the declaration "has the effect of *repealing* all the *laws* operating in a state of peace, so far as they are inconsistent with a state of war." The declaration also has the effect "of *enacting* as *a rule for the executive,* a *new code* adopted to the relation between the society and its foreign enemy." Although Madison did not elaborate, obvious examples from the 1790s are easy to imagine. In times of peace, giving aid and comfort to a foreign nation is permissible, but war would make the same conduct a treasonous violation of a criminal statute. Similarly, war would completely change the applicability of more mundane statutes. For example, in *Bas v. Tingy,* which the Supreme Court decided a few years later, a naval officer sought a salvage award for a ship that he had recaptured from French privateers. The applicable federal statutes, in effect, provided an award of one-eighth the value of the vessel and cargo when the country was at peace and one-half during war. Under this statute, the mere existence of war quadrupled the award.[32]

In addition to explaining the clear and direct legislative effect of a declaration of war, Madison pointed to important policy reasons for barring presidents from starting wars. He introduced his concern in Helvidius No. 1 by

---

31. Ibid., 72–73.

32. Ibid., 69; An Act for the Punishment of Certain Crimes against the United States, 1st Cong., 2nd sess., chap. 9, sec. 1, 1 Stat. 112: Act of March 2, 1799, sec. 7, 1 Stat. 716, applied in *Bas v. Tingy,* 4 U.S. (4 Dall.) 37 (1800).

noting, "Those who are to *conduct a war* cannot in the nature of things, be proper or safe judges, whether *a war ought* to be *commenced, continued,* or *concluded.*" He returned to this theme in a later essay when he warned that if war powers were placed in the executive department, the "trust and the temptation would be too great for any one man." But Madison did not limit himself to vague generalities.[33]

As in all good legal analyses, Madison elaborated upon his vague charges of temptations too great for ordinary people. The founders had a direct and intimate experience with war, and they knew its ugly subplots of personal aggrandizement. "War," he explained, "is in fact the true nurse of executive aggrandizement." War creates unusual concentrations of power that are subject to misuse. "In war a physical force is to be created . . . the public treasures are to be unlocked . . . the honors and emoluments of office are to be multiplied." And these unusual concentrations of power are funneled through the executive. The president directs the physical force and dispenses the public treasures. The honors and emoluments are enjoyed under the executive patronage. In addition to these inordinate powers, war gives the president an unusual opportunity to enhance his personal reputation. "It is in war," Madison concluded, "that laurels are to be gathered, and it is the executive brow they are to encircle."[34]

The passage of two centuries bears out Madison's insight that presidential laurels are to be garnered in war. Many presidents have striven for greatness, but there is a consensus that only three attained it. Each of these three were leaders in the three most important wars in American history. Lincoln brought the nation through the Civil War, and Roosevelt guided us to virtual victory in World War II. The third war was the Revolutionary War, and the third great president was George Washington.

The presence of George Washington at the head of government in 1793 somewhat embarrassed Madison's analysis. Madison knew that President Washington was utterly trustworthy. He was no dictator or would-be king. Like Cincinnatus, he surrendered his powerful wartime office and returned to his farm at the conclusion of the Revolutionary War. Madison believed that "the trust and temptation" of comprehensive war powers "would be too great for any one man," and Washington was the exception that made the rule. With implicit reference to Washington, Madison excepted "such [men]

---

33. Helvidius No. 1, 15:71; Helvidius No. 4, 15:108.

34. Helvidius No. 4, 15:108. For an admirably lucid elaboration of this idea, see William Michael Treanor, "Fame, the Founding, and the Power to Declare War," *Cornell Law Review* 82 (1997): 719–21.

as nature may offer as the prodigy of many centuries." Instead, he was concerned with unknown presidents in the future who "may be expected in the ordinary successions of magistracy."[35]

The solution to the problem of vesting too much power in one individual exemplifies a general idea that Madison had presented during the process of ratifying the Constitution. In Federalist No. 51, with characteristic elegance and insight, he explained:

> If men were angels, no government would be necessary. If angels were to govern men, neither external nor internal controls or government would be necessary. In framing a government which is to be administered by men over men, the great difficulty lies in this: you must first enable the government to control the governed; and in the next place oblige it to control itself. A dependence on the people is, no doubt, the primary control on the government; but experience has taught mankind the necessity of auxiliary precautions.

In the case of war powers, there was an extraordinary need for "auxiliary precautions."[36]

Madison wrote that in monarchies the principal auxiliary precaution was "the personal interest of an hereditary monarch in the government." But in the case of a republic, the executive does not have the same ongoing, permanent personal interest in the government because the executive is "an *elective and temporary* magistrate." Thus there is "an increase of the dangerous temptation" of seeking personal glory through war because a temporary magistrate lacked a monarch's long-term personal stake in government. One of the Constitution's auxiliary precautions against this danger is to take the power to declare war from the executive and place it in the legislative.[37]

Madison's extended analysis of war powers is persuasive, but it in no way refuted Pacificus because Hamilton emphatically agreed that only Congress could declare war. Moreover, Madison introduced his analysis of the differences between an hereditary monarch and an elective and temporary magistrate with an extensive quotation from Federalist No. 75 in which Hamilton had presented precisely the same analysis to explain the decision to require the Senate's advice and consent in the treaty making process.[38]

---

35. Helvidius No. 4, 15:108.
36. Federalist No. 51, 349 (Madison), ed. J. Cooke, ed., 1961.
37. Helvidius No. 4, 15:109–10.
38. Ibid.

Concurrent Powers

Hamilton's analysis of the executive power clause was clear, elaborate, and persuasive, but Pacificus No. 1 makes a second, equally valuable contribution to our understanding of the constitutional relationship between the president and Congress. Hamilton saw that the potential scope of the executive power clause encompasses matters that might with equal plausibility be the subject of valid congressional action. The resulting conflict between potential presidential and potential congressional power might be resolved by defining the powers as mutually exclusive, but Hamilton saw a different solution. He believed that in respect of many matters, Congress and the president are equally empowered to act—that they have concurrent powers.[39]

Hamilton agreed that the Constitution's express grant to Congress of the power "to declare war" excluded an identical presidential power. He also understood that the express congressional power to declare war "includes the right of judging whether the Nation be under obligations to make war or not." He believed, however, that the president has a power, even a "duty ... to preserve Peace till war is declared." In other words, the president has a "right ... to determine the condition of the Nation, though it may consequently affect the proper or improper exercise of the Power of the Legislature to declare war." Hamilton viewed the proclamation as a proper exercise of the president's power "to preserve Peace till war is declared."[40]

In a flash of true brilliance, Hamilton explained the proper resolution of a conflict between the president and Congress on a matter over which each had concurrent authority. Hamilton clearly stated that the executive "cannot control the exercise of [legislative] power." Although the president could veto a declaration of war, the Proclamation of Neutrality did not legally preclude Congress from declaring war. "The Legislature," Hamilton wrote,

> is free to perform its own duties according to its own sense of them—though the Executive in the exercise of its constitutional powers, may establish an antecedent state of things which ought to weigh in the legislative decisions. From the division of the Executive Power there results, in reference to it, a *concurrent* authority, in the distributed cases.

Hamilton's idea of "an antecedent state of things" explains the real-life significance of countless presidential actions.[41]

---

39. Pacificus No. 1, 15:41–42.
40. Ibid., 40–42.
41. Ibid., 42. See chapter 10, this volume.

When Hamilton wrote of "an antecedent state of things," he presumably was thinking of the proclamation. If Congress were subsequently to consider supporting revolutionary France by declaring war upon Great Britain, the president's proclamation, with its implicit finding that the country was not under a treaty obligation to go to war, nevertheless "ought," in Hamilton's words, "to weigh in the legislative decision." Congress nevertheless would be "free to perform its own duties according to its own sense of them." The president's proclamation could not preclude or "control the exercise of that power."[42]

Hamilton's assumption that a congressional declaration of war would override a presidential proclamation of neutrality is obviously correct, but the issue has never been put to a formal test. As a practical matter, presidents and Congresses usually are able to settle their disagreements by negotiation. About a decade after the Neutrality Crisis, however, the federal courts decided two cases that clearly support Hamilton's belief in legislative supremacy. In *United States v. Smith,* a ne'er-do-well in-law of John Adams was prosecuted for violating the Neutrality Act passed by Congress in 1794. When the defendant claimed that President Jefferson had authorized him to violate the act, Justice Paterson responded:

> The President of the United States cannot control the statute, nor dispense with its execution, and still less can he authorize a person to do what the law forbids. . . . Will it be pretended that the President could rightfully grant a dispensation and license to any of our citizens to carry on a war against a nation with whom the United States are at peace?

In *Little v. Barreme,* a conscientious naval officer followed express orders from the executive branch to seize ships sailing from French ports when an act of Congress authorized the capture of ships sailing to French ports but forbade the seizure of ships departing from French ports. When the owner of a ship sued the captain for following orders and violating the act, Chief Justice Marshall held that the captain was personally liable. Marshall explained that "the instructions cannot change the nature of the transaction, or legalize an act which, without these instructions, would have been a plain trespass."[43]

---

42. Ibid.
43. *United States v. Smith,* 27 F. Cas. 1192 (C.C.N.Y 1806) (No. 16, 342), discussed in Louis Fisher, *Presidential War Power* (Lawrence: University of Kansas Press, 1995), 22–24; Robert Reinstein, "An Early View of Executive Powers and Privilege: The

When Madison turned to Hamilton's theory of concurrent powers, he was particularly concerned with the extent to which a presidential action would influence Congress, and he suggested two different models. The president's prior act might be viewed as "impos[ing] a *constitutional obligation* on the *legislative decision.*" More specifically, "the executive may 'lay the *legislature* under an *obligation* to decide in favor of war.'" Under a looser model, the president's power to create an antecedent state of things would have "*an influence* on the *expediency* of this or that decision in the *opinions* of the legislature."[44]

After positing the loose model of influence and the extreme model of obligation, Madison made a surprising concession. Specifically addressing the loose model, Madison wrote, "In this sense the power to establish an antecedent state of things is not contested." In Pacificus, Hamilton stated with utter clarity that he viewed the Constitution as providing for something akin to the loose model, and he clearly eschewed the extreme model. At a fundamental level, therefore, Helvidius embraces Pacificus.[45]

Although Madison actually agreed with most of Hamilton's analysis, he did not write Helvidius as a paean to Pacificus. His purpose was to refute what he saw as undesirable implications in Hamilton's essay. He especially feared that Pacificus could be read as supporting a unilateral presidential power to take the country to war, and he saw the theory of concurrent powers as potentially encompassing presidential war powers. Madison read Pacificus as endorsing a presidential power to require or obligate Congress to declare a war. Hamilton's clear disclaimer of presidential power to obligate Congress to declare war severely complicated Madison's task. Nevertheless, Madison persevered.

Notwithstanding Hamilton's disclaimer, Madison focused upon a single line in Pacificus, which, if wrenched from its context, could be construed as endorsing presidential authority to place Congress under an obligation to declare war. In this part of Pacificus, Hamilton briefly assumed, solely for the purpose of argument, that the Treaty of Alliance required the United States to join France in the war against Great Britain. He then obstinately reiterated the argument, which he had unsuccessfully advanced in cabinet deliberations, that France's change of government suspended the treaty.

Trial of Smith and Odgen," *Hastings Constitutional Law Quarterly* 2 (1975): 309–48; *Little v. Barreme,* 6 U.S. (2 Cranch.) 169 (1804), discussed in Fisher, *Presidential War Power,* 18–20.

44. Helvidius No. 3, 15:102–3.
45. Ibid., 102.

Building on this foundation of sand, Hamilton next stated that the president's express constitutional power to receive ambassadors implicitly empowered the president to recognize the new French government and thereby reinstate the suspended treaty. Therefore, assuming the treaty required the country to go to war, Hamilton concluded that a presidential recognition of France's new government "would have laid the Legislature under an obligation . . . of exercising its power of declaring war."[46]

Madison's insistence that Hamilton was arguing for a presidential power to take the country to war was, to say the least, a stretch. In Hamilton's hypothetical, Congress would be under an obligation to declare war because the treaty, which had been approved by the Continental Congress and was the supreme law of the land, positively required a declaration—not because the president ordained it. The obligation was a treaty obligation. Madison thus presumably agreed that in Hamilton's hypothetical, Congress would be under an obligation to declare war. Madison rejected Hamilton's theory that the treaty might be suspended and then reinstated by the president's recognition of the new French government. Thus unless Congress chose to violate the treaty, Madison surely agreed with Hamilton's conclusion that Congress would be under a treaty obligation to declare war.

Many years later, after Madison had essentially retired from public life, he looked back at Helvidius with regret. He acknowledged that it was a "political tract [that] breathes a spirit which was of no advantage either to the subject, or to the Author." Madison did not identify the portions of Helvidius he regretted, but he surely did not mean to recant his luminous discussion of the reasons for taking the power of declaring war from the executive and vesting it in Congress. On the other hand, Madison's distortion of Hamilton's hypothetical case of a treaty requiring war is indeed regrettable.[47]

In addition to tendentiously distorting a single line from Pacificus, Madison argued that there was no logical basis to cabin Hamilton's argument short of presidential war making. Madison explained that Pacificus had defined war powers to include the right to judge whether or not the nation should go to war. If, therefore, the president is empowered to determine that the nation should remain neutral, Madison claimed that the president must have a parallel power to decide that the nation should go to war.[48]

46. Ibid., 102–3.
47. Madison's detached memoranda, quoted in Powell, "Founders and the President's Authority," 1476.
48. Helvidius No. 2, 15:81–82. See also "Anonymous essay," *National Gazette,* Aug. 7, 1793. Madison advanced additional comparably arid but virtually impenetrable logical analyses. *Papers of James Madison,* 15:84–85, 85–86.

In retrospect, his sterile, logical critique of Hamilton's words without regard to their context seems an unbecoming play on words—a political pun. In fact, Hamilton stated in Pacificus that he was arguing for a presidential power to preserve peace or neutrality and specifically insisted that this power did not extend to a presidential authority to declare war. Given this explicit disclaimer, Madison's logic only makes sense if the power to declare war and the power to preserve peace are monolithic and inseparable. As a general proposition, all the founders, including Madison, sincerely believed that peace is preferable to war. Moreover, the Constitution explicitly addresses the power to declare war but is silent on peace. In other words, Madison's linguistic maneuverings have no credibility.[49]

Madison's entire approach in writing the Helvidius essays is puzzling and gave rise to great confusion in the twentieth century.[50] His overall style suggests that the essays are a systematic refutation of Hamilton, but upon close reading, Helvidius systematically refuses to grapple with Pacificus. Notwithstanding Hamilton's disclaimer of any pretentions to presidential warpowers, Madison devoted much of his efforts to proving that the president lacks authority to take the nation to war. Similarly, on the issue of concurrent powers, Madison limited himself to refuting an extreme model that Hamilton expressly disavowed.

It is probable that Madison simply did not trust Hamilton. We know that Jefferson had an inveterate distrust of Hamilton. From the onset of the Neutrality Crisis, Jefferson consistently viewed him as a puppeteer engaged in all sorts of sinister plots. He believed Hamilton was secretly manipulating the president, that Veritas was written by one of Hamilton's tools, and even that someone might be conspiring to intercept Jefferson's correspondence with Madison. Insofar as Jefferson thought that Hamilton was trying to manipulate the president, he was right. Madison could not help but be influenced by his friend's distrust, which, after all, was at least partially justified. Madison's misgivings about Hamilton came close to the surface when he warned that

> however the consequences flowing from [Pacificus], may be disavowed at this time or by this individual, we are to regard it as morally certain, that in proportion as the doctrines make their way into the creed of the government, and the acquiescence of the public, every power that can be deduced from them, will be deduced and exercised sooner or later by those who may have an interest in so doing.

49. U.S. Constitution, art. 1, sec. 8; Helvidius No. 4, 15:108–9.
50. See chapter 10, this volume.

If Madison actually believed that Hamilton's express disclaimers were false, Helvidius becomes more comprehensible. In addition, Madison's prophesy that Pacificus would be distorted in the future has come to pass. Notwithstanding Hamilton's clear and explicit disclaimers, some two hundred years later, Pacificus is occasionally used to support a unilateral presidential power to start a war.[51]

Selling Prizes

Madison mistrusted Hamilton and wrote Helvidius as an attack on Pacificus, but less than a year later, Madison demonstrated the power of one of Hamilton's brilliant insights. After Congress finally convened in December 1793, the Federalist supporters of strict neutrality proposed the enactment of neutrality legislation. Among other things, the proposed legislation would have outlawed selling "within the United States, any vessel or goods captured from a Prince or State with whom the United States are at peace." The only exception was for vessels and goods that "have been first carried to a port or place within the territory of the Prince or State to which the captors belong."[52]

At first glance this proposed legislation would seem to outlaw the French Consular Courts and require a condemnation in the captor's home country, but that was not the bill's only purpose. The legislation also was aimed at sales without a prior condemnation. Ordinarily prizes were not sold without condemnation because the title to the ship would be in serious doubt. If a captured British ship were purchased without a lawful condemnation, it would be subject to seizure if it later sailed into a British port. The British ambassador was fully aware of this and kept track of the sailings of British ships that had been improperly sold. In the market place, however, there was a substantial difference between ships and their cargoes. The purchaser of a ship would have to use the ship in maritime commerce and expose the ship to being seized. In contrast, the purchase of captured cargo like the fourteen puncheons of Jamaica rum in the *Morning Star* or the huge bolts of rough linen in the *William* was not as problematic. Consumer goods can not be traced as easily as a ship. A contemporary observer explained that without a valid condemnation, the sale of vessels was difficult because "those

---

51. Helvidius No. 1, 15:106. For Jefferson's distrust and modern distortions of Pacificus, see Casto, "Pacificus and Helvidius Reconsidered," 635n60; John Yoo, "War and the Constitutional Text," *University of Chicago Law Review* 69 (2002): 1678.

52. *Annals of the Congress of the United States,* 747 (quoting the bill).

who purchase the vessels, will not easily take them without a previous condemnation." In contrast, consumer goods were different, and the "sale as far as it reflects the cargoes, will be attended with no difficulty."[53]

Although George Washington and his cabinet agreed that the Consular Courts were illegal, they did not object to the French selling prizes, or at least the prize cargoes, without condemnation. In August, Jefferson wrote a long letter outlining to the American minister in Paris the government's various decisions. He explained that "the armed vessels of France have been also admitted to land and sell their prize goods here for consumption" and went on to note that these sales were permitted "tho' unstipulated in our treaties, and unfounded in [France's] own practice, or in that of other nations, as we believe."[54]

When Congress revisited the issue in 1794, William Loughton Smith of South Carolina argued at great length that allowing the French to sell their prizes was contrary to the policy of strict neutrality. Under Article 17 of the Treaty of Amity, the British were forbidden to sell their prizes. To achieve equality of treatment, therefore, the French should be similarly barred. Madison responded that the preferential treatment did not violate the law of nations' principles of neutrality. Although he did not use Hamilton's precise words, he also argued that in this instance the executive had created an antecedent state of things that ought to influence Congress.[55]

Madison noted that the "Executive had expounded the Law of Nations, and our treaties, in this sense, by leaving the sale of French prizes free, and forbidding the sale British prizes." If Congress were to reverse the president's decision and "condemn the exposition of the Executive," the British would be armed "with a charge against the United States, of having violated their neutrality." Madison also insisted that not acquiescing in the president's prior decision "would be the more impolitic and extraordinary, as it could not fail to give extreme disgust to the French Republic, by withdrawing a privilege which it had been determined could be rightfully allowed her." His point was that by permitting the sale of prizes, the president had created an antecedent state of things that ought to weigh in Congress's decision. Although Congress enacted the neutrality legislation, it decided

---

53. *Augusta (Ga.) Chronicle,* Nov. 9, 1793; George Hammond to Lord Grenville, Apr. 14, 15, 1793, PRO:FO 5/4, DLC (transcript).

54. Thomas Jefferson to Gouveneur Morris, Aug. 16, 1793, *Papers of Thomas Jefferson,* 26:705–10.

55. *Annals of the Congress of the United States,* 754; see chapter 9, this volume.

not to reverse the president's decision. The section on the sale of prizes failed to pass.[56]

Pacificus in Retrospect

Hamilton's analysis in Pacificus is a careful and lucid argument that is firmly grounded in the structure and actual words of the Constitution. Simply put, Pacificus No. 1 is one of the best essays ever written on a specific issue of constitutional law. Hamilton's earlier contributions to the Federalist Papers and his 1793 explanation of presidential power establish him, along with James Madison and John Marshall, as the three greatest constitutional theorists of the founding generation. Hamilton explains exactly how the Constitution enables the executive branch to formulate and implement an effective foreign policy, and he forthrightly addresses the apparent conflict in the Constitution between the president's and Congress's powers over foreign affairs. He saw that the executive and legislative branches have overlapping or concurrent powers, and he explained the practical significance of these concurrent powers. The last chapter of this book will revisit Pacificus No. 1 and its relevance to foreign affairs and the Constitution in the twenty-first century.

56. *Annals of the Congress of the United States,* 754, 757; Neutrality Act, 3rd Cong., sess. 1, chap. 50, 1 Stat. 381–84 (An act in addition to the act for the punishment of certain crimes against the United States).

CHAPTER 6

Neutrality in the Courts

> There is an appeal from any determination
> I may give, to a superior tribunal.
> *Findlay v. The William*
>
> The jury, in a general verdict,
> must decide both law and fact.
> *Henfield's Case*

While Hamilton was writing Pacificus No. 1, the federal courts began to take notice of the Neutrality Crisis. From the very outset, Chief Justice Jay lent a willing hand to assist the executive branch. He wrote Hamilton on the advisability of receiving France's new minister and even drafted a neutrality proclamation for the government's use. Jay and Hamilton were fellow New Yorkers, friends, and political allies. During the early years of the federal government, Jay frequently worked with the executive branch, and he continued this relationship throughout the crisis.[1]

Jay's philosophy of cooperation between the judicial branch and other branches of government is neatly summarized in his correspondence with his good friend Alexander Hamilton. Jay saw "no contradiction between separation of powers and cooperation between the branches in achieving national objectives": "Let all the branches of Govt move together, and let the chiefs be committed publicly on one or the other side of the Question." In 1789, he briefly served simultaneously as chief justice and secretary of state, and when a foreign policy crisis involving Nootka Sound erupted the next year, Jay readily complied with the president's request for an advisory opinion on the applicable principles of international law. That same year the president was concerned about Congress's, especially the Senate's, right to establish the grade of American diplomats and to dictate the countries to which they would be assigned. Chief Justice Jay advised him that "they have no Constitutional right to interfere with either." Just a few months before the Neutrality Crisis of 1793, Hamilton suggested to Jay that he should deliver a grand jury charge condemning the actions of the Whiskey Rebels in western Pennsylvania and threatening them with criminal prosecution. Chief Justice Jay had no general objection to supporting the government

---

1. See Casto, *Supreme Court,* 71–72, 74–76, 178–79; Jay, *Most Humble Servants,* 99–101, 167–69.

with a grand jury charge, but he declined to deliver the suggested charge because he did not view it as necessary.[2]

When Hamilton suggested the use of a grand jury charge to bring pressure on the Whiskey Rebels, he was not thinking of a simple communication between a judge and a small group of grand jurors. In the late eighteenth century, American judges routinely used grand jury charges to address a broad range of political and legal issues of general interest to the public. Throughout the 1790s, Supreme Court justices frequently used their grand jury charges to address specific politically sensitive legal issues, and they did so with the knowledge that their charges would be published to the nation in leading newspapers. Everyone in government understood the use of grand jury charges to address important legal issues.[3]

Because so many Americans earnestly believed that the United States should give its full support to France, the Washington administration needed a complete and credible explanation and justification for its announced policy of neutrality. Almost as soon as Chief Justice Jay gave his initial advice to Secretary Hamilton at the outset of the crisis, he began work on a grand jury charge to advise the nation on general issues of neutrality. In his preliminary draft, Jay reminded his intended audience that the law of nations came from God, "*he* from whose *will* proceed all moral obligations," and insisted that in time of war a neutral nation has a duty of "Strict Impartiality in all Cases where prior Treaties do not stipulate for Favors." More specifically, "any persons engaged in fitting out privateers or enlisting Men to serve against either of the Belligerent Powers [were violating] the Laws of Neutrality." He also warned that Americans could not avoid the law by simply renouncing their citizenship and professing French citizenship. He condemned this "novel doctrine" as "ridiculous" and an "absurdity."[4]

As the crisis progressed, Jay had to redraft his planned charge to take into account the president's Proclamation of Neutrality. In his preliminary draft, Jay warned that the "great Questions . . . of peace and War [are] committed exclusively to Congress," and Jefferson had used this idea in cabinet to argue

2. Holt, "Separation of Powers?" in *Neither Separate Nor Equal,* ed. Bowling and Kennon, 194, 199–200; Casto, *Supreme Court,* 71–72; Powell, "Founders and the President's Authority," 1480–85 (discussing the diplomatic corps issue and quoting the president's diary).

3. See Casto, *Supreme Court,* 126–29; Ralph Lerner, "The Supreme Court as Republican Schoolmaster," *Supreme Court Review* 1967 (1967): 127.

4. Draft of John Jay's Charge to the Grand Jury of the Circuit Court for the District of Virginia, before Apr. 22, 1793, *Documentary History of the Supreme Court* 2:359–65.

that Congress's exclusive power precluded presidential authority to issue a neutrality proclamation. Jay's final grand jury charge emphatically endorsed the proclamation. He no doubt knew of Jefferson's argument from conversations with Hamilton and perhaps the president, and he deleted any reference to exclusive congressional powers from his final charge.[5]

The primary thrust of Jay's charge was to insist that under the law of nations, the United States was required "to shew an exact Impartiality between the parties at War." He recognized that the United States had treaties with France but pointed out that the Treaty of Paris, which concluded the Revolutionary War, required the United States to be in "a firm and perpetual peace" with Britain. This treaty provision and similar provisions in treaties with Prussia and the Netherlands supported a policy of exact impartiality.[6]

Chief Justice Jay wrote his charge primarily to support the basic policy of strict neutrality and consciously decided not to address a host of legal issues that were arising in May as the French maritime campaign progressed. He warned that Americans who violated neutrality were subject to criminal prosecution but, with one exception, did not explain the duties of neutrality with "particularized ... detail." Jay did make it clear that the "Right of levying Soldiers is a sovereign Right belonging only to the nation." In other words, the French recruitment activities in Charleston and elsewhere were illegal unless conducted with "previous permission" from the United States. Jay wrote his charge with knowledge that it would be published in newspapers, and the charge was indeed published in Philadelphia and New York. In addition, the administration sent copies of the charge, along with one by Justice Wilson, to Europe to explain and justify the policy of strict neutrality.[7]

The arrival of the *William* with Gideon Henfield, her American prize master, caused quite a stir in the capital. The prize was taken on May 3, and just five days later the British minister, George Hammond, filed his protests with Secretary of State Jefferson. He noted that the *Citoyen Genet* had been "fitted out from" Charleston and that its crew "are for the most part citizens of the United States." Hammond condemned these practices as "breaches of

---

5. Ibid.; see chapter 3, this volume; John Jay's Charge to the Grand Jury of the Circuit Court for the District of Virginia, May 22, 1793, *Documentary History of the Supreme Court* 2:380–91.

6. John Jay's Charge to the Grand Jury, May 22, 1793, *Documentary History of the Supreme Court* 2:380–91.

7. Ibid.; Casto, *Supreme Court,* 131.

neutrality ... and direct contraventions of the [president's neutrality] proclamation." He urged the government to take action "for repressing such practices in future" and to restore any prizes taken by the *Citoyen Genet*. In the second protest, Hammond condemned the French Consular Courts as "not warranted by the usage of nations or ... existing treaties." Needless to say, the French hotly contested Hammond's claims.[8]

Philadelphians assumed that the legal issues raised by the *William*'s capture would be resolved through litigation in the federal courts. Less than two weeks after the capture, Edmond Livingston wrote his brother, "Two very important questions have arisen in Philadelphia—one on the prosecution of sailors on board the privateers and the other on the libeling of prizes." He continued, "These have become much the subject of conversation and occasion much degree of warmth."[9]

Hamilton and Jefferson agreed that the legality of the *William*'s capture should be considered by the judiciary, and Jefferson actually encouraged the British minister to have a suit for the ship's restitution filed in the local federal district court. As for Gideon Henfield and his fellow American crew member, John Singleterry, the cabinet unanimously believed that it was the government's "duty to have prosecutions instituted against them, that the laws [courts?] might pronounce on their case." The government decided to prosecute the two men as a test case "to try the question and to satisfy the complaint of the British Min." On May 15, Jefferson instructed William Rawle, the U.S. attorney for Pennsylvania, to apprehend and prosecute Henfield and Singleterry, and Rawle saw to it that the two men were arraigned before a local city magistrate and confined in the county jail. A special federal grand jury indicted them on July 27.[10]

Findlay v. The William

While the preliminary criminal proceedings against Henfield and Singleterry were moving forward, the British owners filed suit in the federal district court to obtain restitution of the *William* and its cargo. At the same time, the British minister petitioned President Washington to return the ship and cargo by executive decree. A similar diplomatic petition had worked in the case of the *Grange,* and it might work for the *William.* But the cabinet decided to delay consideration of the minister's petition pending the

---

8. See chapter 3.
9. Edward Livingston to Robert Livingston, May 15, 1793, Robert Livingston Papers, NHi.
10. See Casto, "Foreign Affairs Crises," 246–47.

outcome of litigation. Because the suit was a libel in Admiralty, the litigation proceeded apace. Admiralty courts did not use juries and had a tradition of providing speedy justice. District Judge Richard Peters was one of the nation's ablest Admiralty judges, and he promptly scheduled the case for oral argument on June 14.[11]

The suit in Admiralty provided a vehicle for obtaining a timely ruling from the federal courts on many of the legal issues bedeviling the Washington administration. Everyone agreed that the taking of a prize in United States territorial waters was an unlawful violation of American sovereignty, but there was disagreement as to how far American sovereignty extended out to sea. Hamilton believed that the federal courts "had best settle" this specific issue. Similarly, the outfitting of French corsairs in American ports was arguably unlawful and could be viewed as tainting the legality of the corsairs' captures. Finally, a suit for restitution inevitably would require the federal court to assess the legality of a French Consular Court's prior condemnation. A federal court sitting in Admiralty could resolve these legal issues and order restitution of prizes illegally taken.[12]

Although cases such as the *William* might have provided valuable assistance to the Washington administration in divining the applicable principles of law pertinent to neutrality, their potential was never reached. In response to the claimants' suit for restitution, the captors insisted that the federal court lacked subject matter jurisdiction to review the legality of the *William*'s capture. The essence of this defense was that the federal courts were barred from even addressing the legality of a capture. They could neither rule that the capture was lawful nor that the capture was unlawful. They had to stand mute. The captors pointed to a settled principle of customary Admiralty law that in prize cases, no court other than a court of the captor's country had jurisdiction to determine the validity of a capture. In a case involving a prize taken by the French, neither a British court nor

---

11. *Findlay v. The William;* see chapter 3, this volume; Casto, "Foreign Affairs Crises," 247–48.

12. Alexander Hamilton to Rufus King, June 15, 1793, *Papers of Alexander Hamilton* 14:548. See Casto, "Foreign Affairs Crises," 248. Because the French Consular Court in Philadelphia had formally condemned the *William,* the ship could not be restored without considering the validity of the French court's decree. As a general proposition, even an erroneous condemnation by a prize court would not be reviewed by another nation's court. But the French decrees could be attacked if the very existence of the Consular Courts were unlawful violations of American sovereignty. See Casto, "Foreign Affairs Crises," 248n68.

a neutral court was competent to determine this fundamental question of prize or no prize. Only a French court could decide the issue.[13]

Oral argument on the challenge to subject matter jurisdiction commenced on Friday morning, June 14, and the captors' lead attorney, Peter Stephen Du Ponceau spent most of the morning presenting the argument against jurisdiction. Du Ponceau was a polymath who among other things was one of the nation's most capable and highly regarded international lawyers. He had come to America during the Revolutionary War as an aide to Baron Von Steuben. With the "slightest imaginable accent [that] revealed his French origin," Du Ponceau argued that

> prizes should be tried in the court of the country to whom the captor belongs; that a neutral power has no right to enquire into the validity of prizes brought into their ports, and expressly so by treaty, as it relates to France and the United States; and that questions in which the sovereignty of States is involved can only be settled by negotiation [between the interested governments].

Du Ponceau based his argument upon settled prize law and supported it with extensive citation to pertinent authority and precedent. He closed with a policy argument "on the importance of keeping clear of the disturbances which agitate Europe." Then his co-counsel, Jonathan Dickson Sergeant, added "some authorities omitted by his colleague." Like Du Ponceau, Sergeant was a highly regarded attorney. At this point, Judge Peters adjourned for lunch. In the afternoon, the British owners' counsel began their argument. They were also distinguished members of the bar. First up was William Rawle. Although he was also the lead prosecutor in *Henfield's Case,* the office of U.S. attorney was a part-time job in the 1790s. He appeared in *William* in his private capacity. He agreed with the general proposition that the courts of a neutral power lacked subject matter jurisdiction over the fundamental question of prize or no prize, but he argued that an exception should be made for captures made in the neutral country's waters in violation of the neutral power's sovereignty. After a long day, Judge Peters adjourned court for the evening.[14]

---

13. Captor's Plea, *Federal Gazette,* June 24, 1793. See also *General Advertiser* (Philadelphia), June 19, 21, 1793 (argument of captor's counsel).

14. *General Advertiser,* June 19, 1793; Thomas Wharton, "Peter S. Duponceau," in *Lives of Eminent Philadelphians, Now Deceased,* by Henry Simpson (Philadelphia: W. Brotherhead, 1859), 331. See Casto, "Foreign Affairs Crises," 249–50.

The next morning, a Saturday, Jared Ingersol presented additional arguments for the French captors. When Ingersol started edging into the merits with an argument that "a 24 pounder will not throw a ball to the distance of quite 3 miles," Judge Peters broke in and reminded counsel that "the point, before the court [is] whether *if* the capture was made on neutral territory, then can the court take cognizance." And so the argument continued until the noon adjournment. When everyone returned after lunch, William Lewis, who had preceded Judge Peters as the U.S. district judge for Pennsylvania, concluded the British owners' case. His argument, which lasted into the evening, was based entirely upon policy and extrapolation from precedent and authority not directly on point. Like his co-counsel, he urged that in cases in which a capture violated a neutral country's sovereignty, an exception should be created to the general rule against jurisdiction. At one point he conceded that "no instance can be produced of a similar case being brought in a [neutral country's] court of admiralty." After two solid days of detailed argument by the best lawyers in Philadelphia, Judge Peters took the case under advisement.[15]

Peters devoted great care and attention to the issue, and about a week later, he announced his decision in a lengthy opinion. He concluded that the British owners' arguments were without precedent and contrary to the settled rule that "affairs of prizes are only cognizable in the courts of the power making the capture." He understood that a capture in American waters implicated the nation's sovereignty interests, and both sides had addressed this point at great length. The French captors' attorneys insisted that the nation's sovereignty interests had to be vindicated through diplomacy, and the British owners' attorneys responded that litigation provided a more just and effective mode of vindication. Insofar as the case involved the United States' interest as a sovereign, Peters concluded, "this is a matter, not of judicial, but political arrangement." As a trial judge, he felt that he could not ignore the settled precedent. At the conclusion of his opinion, however, he strongly hinted that the Supreme Court might be willing to ignore the precedent. "There is an appeal," noted Peters, "from any determination I may give, to a superior tribunal."[16]

Notwithstanding Judge Peters's broad hint that the British owners should appeal his decision, a funny thing happened on the way to the Supreme Court. The owners decided not to appeal. They instead relied upon their petition to the executive branch for a remedy, and their petition

15. *General Advertiser,* June 21 1793. See Casto, "Foreign Affairs Crises," 250.
16. *Findlay v. The William.* See Casto, "Foreign Affairs Crises," 250–51.

was denied a year later. Soon after Peters's decision, a second case for restitution of an allegedly unlawful prize was filed in his court, and the cabinet expected that he would "very shortly reconsider" his decision in *Findlay*. But in *Moxon v. The Fanny,* Peters cleaved to his original analysis. Within half a year, at least four other district judges followed his lead. One of the owners in these other four cases was "unwilling to appeal if Govt will afford any Extrajudicial [executive] Relief." Judge Lowell in Massachusetts was the only lower federal judge who was willing to carve out a narrow exception to the general rule against jurisdiction. Following an idea initially advanced by the executive branch, Judge Lowell held that the courts had jurisdiction in the case of prizes and cargoes belonging to American citizens and other neutrals. The upshot of all this litigation was that the federal courts denied timely legal advice to the nation and the Washington administration.[17]

Ordinarily, trial court errors may be corrected by an appeal, as Judge Peters strongly hinted in his opinion. An appeal to the Supreme Court would have provided precisely the legal advice that the nation sorely needed, but such an appeal was captive to the British owners' personal financial interest, and they decided not to pursue it. As a result, the question of the federal courts' jurisdiction to review the validity of captures was not resolved until February of the next year, when a case finally reached the Supreme Court. In *Glass v. The Betsy,* the Court announced without explanation that it was "decidedly of opinion" that the federal district courts have jurisdiction to examine the legality of a capture and order restitution in an appropriate case. The justices did not deliver opinions in support of their decision probably because they knew that Admiralty precedents and authorities were so decidedly to the contrary. The Court's opinion, however, was too late to assist the Washington administration in dealing with the Neutrality Crisis of the prior year. By the time the Court had decided *Glass,* the country was involved in a new crisis that threatened war with Great Britain.[18]

17. *Moxon v. The Fanny,* 17 F. Cas. 942 (D. Pa. 1793) (No. 9895); unnamed case (D.N.C. 1793), *Salem Gazette,* Aug. 6, 1793; *The Catherine* (D.N.Y. 1794), reprinted in *Decree on the Admiralty Side of the District Court of New York* (1794) (Evans No. 26, 915); *Castello v. Boutelle,* 5 F. Cas. 278 (D.S.C. 1794) (No. 2504); *Glass v. Sloop Betsy, Documentary History of the Supreme Court* 6:324 (D. Md. 1793), rev'd 3 U.S (3 Dall.) 6 (1794); *Folger v. Lecuyer, Boston Centinel,* Jan. 4, 1794 (D. Mass. 1793). *Richard Harison v. Edmund Randolph,* Mar. 6, 1794, Harison Letterbook, NHi (describing owners decision not to appeal). See Casto, "Foreign Affairs Crises," 250–52.

18. 3 U.S. (3 Dall.) 6 (1794), discussed in Casto, *Supreme Court,* 82–87, and *Documentary History of the Supreme Court,* 6:296–355. For the new crisis, see chapter 9, this volume.

Henfield's Case

While Judge Peters was crafting his opinions in *Findlay* and *Moxon,* the criminal case against the *William*'s prize crew moved forward. Henfield was on board the corsair *Citoyen Genet* when he was arrested, and he was quickly arraigned before Hilary Baker, a local alderman with judicial powers. In his defense, he initially explained to Alderman Baker that he had been a sailor without a ship in Charleston and was looking for a ride north. Because he could not afford to pay his passage, he struck a bargain with Captain Johannene. He agreed to sail with the *Citoyen Genet,* and the captain agreed to make him prize master of the first capture sent into an American port. During the initial arraignment, Henfield "protested himself an American, that as such he would die, and therefore could not be supposed likely to intend anything to her prejudice." Moreover, he joined the corsair without knowledge of the Proclamation of Neutrality, which had been issued three days after the *Citoyen Genet* departed Charleston. He earnestly "declared if he had known it to be contrary to the President's proclamation, or even the wishes of the President, for whom he had the greatest respect, he could not have entered on board."[19]

A month later, at a second preliminary hearing, Henfield told a different story. Ambassador Genet had retained counsel for Henfield and was participating in shaping trial strategy. Now Henfield insisted that he had become a French citizen and "meant to move his family within their [i.e., French] dominions." If so, Henfield's service on the *Citoyen Genet* could not be a violation of American neutrality. As Genet vigorously argued in a June 1 letter to the executive branch, there could be nothing wrong with a French citizen fighting for his own country.[20]

Henfield's Case was a high-profile, politically controversial prosecution. In the June 1 letter, Genet indignantly and with angry irony protested Henfield's arrest and urged two technical legal defenses. First, he stated that he was "ignorant of any positive law [i.e., an act of Congress] which deprives Americans of this privilege" of helping France. Second, he noted that Henfield had become a French citizen before joining the *Citoyen Genet* and thus had "the right of French citizens" to defend France. In a letter carefully vetted by Alexander Hamilton and Attorney General Randolph, Jefferson

---

19. *Henfield's Case,* 11 F. Cas. 1099 (C.C.D. Pa. 1793) (No. 6360). See Casto, "Foreign Affairs Crises," 253–54.

20. *Henfield's Case,* 78; Thomas Jefferson to James Madison, Aug. 11, 1793, *Papers of Thomas Jefferson,* 26:653; Edmond Genet to Thomas Jefferson, June 1, 1793, *Papers of Thomas Jefferson,* 26:158 (discussed in chapter 4).

replied that the matter was now with the judiciary, "over whose proceedings the Executive has no control."[21]

The defenses Genet raised on behalf of Henfield were not frivolous. In fact, there was no act of Congress making his conduct a crime or forbidding American citizens from violating American neutrality. The cabinet referred the matter to Attorney General Randolph, who quickly came up with a common-law solution to the problem. Randolph believed that Henfield had violated treaties that established a condition of peace between the United States and some of the powers at war with France. Although the treaties made no reference to criminal prosecutions, there was a well-established common-law doctrine that the law of nations was incorporated into the common law and that violations of the law of nations were common-law misdemeanors. Randolph concluded that Henfield "is indictable at the common Law; because his conduct comes within the description of disturbing the Peace of the United States." Jefferson assured James Monroe that Randolph's opinion "coincided with all our private opinions, and the lawyers of this state, New York and Maryland who were applied to, were unanimously of the same opinion." He noted, however, that Rawle "supposes the law more doubtful. New Acts therefore of the same kind are left unprosecuted till the question is determined by the proper court."[22]

In addition to the matter of common-law prosecutions, there was some doubt whether the law of nations had even been violated. Today, American citizens' participation in fitting out French commerce raiders and crewing them may seem obvious neutrality violations, but in 1793 the issue was not

21. Edmond Genet, Report on the Arming of Privateers, n.d. ("indignant"), Edmond Genet Papers, DLC; Edmond Genet to Thomas Jefferson, June 1, 1793, *Papers of Thomas Jefferson,* 26:159, and *American State Papers,* 151 (English translation).

22. Edmund Randolph's Opinion on the Case of Gideon Henfield, May 30, 1793, *Papers of Thomas Jefferson,* 26:145–46; Thomas Jefferson to James Monroe, July 14, 1793, *Papers of Thomas Jefferson,* 26:501–2; *Dunlap's American Daily Advertiser,* June 12, 1793 (espousing common law crimes); see generally Casto, *Supreme Court,* 130–41. For additional excellent discussion of this topic, see John Gordan, "United States v. Ravara, 'Presumptuous Evidences,' 'Too Many Lawyers,' and a Federal Common Law," in *Origins of the Federal Judiciary,* ed. Maeva Marcus (New York: Oxford University Press, 1992), 106–72; Stephen B. Presser, *The Original Misunderstanding: The English, the Americans, and the Dialectic of Federalist Jurisprudence* (Durham, N.C.: Carolina Academic Press, 1991), chap. 6; Stewart Jay, "Origins of Federal Common Law," *Univ. Penn. L. Review* 133 (1985): 1003, 1231. Kathryn Preyer, "Jurisdiction to Punish: Federal Authority, Federalism and the Common Law of Crimes in the Early Republic," *Law & History Review* 4 (1986): 223.

so clear cut. In the late eighteenth century, the rights and duties under international law of a neutral country had yet to be clearly established. "The direct supply of troops and of actual or potential warships by neutral powers to belligerent States," for example, "was in frequent use in the 16th–18th centuries." The policies the United States crafted in response to the 1793 crisis eventually played a significant role in the development of the international law of neutrality. But "not all of [the American policies] reflected mandatory rules of international law in force at that time." Finally, the argument that Americans were free to expatriate themselves and become French citizens was consistent with the American Revolution in which the rebelling colonists expatriated themselves from Great Britain.[23]

When a special circuit court was convened in July to consider the government's test case, Justice Wilson, the senior circuit judge, was well aware of the issues that would be raised in the case, but his charge to the grand jury, like Chief Justice Jay's earlier charge, was somewhat vague on the applicable legal rules. In ten pages replete with numerous references to obscure and well-known lawyers and philosophers from Plato to Blackstone, Wilson extolled the common law that Americans had inherited from their Saxon forefathers. In particular, Wilson explained that the common law included the law of nations and that by the law of nations, countries not at war were required not to harm each other. Moreover, violations of this duty by individual citizens were punishable as common-law crimes. If the United States did not take steps to punish citizens such as Henfield who attacked Great Britain, the nation would be in violation of the law of nations. The United States would become responsible for injuries caused by citizens such as Henfield, which could lead "to *Reprisals certainly:* And if so; *probably* to War." Wilson concluded with a lengthy explanation that under the Constitution, only Congress, and certainly not private citizens such as Henfield, had authority to declare war.[24]

Judge Wilson's solemn predictions of dire consequences flowing from Americans joining the French cause struck many as unrealistic. At the outset

23. J. H. W. Verzijl, *International Law in Historical Perspective* (Alphen Aan Den Rijn, Netherlands: Sijthoff & Noordhoff, 1979), 10:51–58, 86. See, for example, E. de Vattel, *The Law of Nations or the Principles of Natural Law* (1758; reprint, Washington, D.C.: Carnegie Institute Translation, 1916), 265, quoted in Prakash and Ramsey, "Executive Power over Foreign Affairs," 333n447. See also Hyneman, *First American Neutrality,* 14–19, 96–98.

24. James Wilson's charge to the Grand Jury of a Special Session of the Circuit Court for the District of Pennsylvania, July 22, 1793 (citations omitted), *Documentary History of the Supreme Court,* 2:414.

of the Neutrality Crisis, a pro-French American writing under the pen name Americanus pointed out that individuals commonly served in the armed forces of other countries. A correspondent in South Carolina concurred. Americanus insisted, "I am free to enter into any service, or become a citizen in any nation who will receive me." "A Republican" in Boston attacked Wilson by name and condemned his analysis as a "sophistry."[25]

In addition to rejecting Genet's argument that there was no law forbidding Americans from helping the French, Wilson addressed Genet's claim that Article 22 of the Treaty of Amity gave France a right to fit out privateers in American ports. He pointed out that the provision prohibited enemies of France from fitting out privateers and that the article literally was silent on the rights of France. He understood that it might be claimed that prohibiting British use of ports *"implies* [by negative implication] a *permission* to fit the Ships of Privateers belonging to *France,"* but he rejected the claim. The treaty was simply silent on this right, and "it remains in our *Option* whether we will or will not *grant* it to *France."*[26]

The grand jury returned a long, prolix, and virtually unreadable indictment that was drafted by Rawle. As befitted a political prosecution, the attorney general and Secretary Hamilton assisted in drawing up this masterpiece of legal jargon. To this day, capable lawyers find the indictment puzzling and daunting.[27]

Trial commenced on Friday, July 26. Henfield pleaded "non cul[pabilis]," but Singleterry "being called came not." The two men were out on bail, and at the last moment, Singleterry fled the jurisdiction. The trial proceeded against Henfield as the sole defendant.[28]

The judges were Wilson and James Iredell of the Supreme Court and Peters, the local federal district judge. In 1793, the circuit court, which was the primary federal trial court, consisted of the local federal district judge and two Supreme Court justices riding circuit. The opposing counsel from *Findlay v. The William* were again present. Du Ponceau, Ingersoll, and

---

25. Americanus, *Federal Gazette,* May 31, 1793; *Charleston (S.C.) City Gazette,* May 2 and 3, 1793; "A Republican," *Virginia Chronicle* (Norfolk), Aug. 31, 1793 (reprinted from *Independent Chronicle* [Boston]).

26. James Wilson's charge to the Grand Jury of a Special Session of the Circuit Court for the District of Pennsylvania, July 22, 1793, *Documentary History of the Supreme Court,* 2:414.

27. *Henfield's Case,* 66–71. See Casto, "Foreign Affairs Crises," 257.

28. Circuit Court of the United States for the District of Pennsylvania Minutes, Apr. 1793–Oct. 1975, National Archives Regional Archive, Philadelphia, Pa., 16–17, 25; *Carlisle (Pa.) Gazette,* Aug. 21, 1793.

Sergeant represented Henfield, and Rawle represented the United States with the assistance of Attorney General Randolph. William Lewis was not a prosecutor and did not appear as counsel for the government. Nevertheless, he and Alexander Hamilton took an active role in assisting the prosecution. The facts of the case were fairly straightforward and uncomplicated. Henfield's service with the French and the taking of the *William* were not in dispute. With the exception of the question whether Henfield had actually intended to become a French citizen, all the issues in the case were legal rather than factual. The principal witnesses for the prosecution were Jonas Simmons, John Morgan, Lewis Deblois, and Hilary Baker, who presided at Henfield's arraignment. There is no indication that the defense called any witnesses. On Saturday, the attorneys made their closing arguments, the judge charged the jury, and the jurors commenced their deliberations.[29]

Some two hundred years later, the attorneys' closing arguments to the jury are puzzling and seem irrelevant. Both sides devoted most of their arguments to conflicting views of the applicable legal principles. Today these legal arguments would be reserved for the judge's ears, but this approach made sense in the late eighteenth century. At that time, the jury in a criminal case had final authority to determine both the facts and the law. Judge Wilson specifically explained to the petit jurors in his charge that "the jury, in a general verdict, must decide both law and fact." Although he charged the jury on the law, his charge was advisory. The jury had no obligation to follow his instructions if they believed he was mistaken. But the jury did not have an unfettered discretion to make law. As Wilson explained, they were not authorized "to decide it as they pleased; they were as much bound to decide by law as the judges: the responsibility was equal upon both."[30]

Judge Wilson's idea that the jurors "were as much bound to decide by law as the judges: the responsibility was equal upon both" rings strange to modern ears, but his charge was not for modern ears. The predominant eighteenth-century understanding of the judicial process denied that judges

29. *Dunlap's American Daily Advertiser,* Aug. 8, 1793; Circuit Court Minutes, 29. See Casto, "Foreign Affairs Crises," 257–58.

30. *Henfield's Case,* 78–83, 87–88. On the jury's final authority to determine the law, see John Gordan, "Juries as Judges of the Law; The American Experience," *Law Quarterly Review* 108 (1992): 272; Daniel Blinka, "'This Germ of Rottedness': Federal Trials in the New Republic, 1789–1807," *Creighton Law Review* 36 (2003): 135–89; William Nelson, *Americanization of the Common Law* (Cambridge, Mass.: Harvard University Press, 1975), 28–29, 165–66. See also *Georgia v. Brailsford,* Chief Justice Jay's Charge to the Petit Jury (U.S. 1799) (civil action), *Documentary History of the Supreme Court,* 6:173.

had any lawmaking authority.[31] They merely applied preexisting legal rules to the cases that came before their courts. In the case of positive laws such as statutes and treaties, the rules came from legislatures and treaty makers. In the case of unwritten laws such as the common law or the law of nations, virtually all eighteenth-century attorneys believed that the applicable rules existed in nature. Under this natural-law vision, judges did not make laws but used their experience and intellect to find the applicable rules that preexisted in nature. In searching for the pertinent legal principles, then, the judges and the jurors performed parallel and comparable functions. The "responsibility was equal upon both" to discover the applicable, preexisting law.

Under this natural-law understanding of the legal process, the purpose of a judge's charge to a jury was to give the untutored jurors the benefit of the judge's experience and wisdom. Judge Wilson, then, addressed the pertinent legal issues. He emphatically rejected the argument that Henfield should be acquitted because there was no act of Congress making his conduct a crime. He explained that it "is the joint and unanimous opinion of the Court" that Henfield's conduct was "an offense against this country, and punishable by its laws." He specifically explained that this was "not an *ex post facto* law" that was made up after Henfield joined the *Citoyen Genet*. Henfield's conduct was in violation of the law of nations and treaties of the United States, which predated the Neutrality Crisis.[32]

In respect of the expatriation defense, that Henfield had changed his citizenship, Judge Wilson narrowed his analysis to the specific facts of the case. Given the American Revolution, Wilson could hardly deny the possibility of changing citizenship. One American colorfully stated that a complete bar to expatriation "is better adapted to the meridian of Turkey than to that of America." Wilson agreed. "Emigration [i.e., change of citizenship] is, undoubtedly one of the natural rights of man," he wrote. But he insisted that something other than conduct inconsistent with citizenship was necessary to accomplish a change of citizenship. Otherwise, he noted, there could seldom be a prosecution for treason: "Nothing is more inconsistent with the duty of a citizen than treason; but it is because he still continues a citizen that he is liable to punishment." A few weeks later, Thomas Jefferson elaborated upon this idea, noting that American "citizens are certainly free to divest themselves of that character, by emigration, and other acts manifesting their

---

31. See William Casto, "The Erie Doctrine and the Structure of Constitutional Revolutions," *Tulane Law Review* 62 (1988): 907.

32. *Henfield's Case,* 1120.

intention." There must, however, be some evidence to support an intent to change citizenship, and "the laws do not admit that the bare Commission of a crime amounts of itself to a divestment of the character of citizen." Given Henfield's firm insistence at the first preliminary hearing that he was "an American [and] as such he would die," his subsequent expatriation defense seems implausible.[33]

The jury began their deliberations at nine o'clock Saturday evening and after two and a half hours reported they were unable to agree. The judges asked them to try again and adjourned court at midnight while the jurors continued their deliberations. Sometime early Sunday morning, they gave a tentative privy verdict, which was unofficial and lacked validity until affirmed by a public verdict in court. Judge Wilson, who had remained at the courthouse while his fellow judges went to bed, accepted the privy verdict and excused the jurors until Monday. When court was reconvened on Monday, one of the jurors expressed some doubts about the privy verdict, which made the vote eleven to one for acquittal. Apparently, many of the jurors were persuaded by the change of citizenship defense, notwithstanding Henfield's earlier testimony, but the lone dissenter was not. He also stated that "he was induced to agree to the verdict which acquitted Henfield because he heard threats made out of doors against any one who should be against the acquittal." All three judges separately gave their opinions on the applicable law "particularly as to the change of political relation in the defendant." The jury then returned to their deliberations, and as an inducement, the judges decided that they would receive no food. The "constable" was to "supply them with water merely."[34]

Late in the afternoon, the jurors finally reached an agreement for acquittal and presented a written verdict that apparently attempted to explain the reasons for their decision. But the judges refused to accept the verdict because it was "neither general nor special." In other words, it was neither a simple recitation of guilty or not guilty nor a bare determination of specific facts. And so the jurors returned to their water, and finally, at seven o'clock Monday evening, they returned a general verdict of "Not Guilty."[35]

33. Ibid.; John Dawson to James Monroe, July 12, 1793, James Monroe Papers, NN; Thomas Jefferson to Gouverneur Morris, Aug. 16, 1793, *Papers of Thomas Jefferson,* 26:701.

34. Circuit Court Minutes, 31; *Henfield's Case,* 88; Henry Campbell Black, *Black's Law Dictionary,* 5th ed. (St. Paul, Minn.: West Publishing, 1979); *Federal Gazette,* July 29, 1793; *General Advertiser,* July 30, 1793.

35. *Henfield's Case,* 88.

As soon as the verdict was announced, someone published a scurrilous cartoon in Philadelphia to celebrate the victory. The cartoon portrayed the verdict as a symbolic execution and showed President Washington and Judge Wilson being guillotined. Hamilton and Knox must have been shocked and delighted. Although Knox was an old friend of the president, he had a sly habit of needling Washington during cabinet meetings. At one cabinet meeting before Henfield's trial, he noted some people were saying that "the Pr. was as great a tyrant as any of them and that it would soon be time to chase him out of the city." Jefferson reports that at the next cabinet meeting after the cartoon was published, Knox brought up the "pasquinade," or political lampoon, in "a foolish incoherent sort of speech." Washington was customarily a reserved man, but he was notorious for occasional outbursts of unbridled rage. Knox's foolish speech unleashed a torrent of suppressed presidential fury.[36]

It was like lighting a roman candle. As the cabinet members tried to blend into the room, the "Presidt. was much inflamed [and] got into one of those passions when he cannot command himself." He railed against "the personal abuse which had been bestowed on him" and furiously swore that *"by god* he had rather be in his grave than in his present situation." He deeply resented the public attacks against him and angrily insisted that "he had rather be on his farm than be made *emperor of the world* and yet that they were charging him with wanting to be a king." As the president's anger dissipated, no one knew what to do. "There was a pause [and] some difficulty in resuming our question." The meeting was at an end.[37]

Needless to say, the cartoon was not the only public reaction to Henfield's acquittal. Although Henfield quickly faded from history, he experienced a brief period of national acclaim, as most of the nation exulted in the jury's verdict. Many years later, Chief Justice Marshall reminisced "the verdict in favor of Henfield was celebrated with extravagant marks of joy and exultation." In Boston, the toast of the day was, "The virtuous and Independent jury of Pennsylvania, who acquitted Henfield." In addition to celebrating the acquittal, supporters of France vigorously attacked the judges' analyses of the applicable law. In a criticism resonating with natural-law philosophy,

---

36. Notes of Cabinet Meeting on Edmond Charles Genet, July 23, 1793, *Papers of Thomas Jefferson,* 26:554–55; John Hamilton to Lord Grenville, Aug. 8, 1793 (describing the cartoon), PRO:FO 5/2, Consular Correspondence, quoted in Casto, "Foreign Affairs Crises," 260–61n154; Notes of Cabinet Meeting, Aug. 2, 1793, *Papers of Thomas Jefferson,* 26:602.

37. Notes of Cabinet Meeting, Aug. 2, 1793, *Papers of Thomas Jefferson,* 26:602–3.

a writer in Philadelphia "lament[ed] that any occasion should arise for introducing motives of policy, to influence the decisions of our courts of justice." Further, the argument was made that "by this verdict, which according to the charge of the court, indicates a decision on the *law* as well as the *facts,* it is now established that a citizen of the United States may by law enter on board a French Privateer and it is presumable that no other prosecution for this same cause can be sustained." An "Archy Simple" in South Carolina presented a more narrowly focused legal analysis. Despite his unassuming pseudonym, Archy was a very capable lawyer. He elaborately argued that the verdict supported Americans' rights to expatriate themselves and become French citizens.[38]

In anticipation of this kind of talk, Attorney General Randolph placed an anonymous note in the *Federal Gazette* emphatically stating that "the court, with whom the law rests, most explicitly and unanimously declared that [Henfield's] conduct is in violation of our treaty with his Britannic majesty . . . and . . . is criminal." He explained that the acquittal "was owing to some deficiency in point of fact, or some *equitable* circumstances." Randolph later told President Washington that "the leading man among" the jury told Randolph that Henfield's "declaration that he would never have enlisted, had he known it to be against General Washington's opinion, was the reason of my voting for his acquittal." Alexander Hamilton also believed that the acquittal could not be fairly read as a refutation of the judges' charges on the applicable legal principles. "The Jury," he wrote, "was universally believed in this city to have been selected for the purpose of acquittal; so as to take off much the force of example." Because of this, the verdict could "afford no evidence that other juries would pursue the same course."[39]

About two weeks after the acquittal, Jefferson followed Attorney General Randolph's analysis and stated in official correspondence to the American minister in Paris that the jury acquitted Henfield because he "was ignorant of the unlawfulness of his undertaking; that in the moment he was apprised of it, he shewed real contrition." Jefferson also believed that the

38. John Marshall, *Life and Washington* (1807), 274, quoted in *Henfield's Case,* 89n*; *National Gazette,* Aug. 17, 1793; *National Gazette,* Aug. 3, 1793; "Archy Simple," *Columbia Herald,* Aug. 29, 1793. For citations to additional commentary, see Casto, "Foreign Affairs Crises," 260–61.

39. *Federal Gazette,* July 30, 1793, discussed in *Papers of Thomas Jefferson,* 26:653–54; Edmond Randolph to George Washington, Aug. 21, 1793, quoted in *Papers of Thomas Jefferson,* 26:713n; Alexander Hamilton to George Washington, Aug. 5, 1793, *Papers of Alexander Hamilton,* 15:194.

verdict was influenced by Henfield's "meritorious services" during the Revolutionary War. No other surviving records from the time of the trial even hint at these "services," but Jefferson's letter indicates that the jury knew about them.[40]

Henfield was an experienced captain and not a simple impecunious seaman seeking a ride home. He was from Salem, Massachusetts, which during the Revolutionary War was a major privateering port. In early April 1793, a respected Boston merchant had warned Alexander Hamilton that "some of our old adventurers in privateering who are again reduced will require a tight rein to prevent them" from attacking British commerce. During the Revolution, Henfield was the "very successful" commander of the privateer *Centipede,* which was almost identical in size, armament, and crew to the *Citoyen Genet.* He commanded several other privateers during the war, but in January 1781 he was captured and confined in Old Mill prison in England. John Singleterry, Henfield's co-defendant, who jumped bail, was one of Henfield's fellow prisoners at Old Mill. After the acquittal the French made Henfield captain of the sloop *Spry,* which they were fitting out as a corsair. Little is known of his subsequent career, except that he was captured by a British cruiser and died about seven years later in his home town of Salem.[41]

Although the government brought other common-law prosecutions for neutrality violations, none was successful. *Henfield's Case* was replayed in Augusta, Georgia, when the government prosecuted Joseph Rivers and three others, who served on the ill-fated corsair *Anti-George.* At an arraignment before federal district judge Nathaniel Pendleton, one of the accused turned out to be British, and he was "taken under the protection of a number of spirited gentlemen who gave him a compleat new suit of tar and feathers." The others were incarcerated, and Judge Pendleton subsequently was criticized for ignoring Rivers's right to change his citizenship. When the defendants were indicted and tried in November, the jury found them not guilty, "contrary to the opinion of the judges." Rivers then boasted that the Georgia jurors, like those in "Philadelphia, [had] established the rights of man, by a judicial and well reasoned verdict."[42]

The most flagrant breach of neutrality involved Gideon Olmstead, another one of the "old adventurers in privateering." In fact, he was one of

---

40. Thomas Jefferson to Gouverneur Morris, Aug. 16, 1793, *Papers of Thomas Jefferson,* 26:702.

41. Casto, "Foreign Affairs Crises," 262–63.

42. *United States v. Rivers,* Minute Book (C.C.D. Ga. 1793), NARA–Atlanta Branch, discussed in *Augusta (Ga.) Chronicle,* July 20, Aug. 3, Nov. 23, Dec. 4, 1743;

America's best privateer captains during the Revolutionary War. In May, Captain Olmstead sailed his schooner the *Hector* from the West Indies to Charleston and refitted her as a corsair. He ostensibly sold the ship to François Hervieux, a twenty-five-year-old Frenchman who had a privateer's commission. The *Hector* cleared Charleston as a merchant vessel under Hervieux's command, but Olmstead remained on board as an officer. The French claimed that, like Henfield, Olmstead was simply "going to Philadelphia." One of the crew, however, swore that Olmstead "appeared to have the . . . command." Olmstead also claimed that he had become a French citizen. After the *Hector* cleared the Charleston bar, "the name on her stern was defaced" and she was rechristened *Vainquer de la Bastille.* The new corsair quickly captured the sloop *Belle* with a cargo of thirty-seven puncheons of rum and eighteen hundred dollars and sent her into Charleston. Next the *Vainquer* took the sloop *Providence* and sailed for Wilmington, North Carolina.[43]

When the *Hector / Vainquer de la Bastille* put into Wilmington, North Carolina, with her prize, litigation ensued. The British captain of the prize filed suit in federal court for restitution, but as in the case of the *William,* the local federal judge decided that his court lacked subject matter jurisdiction. The authorities also decided to prosecute Olmstead for violating American neutrality, but there was a problem: the next federal circuit court was not scheduled to commence until November, five months later. Rather than spend half a year in jail, Olmstead posted a one-thousand-dollar recognizance bond to secure his appearance in court. Ten other American sailors posted bonds of fifty dollars each.[44]

Dunlap's American Daily Advertiser, Dec, 10, 1793; *Federal Gazette,* Aug. 9, 1793; Jackson, "Consular Privateers," 97–98.

43. See Louis F. Middlebrook, *Captain Gideon Olmstead* (Salem, Mass.: Newcomb & Gauss, 1933), chap. 19; Affidavit of Severin Erickson, June 14, 1793, *United States v. Olmstead,* Case File (C.C.D.N.C. 1793), NARA–Atlanta Branch; Affadivit of James Lockwood, June 14, 1793, *United States v. Olmstead;* Deposition of David Bowley, June 14, 1793, *United States v. Olmstead;* Alan Watson, *Wilmington: Port of North Carolina* (Columbia: University of South Carolina Press, 1992), 40; Jackson, *Privateers in Charleston,* 130–31. For the *Belle,* see *Federal Gazette,* Aug. 9, 1793; Jackson, *Privateers in Charleston,* 130–31.

44. *United States v. Olmstead,* order allowing the posting of bonds (C.C.D.N.C. July 3, 1793); Middlebrook, *Captain Gideon Olmstead,* chap. 19. Contemporary newspapers erroneously reported the bond as being two thousand pounds (Middlebrook, *Captain Gideon Olmstead,* chap. 19). For the decision on subject matter jurisdiction, see *Salem Gazette,* Aug. 6, 1793; *Boston Gazette,* Aug. 5, 1793.

Meanwhile, Captain Hervieux decided to convert the *Providence* to a corsair. Using funds supplied by the acting French vice consul, local shipwrights fitted her out with six carriage guns, swivels, and muskets taken from the *Vainquer de la Bastille*. Hervieux renamed his new ship *L'Aimée Marguerite,* and she became a controversial corsair. As for Olmstead, soon after he posted bond, he and presumably his crew took possession of his old ship, the *Hector,* and sailed to the West Indies. He rearmed her, renamed her the *Port-de-Paix,* and the next year he was again sailing as a corsair. The *Hector/Port-de-Paix* had a successful career, and of course Olmstead described himself and his crew as French citizens.[45]

Between Olmstead's posting of his recognizance bond in July and his scheduled reappearance in the late fall, the juries in *Henfield's Case* and *United States v. Rivers* returned their verdicts of acquittal. When the federal court finally met in Wilmington in November, a grand jury was convened, but there is no indication in the minute books that the Olmstead case was even presented to the grand jurors. After the *Henfield* and *Rivers* verdicts, the U.S. attorney probably abandoned the prosecution as unlikely to succeed. Perhaps Olmstead did not even return to North Carolina. He did, however, retain William Davie, a staunch Federalist who was elected governor of North Carolina in 1798, to appear as his counsel. On motion by Davie, the court discharged the recognizance bond, and so the grand idea of common-law prosecutions ended with a whimper.[46]

45. For the *Providence / L'Aimée Marguerite,* see Affidavit of William Reddie and John Telfair, Nov. 24, 1793, *Papers of Thomas Jefferson,* 27:627 (synopsis); Affidavit of James Robertson, Nov. 24, 1793, *Papers of Thomas Jefferson,* 27:627–28 (synopsis); Joseph de Jaudenes and Joseph Ignacio de Viar to Thomas Jefferson, Oct. 23, 1793; Thomas Jefferson to Henry Knox, Nov. 10, 1793; Thomas Jefferson to Josef Ignacio de Viar and Josef de Jaudenes, Nov. 10, 1793; Joseph de Jaudenes and Josef Ignacio de Viar to Thomas Jefferson, Dec. 26, 1793, all in *Papers of Thomas Jefferson,* 27:268–69, 343–44, 345–46, 625–28; *Castello v. Boutelle* (referring to *L'Aimée Marguerite* as *Fair Margaret*). For the *Hector / Port-de-Paix,* see *Williamson v. Brig Betsy,* 30 F. Cas.7 (D.S.C. 1795) (No. 17,750); Jackson, *Privateers in Charleston,* 130–33, 138–39, 146–47.

46. Motion by Col. W. R. Davie, Dec. 6, 1793, Circuit Court Minute Book for the District of North Carolina, NARA–Atlanta Branch.

CHAPTER 7

Consulting the Supreme Court

> Is the Minister of the French Republic to set the Acts of this Government at defiance—with impunity?
> *George Washington*
>
> The whole is an affair between the Governments of the Parties concerned—to be settled by reasons of state, not rules of law.
> *Alexander Hamilton*

The capture of the *William* sparked important litigation, but another prize proved to be more significant. In late April, *L'Embuscade* came upon the British brig *Little Sarah* off the capes of Delaware. The wind was blowing from the *Little Sarah* toward *L'Embuscade,* so Bompard could not reach his prey. He immediately launched a large boat carrying sixty armed sailors. Meanwhile, Bompard searched for a good breeze and found one. As the sailors steadily rowed toward the brig, the wind shifted and the British captain tried to reach the shore. But *L'Embuscade* was the faster ship, and Bompard took another prize. He sent her into Philadelphia, where the French consul quickly condemned her, but instead of having a public sale, agents of the French government bought her with an eye toward converting her to a commerce raider. "She was a superior sailor, copper bottomed [and] she had some cannon," Genet wrote. The plan to refit her soon became an open secret. In Philadelphia, apprentices began running away to join the *Little Sarah*. One George Leaycraft came down from New York for the "very purpose" of joining the new privateer's crew. He assured the French minister that he would "be happy in becoming a French Subject and going in her."[1]

Although the *Little Sarah* posed a host of legal problems, Genet reported, "I did not receive any complaint during the arming." In late June, however, Governor Thomas Mifflin of Pennsylvania forwarded a report to President Washington that the *Little Sarah* had been refitted. Shortly afterward, the imminent death of the president's manager at Mount Vernon required him

---

1. *Boston Gazette,* May 6, 1793; Memorial of Benjamin Holland and Peter Mackie, May 24, 1793, *Papers of Thomas Jefferson,* 26:106; *Counter Case of Great Britain,* 609–10; Genet, "Report on the Arming of Privateers" (describing the brig's qualities); Thomas Jefferson to Edmond Genet, July 11, 1793, *Papers of Thomas Jefferson,* 26:468; George Leaycraft to Edmond Genet, May 17, 1793, Genet Papers, DLC.

to return to Virginia, and while he was away, the affair exploded into a cause célèbre. On July 5, Hamilton raised the matter at a specially convened rump cabinet meeting, and the issue was referred for immediate investigation to Governor Mifflin. The very next day the master warden of Philadelphia reported that the brig originally had "four Iron Cannon Mounted, and a number of wooden." Presumably the wooden cannon were replicas intended to deceive other ships. The French, however, had augmented the brig's armament to "14 Iron Cannon and Six Swivels now mounted," and the crew had been enlarged to 120 officers, men and boys. In response to the warden's report, Mifflin called out the militia and, on Sunday, July 7, wrote Jefferson by express letter that the privateer "will probably sail this day."[2]

That Sunday was a busy day for Jefferson. He immediately rushed to the governor's house, and Mifflin told him that the previous night Alexander Dallas had a midnight consultation with Genet. Dallas, who was the Pennsylvania secretary of state, was an attorney well known for his support of the French cause. When Dallas spoke to Genet about the possibility of delaying the *Little Sarah*'s departure, Genet "flew into a great passion, talked extravagantly and concluded by refusing to order the vessel to stay."[3]

As soon as Jefferson learned of this debacle, he asked Genet to visit with him, and Genet did so that afternoon. Jefferson raised the issue of the *Little Sarah*'s impending departure, and Genet launched into "an immense feild [sic] of declaration and complaint." Genet angrily rehearsed all of his objections to the Washington administration's policy of neutrality and "charged us with violating the treaties between the two nations." During Genet's rant, Jefferson could do nothing but "let him go on." Indeed, Jefferson told Washington that "the few efforts which I made to take part in the conversation were quite ineffectual." Eventually Genet calmed down, and the two men were able to discuss the *Little Sarah*. Genet said that the brig was not yet ready to sail, and when Jefferson pressed him for assurances that she would not sail until the president returned, Genet's response was vague but reassuring. The most he was able to offer was a "look and gesture which showed he meant [Jefferson] should understand she would not be gone before" the president returned. After Jefferson left, Genet ordered the captain of

---

2. Editorial note, *Papers of Thomas Jefferson*, 26:447; Thomas Jefferson to James Madison, June 23, 1793; Nathaniel Falconer to Thomas Mifflin, July 6, 1793; and Thomas Mifflin to Thomas Jefferson, July 7, 1793, all in *Papers of Thomas Jefferson*, 26:346, 445, 444–45; Casto, "Justices' Most Significant Opinion," 177.

3. Jefferson's Memorandum, July 10, 1793, *Papers of Thomas Jefferson*, 26:463–64.

the *Little Sarah* "to receive no one on board and to go out." The next day the ship set sail.[4]

After the conference with Genet, Jefferson hurried back to Governor Mifflin's house, and Mifflin agreed to dismiss the militia. Dallas was also present, and as Jefferson described his meeting with the French minister, Dallas made a startling revelation. He said that although Genet did not "use disrespectful expressions of the President," he nevertheless had stated that if the president did not change his administration's policy of strict neutrality, Genet "would appeal from the President to the people." The day had racked Jefferson with frustration and anger, and that evening he dashed off a quick letter to James Madison condemning Genet's conduct as "calamitous." Genet, continued Jefferson, is

> hotheaded, all imagination, no judgment, passionate, disrespectful and even indecent towards the P. in his written as well as verbal communications, talking of appeals from him to Congress, from them to the people, urging the most unreasonable and groundless propositions, and in the most dictatorial style &c. &c. &c.

Jefferson bemoaned that if Genet's communications were ever placed "before Congress or the public, they will excite universal indignation."[5]

Meanwhile, Genet actually believed that the people would support him in a conflict with the president. In drafting a letter to his minister of foreign affairs, he confidently predicted, "We will soon be avenged. The people see that the behavior of its government is not similar to ours, that it encourages the arrogance of the English, and [the people] can no longer suppress its indignation." In a laughable flight of fancy, he cautioned, "That is where my moderation has been valuable." Although these passages undoubtedly reflected his true beliefs, even Genet understood that they might cause a raised eyebrow back in Paris. So he struck them from his draft.[6]

The next day, the rump cabinet of Hamilton, Jefferson, and Knox reconvened for a stormy session. Hamilton and Knox did not trust Genet and were for mounting a battery of cannon downriver at Mud Island to prevent the *Little Sarah* from sailing. Jefferson strongly dissented. The French ship was now fully armed, he declared, and if the proposed battery actually fired

4. Ibid.; Genet, "Report on the Arming of Privateers."
5. Jefferson's Memorandum, July 10, 1793, *Papers of Thomas Jefferson,* 26:463–64; Thomas Jefferson to James Madison, July 7, 1793, *Papers of Thomas Jefferson,* 26:449.
6. Genet to Minister of Foreign Affairs, July 30, 1793, "Correspondence of the French Ministers," 228–31, Minnigerode, *Genet,* 273 (translation).

upon her, "it is morally certain that bloody consequences would follow." Moreover, a powerful French squadron was expected to appear any day from the West Indies. The squadron might "arrive at the scene of blood in time to continue it, if not to partake in it." Finally, Jefferson assured Hamilton and Knox that he was "satisfied from what passed between Mr. Genet and myself at our personal interview yesterday, that the vessel will not be ordered to sail till the return of the President."[7]

By the time the president got back to Philadelphia, on Thursday, July 11, concern over the *Little Sarah* had reached a fever pitch. Jefferson was ill and had retired to a house outside Philadelphia, but he left Washington a stack of papers detailing the recent course of events. Among other things, Jefferson included a memorandum detailing his conversations with Governor Mifflin, Genet, and Dallas and specifically recounting Genet's threat that if the president did not amend the policy of strict neutrality, Genet "would appeal from the President to the people."[8]

President Washington was appalled. For weeks Genet had claimed that the government was not acting in accordance with "the people of America," but he had not threatened to go over Washington's head to the people. The threat was particularly ominous given the fact that the French Revolution and execution of Louis XVI could be viewed as an appeal of the king's reign to the people. A month later, William Willcocks, a New York Federalist, publicly charged that the threatened appeal might take the form of inciting the people "to insurrection, riot and treason," and Hamilton and Knox were saying the same thing within the cabinet. Washington furiously penned a letter to Jefferson. "What is to be done in the case of the Little Sarah?" he asked. Washington continued with two rhetorical questions dripping with anger:

> Is the Minister of the French Republic to set the Acts of this Government at defiance—*with impunity?* and then threaten the Executive with an appeal to the People. What must the World think of such conduct, and of the Government of the U. States in submitting to it?

---

7. Cabinet Opinions on the *Little Sarah*, July 8, 1793, *Papers of Thomas Jefferson*, 26:446–49; Jefferson's Memorandum, July 10, 1793, *Papers of Thomas Jefferson*, 26:467; Dissenting Opinion on the *Little Sarah*, July 8, 1793, *Papers of Thomas Jefferson*, 26:449–52.

8. Memoranda from Thomas Jefferson to George Washington, July 11–13, 1793, *Papers of Thomas Jefferson*, 26:476–81; Memorandum of a Conversation with Edmond Genet, July 10, 1793, *Papers of Thomas Jefferson*, 26:463–66.

The president's concern about what the world would think was justified. A few months later the British minister complained to his Foreign Office that the American government's policy amounted to "half measures and Palliatives, that would disgrace the miserable republic of San Marino." The president was mortified and wished to resolve these "serious questions" as soon as possible.[9]

The cabinet met the next day and discussed many of the legal issues involved in the refitting of the *Little Sarah*. Genet's threat against the president hung over the meeting, and the cabinet decided to refer all the legal issues to the justices of the Supreme Court, who were described as "persons learned in the law." Formal advice from the Court would finally settle the legal issues in dispute within the cabinet, and in the event that Genet truly launched his "appeal to the people," a Supreme Court opinion would provide valuable political support. The same day Jefferson wrote a circular letter to the justices informing them that Washington was "desirous of asking the advice of the Judges of the Supreme Court of the United States on certain matters of great public concern." Jefferson simultaneously wrote the British and French ministers informing them of the decision to consult the Supreme Court and noting that the president "will expect" that the *Little Sarah*'s departure would be delayed "until his ultimate determination." Notwithstanding Jefferson's request, the *Little Sarah,* which was renamed the *Petite Democrate,* sailed pursuant to Genet's previous order and embarked upon a successful career against British commerce.[10]

While waiting for the justices to come to Philadelphia, the cabinet members worked out a comprehensive set of twenty-nine legal questions for the Court. At about the same time, Jefferson reviewed in his mind a number of specific issues that the cabinet had considered over the previous few months and recorded his understanding of the cabinet's deliberations in a set of

---

9. William Willcock's Address, *United States Chronicle,* Aug. 15, 1793, reprinted from *Daily Advertiser;* Thomas Jefferson to James Madison, Aug. 11, 1793, and George Washington to Thomas Jefferson, July 11, 1793, *Papers of Thomas Jefferson,* 26:560, 481; George Hammond to James Bland Burges, Oct. 12, 1793, James Bland Burges Papers, Bodleian Library, Oxford University.

10. Cabinet Opinion on Consulting the Supreme Court, July 12, 1793, *Papers of Thomas Jefferson,* 26:484–85; Thomas Jefferson to John Jay, July 12, 1793, *Documentary History of the Supreme Court,* 6:744 (app.); Thomas Jefferson to Edmond Genet and George Hammond, July 12, 1793, *Papers of Thomas Jefferson,* 26:487–88; Edmond Genet, "Report on Arming of Privateers," n.d., Edmond Genet Papers, DLC; Maud Woodfin, "Citizen Genet and his Mission" (Ph.D. diss., University of Chicago, 1928), D-5 (app.).

rough notes. These notes are particularly valuable because they indicate the specific issues on which there was actual disagreement within the cabinet. A comparison of Jefferson's notes and some of the final questions provides clues to the motivation for posing the questions.[11]

The first question that the cabinet wished answered was

> Do the treaties between the U.S. & France give to France or her citizens a *right,* when at war with a power with whom the U.S. are at peace, to fit out originally in and from the ports of the U.S., vessels armed for war, with or without a commission?

Although the French minister insisted that the treaties by negative implication gave France such a right, the cabinet had reached the unanimous conclusion that the treaties left the United States "free to prohibit her from arming vessels in our ports." In other words, the cabinet wished to pose a question to the Court in which there was no dispute whatsoever within the government as to the proper answer.[12]

There was, however, clear disagreement within the cabinet as to the proper resolution of other issues that would be presented to the Court. The cabinet's sixteenth question is illustrative. Although there was complete agreement that commerce raiders should not be fitted out in American ports, there was disagreement as to the propriety of French ships being sailed into American ports and outfitted with French cannon brought to America from France. Jefferson was "of the opinion they [the French] are free to use their own means, i.e., to mount their guns &c.," but Hamilton and Knox were "of opinion they are not to put even their own implements or means into a posture of annoyance."[13]

This precise issue was implicated in the case of the *Little Sarah.* Although ten iron cannon and six swivels had been added to her armament, all but two of these additional guns were France's "own property." Accordingly, the cabinet wished to ask the Supreme Court,

---

11. Questions Proposed to be Submitted to the Chief Justice and Judges of the Supreme Court, July 18, 1793, *Documentary History of the Supreme Court,* 6:747–51 (app.); Notes on Neutrality, July 13, 1793, *Papers of Thomas Jefferson,* 26:498–500. See generally The Referral of Neutrality Questions to the Supreme Court, *Papers of Thomas Jefferson,* 26:525–37.

12. Question 1, *Documentary History of the Supreme Court,* 6:747 (app.); Notes on Neutrality Questions, July 13, 1793, *Papers of Thomas Jefferson,* 26:498–500.

13. Notes on Neutrality Questions, July 13, 1793, *Papers of Thomas Jefferson,* 26:499.

Does it make any difference in point of principle, whether a vessel be armed for war, or the force of an armed vessel be augmented, in the ports of the U.S. with *means* procured in the U.S. or with means brought into them by the party who shall so arm or augment the force of such vessel?

This question was particularly important because the president had yet to resolve the disagreement on this precise issue between Hamilton and Jefferson.[14]

In seeking advice from the Court, President Washington undoubtedly was motivated in part by a desire to obtain political support for his decisions. The president and his cabinet had unanimously concluded that French commerce raiders could not be completely fitted out in American ports, and Genet had vehemently objected to this policy. Given the cabinet's unanimity, an important reason for referring this issue to the Court was undoubtedly to secure political support in dealing with Genet's threatened appeal to the people. Surely there was no thought that a Supreme Court opinion would persuade Genet of the error of his ways. Just a few weeks earlier, Genet had sneered at Jefferson's suggestion that the federal judiciary would resolve many of the disputed issues in criminal prosecutions and suits for restitution. Genet dismissed the federal judiciary as mere "counsellors, since no particular tribunal has the right or the power to interpose between two nations." In seeking the justices' advice, Jefferson specifically asked "whether the public may, with propriety, be availed of their [the justices'] *advice.*" In other words, Washington was not seeking confidential advice but had planned from the outset to make the justices' advice available to the public.[15]

In addition, some of the legal issues, like the augmentation of a ship's armament using French rather than American cannon, were hotly disputed within the president's cabinet. Two days after the president and the cabinet resolved to seek the Court's advice, the attorney general of Pennsylvania, who was soon to become the attorney general of the United States, told his

---

14. Nathaniel Falconer to Thomas Mifflin, July 6, 1793, *Papers of Thomas Jefferson*, 26:445; Question 16, *Documentary History of the Supreme Court*, 6:749 (app.); Notes on Neutrality Questions, July 13, 1793, *Papers of Thomas Jefferson*, 26:500.

15. Thomas Jefferson to Justices, July 18, 1793, *Documentary History of the Supreme Court*, 6:747 (app.); Thomas Jefferson to Edmund Genet, June 17, 1793, *Papers of Thomas Jefferson*, 26:300; Edmund Genet to Thomas Jefferson, June 22, 1793, *Papers of Thomas Jefferson*, 26:341, and *American State Papers*, 156 (English translation).

father-in-law that the decision was the result of "some difference in the construction of the treaty [that] has taken place among the President's advisers." Although Hamilton and Jefferson agreed that the United States should remain neutral, their differing attitudes toward France and Great Britain placed them in conflict in respect to some of the details of neutrality. A Supreme Court advisory opinion would be a good way to resolve these conflicts.[16]

The justices, however, were not available for immediate consultation. Justice Wilson lived in Philadelphia, but Chief Justice Jay and Justices Iredell, Paterson, and Cushing were out of town. Jefferson immediately sent letters to the absent justices requesting their return by July 18, the following week, to advise the president. By July 17, Chief Justice Jay and Justice Paterson had arrived, and Jay immediately consulted with the president. Apparently Jay expressed some private qualms about the propriety of the justices providing an advisory opinion. After talking with Jay, the president wrote Jefferson that "the Judges will have to decide whether the business which, it is proposed to ask their opinion upon is, in their judgment, of such a nature as that they can comply."[17]

Jefferson then sent a formal request for the justices' opinions. He noted that the war had given rise to many legal questions "of considerable difficulty, and of greater importance to the peace of the US." Ordinarily the Supreme Court would be expected to address these kinds of questions in the context of specific litigation, but Judge Peters's recent decision in *Findlay* indicated that the federal courts were not authorized to hear cases involving French prizes. Jefferson, therefore, explained that the questions were "often presented under circumstances *which do not give a cognisance of them to the tribunals of the country.*" He specifically emphasized what the justices already knew—that the request was from the president himself.[18]

Jefferson explained that the president had two distinct purposes for seeking the justices' opinions. First, he wanted to do the right thing and wished to avoid placing the United States in violation of the law. The justices' opinion "would secure us against errors dangerous to the peace of the US." In

---

16. William Bradford Jr. to Elias Boudinot, July 14, 1793, *Documentary History of the Supreme Court,* 6:744 (app.).

17. Thomas Jefferson to John Jay, July 12, 1793, and George Washington to Thomas Jefferson, July 18, 1793, *Documentary History of the Supreme Court,* 6:744, 745 (app.); see Casto, "Justices' Most Significant Opinion," 183.

18. Thomas Jefferson to the Justices, July 18, 1793, *Documentary History of the Supreme Court,* 6:747 (app.).

addition, Jefferson explained, an opinion from the justices would provide the president with important political support. Their "authority [would] ensure the respect of all parties." Jefferson did not state who "all parties" were, but he clearly had in mind France and Great Britain. He had already informed the British and French ministers of the cabinet's decision to seek judicial advice. It is doubtful, however, whether anyone seriously believed that Genet would have been persuaded by a Supreme Court decision contrary to France's interests. In addition, Jefferson undoubtedly anticipated using the justices' advice to resolve some of his disputes with Hamilton. Jefferson also had in mind the American public. In seeking an opinion that would be made available to the public, Jefferson proposed a two-step process. First, he sought the justices' "opinion, whether the public may, with propriety, be availed of their *advice on these questions*." Second, "if they [the public] may, to present, for their [the justices'] advice, the abstract questions."[19]

The justices immediately responded as most lawyers do. They asked for more time. Only four of the six justices had reached Philadelphia by July 20. Because the request "affects the judicial Department," the justices felt "a reluctance to decide it, without the advice and participation of our absent Brethren." In response, the president acquiesced in the justices' desire to await the arrival of their "absent Brethren."[20]

On August 8, about three weeks after Jefferson formally broached the matter, the justices politely declined to provide the requested advisory opinion. In a letter addressed to the president, they wrote that they were specifically concerned about maintaining the "Lines of Separation drawn by the Constitution between the three Departments of Government" and the fact that the three departments are "in certain Respects checks on each other." The justices also noted that they were "Judges of a court in the last Resort." They did not present these considerations as a flat bar to advisory opinions but simply stated without elaboration that these "considerations . . . afford strong arguments against the Propriety of our extrajudicially deciding the [president's] questions." They reached their conclusion "especially as the Power given by the Constitution to the President of calling on the Heads of

---

19. Ibid.; Jay, *Most Humble Servants,* 158–59; Edmund Genet to Thomas Jefferson, June 22, 1793, *Papers of Thomas Jefferson,* 26:341, and *American State Papers,* 156 (English translation).

20. Justices of the Supreme Court to George Washington, July 20, 1793, and George Washington to Justices, July 23, 1793, *Documentary History of the Supreme Court,* 6:752, 753 (app.).

Departments for opinions, seems to have been *purposely* as well as expressly limited to *executive* Departments."[21]

The justices' references to the Constitution's "Lines of Separation" and the fact that the executive, legislative, and judicial branches are expected to be "in certain Respects checks on each other" are vague, but we have some idea of what Chief Justice Jay had in mind when he penned these phrases. Obviously he was referring to the general constitutional theory of separation of powers, and three years earlier, in his first grand jury charge, he had explained his understanding of this theory: "Wise and virtuous men have thought and reasoned very differently respecting Government," but they have "unanimously agreed . . . that [its] powers should be divided into three distinct, independent Departments—The Executive legislative and judicial." The purpose of this separation of powers is "to guard against Abuse and Fluctuation, & preserve the Constitution from Encroachments." To accomplish this purpose, "much Pains have been taken so to form and define [the three branches of government] so that they may operate as Checks one on the other."[22]

Jay's earlier grand jury charge on separation of powers tells us how he thought that separation of powers issues should be decided. Jay was a pragmatic man who began his grand jury charge by frankly stating that the new national government is an "Experiment," and the "the good Sense of the People will be enabled by Experience to discover and correct its Imperfections." He continued:

> If the most discerning and enlightened minds may be mistaken relative to theories unconfirmed by Practice—if on such difficult Questions men may differ in opinion and yet be Patriots—and if the Merits of our opinions can only be ascertained by Experience, let us patiently abide the Tryal, and unite our Endeavors to render it a fair and an impartial one.

The president's 1793 request for advice was part of the ongoing experience under the Constitution.[23]

---

21. Justices to George Washington, Aug. 8, 1793, *Documentary History of the Supreme Court,* 6:755 (app.).

22. John Jay's Charge to the Grand Jury of the Circuit Court for the District of New York, Apr. 12, 1790, *Documentary History of the Supreme Court,* 2:25–30; Casto, *Supreme Court,* 125–29.

23. John Jay's Charge to the Grand Jury, Apr. 12, 1790, *Documentary History of the Supreme Court,* 2:25–30.

The justices' reference to the doctrine of separation of powers as a reason for declining to advise the president is at first glance somewhat puzzling. As the justices noted, the purpose of this doctrine is to enable the independent departments to serve as "checks on each other" or, to use Jay's earlier words, "to guard against Abuse and Fluctuation, & preserve the Constitution from Encroachments." The president's request was not inconsistent with this purpose. To the contrary, he was offering the Court a chance to review executive action before it was taken. This proffered opportunity would have permitted the justices to check executive action before government resources were committed and before anyone was harmed by a good faith but erroneous presidential decision regarding the requirements of the law. On the other hand, if the justices were primarily concerned about the president's power to order them to provide advice, their references to separation of powers makes more sense.

The justices also referred to "our being Judges of a court in the last Resort" but again failed to elaborate. Perhaps they had in mind the fact that the very questions that the president might pose probably would come before the Court in actual litigation. In administering the Invalid Pensions Act a year earlier, Justice Iredell and District Judge John Sitgreaves had expressed reservations about providing advisory opinions. They explained that judges, "in general," should be "extremely cautious in not intimating an opinion in any case extra-judicially." Caution was necessary "because we well know how liable the best minds are, notwithstanding their utmost care, to a bias which may arise from a preconceived opinion, even unjudicially, much more deliberately given." In a subsequent formal opinion, which Iredell announced to the public, he stated that if a question came before him in a nonjudicial capacity that "could by any possibility come before me as a Judge, either in the circuit or the Supreme Court, I ought not to exercise the authority [to decide it extrajudicially]." Chief Justice Jay expressed a similar sensitivity to this problem in private correspondence with a fellow justice in 1792.[24]

For the last hundred years, everyone who has focused upon the justices' reference to having final appellate authority has assumed that they were raising a concern about prejudging an issue that might later come before them in litigation. If so, they did not expressly state their concern on this

---

24. James Iredell and John Sitgreaves to George Washington, June 8, 1792, *Documentary History of the Supreme Court,* 6:287; Reasons for Acting as a Commissioner on the Invalid Act, Sept 26, 1792, *Documentary History of the Supreme Court,* 6:291. See Casto, "Justices' Most Significant Opinion," 187.

occasion. Rather, they placed emphasis on the fact that they constituted a court of "last resort" rather than a lower trial court. They may have intended simply to describe the particular nature of their judicial office, but their choice of words indicates that they viewed their possession of final appellate authority as having special significance. Perhaps they thought that a judge of a lower court might have a broader discretion to provide advisory opinions because an inferior court would be subject to appellate review by a higher court whose judges would be unembarrassed by preconceived ideas about a particular legal issue. Justice Iredell, however, explicitly rejected this distinction a year earlier. The most plausible explanation for the justices' emphasis upon their being a court of last resort lies in their knowledge of the English practice in respect of extrajudicial advisory opinions. In fact, English judges had been giving advisory opinions to the Crown for over a hundred years. American lawyers were fully aware of this practice, and the practice undoubtedly informed the cabinet's decision to seek an advisory opinion. When Thomas Jefferson informed James Madison of the justices' refusal, he could not resist noting that "in England you know such questions are referred regularly to the judge of Admiralty." In light of this well-known practice, the justices may have emphasized their being a court of last resort in order to distinguish the English precedent. In England, advisory opinions were rendered by the common law and Admiralty judges, but not by the House of Lords, which was the English court of last resort. Perhaps the justices simply meant that like the House of Lords, they were not bound to comply with a request by the executive.[25]

The justices' concluding argument was a reference to the provision in Article II, Section 2, of the Constitution, which provides that the president "may require the Opinion, in writing of the principal Officer in each of the executive Departments, upon any Subject relating to the Parties of their respective Offices." As the justices emphasized, this provision is "expressly limited to *executive* Departments" and therefore does not address the issue of judicial advisory opinions. Apparently, however, the justices believed that the provision implicitly limits the practice of judicial advisory opinions by negative inference. In other words, the president "may require" executive branch officers to provide opinions but may not require the judicial to provide an opinion.[26]

---

25. See Casto, "Justices' Most Significant Opinion," 188–89; Thomas Jefferson to James Madison, Aug. 11, 1793, *Papers of Thomas Jefferson,* 26:651–53; Jay, *Most Humble Servants,* chap. 1.

26. U.S. Constitution, art. 2, sec. 2.

This final consideration also supports a narrow reading of their refusal to provide an advisory opinion. The Constitution clearly empowers the president to require department heads to provide written opinions but does not expressly address a comparable presidential power in respect of the judiciary. If a negative inference is to be drawn from this provision, the inference would be that the president does not have a similar power to require the Supreme Court to provide an advisory opinion. This narrow reading is consistent with the other arguments adduced by the justices. A presidential power to compel action from the Courts detracts from the Court's independent stature under the plan of the Constitution. To the extent that the president is given power over the Court, the "Lines of Separation drawn by the . . . Constitution" are blurred. The diminution in the Court's independent statute would reduce its ability to serve as a check upon the executive. Similarly, the justices' reference to their being a court of "last resort" easily could be read as addressing the narrow issue of whether the president had power to compel the Court to render advice. By emphasizing the Supreme Court's status as a court of last resort, the justices may have been thinking about the well-established English practice, under which the king lacked authority to compel the House of Lords to take action.[27]

In other words, the justices quite possibly wrote their opinion solely to address the narrow issue of presidential authority to compel the rendering of an advisory opinion. Nothing in their letter expressly addresses the issue of whether the justices had a discretionary power to render an advisory opinion. Their 1793 refusal to provide advice to President Washington cannot plausibly be read as precedent for an absolute bar to advisory opinions. Certainly the opinion itself is not written in absolute terms. The justices did not state their "considerations" as an absolute bar to the president's request. Instead, they described them as "strong arguments."[28]

The justices' refusal must be considered in the context of their willingness to provide advisory opinions on many other occasions before and after the summer of 1793. Chief Justice Jay evidenced no qualms about advising the president during the Nootka Sound Crisis. After the crisis, the next chief justice, Oliver Ellsworth, wrote advisory opinions on issues of immense national importance. When a dispute erupted between the president and the House of Representatives over executive privilege and the Jay Treaty, Chief Justice Ellsworth wrote a lengthy opinion advising that the president was

27. The Justices to George Washington, Aug. 8, 1793, *Documentary History of the Supreme Court*, 6:755.
28. Ibid.

not obligated to provide the House with confidential papers related to the treaty. Ellsworth also advised Secretary of State Timothy Pickering on the constitutionality of the Sedition Act. This latter advisory opinion is particularly noteworthy because Pickering was the cabinet officer charged with supervising the U.S. attorneys who would bring prosecutions under the act, and Ellsworth's circuit riding duties required him to preside over prosecutions. Throughout the 1790s, the justices were also happy to provide advisory opinions on more mundane matters. When the justices' 1793 refusal is considered in this context, their refusal is difficult to explain except in prudential terms.[29]

The argument has been made that the early justices drew a distinction between institutional advisory opinions, which as a court they were not allowed to render, and private opinions that they might render as individuals. If so, none of the early justices ever stated such a distinction. Moreover, on at least one occasion Chief Justice Jay, Justice Cushing, and District Judge Duane, sitting as a circuit court, rendered an advisory opinion and formally entered it on the minutes of the court. This action looks for all the world like an institutional advisory opinion and was viewed as a decision of the court by a sophisticated contemporary observer.[30]

Although the justices seem to have written their letter of refusal primarily to address the issue of raw presidential power over the Court, the fact remains that they could have denied that the president had constitutional power to compel the rendering of an advisory opinion and then proceeded to provide an opinion in the exercise of their own sound discretion. Such peekaboo strategies were not unknown to the Court. About a year earlier, when the justices decided that duties assigned to them as circuit judges under the Invalid Pensioners Act were unconstitutional, most of them decided nevertheless to perform those duties as commissioners rather than judges. But the justices clearly decided against a peekaboo approach in 1793 and refused to render the requested advice.[31]

Some have speculated that the justices were dissatisfied with the extent to which they were required to perform extrajudicial services and that their refusal "was part of a broader attempt by the early Supreme Court to

29. See chapter 6, this volume; Casto, *Supreme Court,* 97–98, 147–57, 178–83; William R. Casto, "Two Advisory Opinions by Chief Justice Oliver Ellsworth," *Greenbag 2d* 6 (2003): 413–16; Jay, *Humble Servants.*

30. Maeva Marcus, "Separation of Powers in the Early National Period," *William & Mary Law Review* 30 (1989): 269; Casto, *Supreme Court,* 180–81.

31. Casto, *Early Supreme Court,* 175–78.

deemphasize the obligatory extrajudicial service concept."[32] If so, there is no surviving evidence that directly supports this speculation. More significantly if the justices were especially upset by some of the picayune nonjudicial duties assigned to them, they picked a strange time to assert their independence. George Washington was the most respected man in the United States, and he had personally appointed each of the justices to their office. The United States was in the throes of a major foreign affairs crisis, and the French minister was threatening to challenge Washington's judgment in the court of public opinion. That the justices, who were mature and responsible public servants, would have used the occasion to score political points in an effort "to deemphasize the obligatory extrajudicial service concept" is highly unlikely.

Others have speculated that the justices' refusal was motivated in significant part by the formidable extent and magnitude of the questions. Had they "been brief and easily answered the Court might, not improbably, have slipped into the adoption of a precedent that would have engrafted the English usage upon our national system."[33] Aside from the formidable nature of the questions, there is nothing in the extant historical record to support this speculation. Perhaps some of the justices were happy not to have to answer the questions. At the same time, however, some of the justices —Iredell and Wilson, for example—prided themselves on their ability to engage in rigorous, exhaustive, and exhausting legal analysis. On balance, there is little likelihood that the justices were motivated primarily by a desire to avoid an arduous task. Certainly they would not have done so if they believed that the president really needed their advice.

So why did the justices not come to the assistance of their president in his hour of need? Given their willingness on other occasions to write advisory opinions on a wide range of issues, the answer must surely be that they did not believe their assistance was vital. The justices were experienced politicians, and they undoubtedly had ex parte conferences with President Washington and his cabinet. We know that as soon as Chief Justice Jay returned to the capital, he consulted in private with the president. Jay apparently asked Washington for a copy of the questions that needed to be answered, and the president "was embarrassed" to respond that the questions had yet

---

32. Wheeler, "Extrajudicial Activities," 158.
33. James Thayer, "Advisory Opinions," in *Legal Essays,* by James Thayer (Boston: Chipman Law, 1908), 54; Hershkoff, "State Courts and the 'Passive Virtues': Rethinking the Judicial Function," *Harvard Law Review* 114 (2001): 1844n62; Casto, *Supreme Court,* 250; Wheeler, "Extrajudicial Activities," 154n141.

to be drafted. In addition, Jay told the president that the justices might be unwilling to answer the questions.[34]

Following Jay's premonitory suggestion that an advisory opinion might not be forthcoming, no advisory opinion was ever requested. Instead, the president, through Jefferson, wound up asking the justices only the preliminary question of whether the justices would answer questions if questions were proffered. By the end of July, all the justices, save Cushing, were in town and had decided not to render an advisory opinion. Although their formal letter of refusal was not written until August 8, they clearly informed the president of their decision much earlier through informal channels. As early as July 29, the cabinet knew that no advisory opinion would be forthcoming and commenced working out an executive branch answer to the questions that they would have submitted to the Court.[35]

The most likely explanation for the justices' refusal lies with Alexander Hamilton. We know that Chief Justice Jay conferred with the president on this issue. Moreover, Jay and Justice Wilson conferred with Jefferson on at least one occasion. It is inconceivable that they did not also speak with Alexander Hamilton. After all, Jay and Hamilton were close political allies, and the two had frequently conferred with each other in the past.[36]

We do not know what Hamilton told the justices in private, but we do know that Hamilton believed that the resolution of many issues related to the Neutrality Crisis should be based upon reasons of state rather than legal principles, and so he opposed referring some questions to the Court. In addition to this theoretical concern, Hamilton had reason to believe that he had a significant practical advantage if issues were resolved within the cabinet. Throughout the Neutrality Crisis, President Washington showed a clear preference for resolving disputes within the cabinet by taking informal votes. Because there were only four cabinet members and because Secretary of War Knox always voted with Hamilton, Jefferson could not manage a majority vote on a disputed question.[37]

Jefferson fully understood that all disputes began with a vote of two (Hamilton and Knox) to one (Jefferson), which left Attorney General Randolph as an

---

34. George Washington to Thomas Jefferson, July 18, 1793, *Documentary History of the Supreme Court,* 6:745 (app.).

35. Notes on Cabinet Meeting on Neutrality, July 29, 1793, *Papers of Thomas Jefferson,* 26:579.

36. Thomas Jefferson to George Washington, July 29, 1793, *Documentary History of the Supreme Court,* 6:751 (app.); see chapter 3, this volume.

37. See Casto, "Justices' Most Significant Opinion," 198–99.

unreliable swing vote. During the first month of the crisis, Jefferson bitterly complained to James Monroe that "our votes are generally 2½ against 1½." Jefferson was more blunt when he described Randolph's vacillations to James Madison:

> Every thing my dear Sir, now hangs on the opinion of a single person, and that the most indecisive one I ever had to do business with. He always continues to agree in principle with one, but in conclusion with the other. . . . If anything prevents [the administration's policy] from being a mere English neutrality, it will be that the penchant of the P[resident] is not that way, and above all, the ardent spirit of our constituents.

Given this voting trend within the cabinet, Jefferson probably viewed the prospect of an advisory opinion from the justices as more desirable than a likely defeat within the cabinet.[38]

The issue of whether the French could arm raiders in American ports with cannon brought from France is illustrative. In Randolph's absence from the capital, Hamilton and Knox outvoted Jefferson two to one, and the president had yet to decide the matter. The justices might have decided this narrow issue in Jefferson's favor, but their refusal to provide an advisory opinion remanded the issue to the cabinet. When Randolph returned, the cabinet and President Washington decided the issue along the line proposed by Hamilton. About two weeks later, Jefferson bitterly complained that Randolph "is the poorest Cameleon I ever saw [and] his opinion always makes the majority, and that the president acquiesces *always* in the majority."[39]

Hamilton also may have lobbied the justices because he knew that the answers to some of the questions would embarrass the government. Questions one and three asked whether the treaties gave France a *"right"* to fit out originally or refit corsairs in American ports, and there was unanimous agreement within the cabinet that the treaties conferred no such right. Questions eleven and thirteen asked the same question in a subtlety different way. The latter two questions shifted from questions of absolute right to whether the United States could in its discretion "allow" France to fit out or refit corsairs in American ports. The answer to these later questions was not

---

38. Thomas Jefferson to James Monroe, May 5, 1793, and Thomas Jefferson to James Madison, May 15, 1793, both in *Papers of Thomas Jefferson,* 25:661, 26:26.

39. Rules on Neutrality, Aug. 3, 1793 (item 6), *Papers of Thomas Jefferson,* 26:608; Thomas Jefferson to James Madison, Aug 11, 1793, *Papers of Thomas Jefferson,* 26:651–53.

entirely clear, and the justices may very well have responded that the government had this authority.[40]

Four days after the questions were put in final form, Justice Wilson addressed these questions in his charge to the grand jury that indicted Henfield. Wilson emphatically rejected Genet's argument that by negative implication the treaties established a right to fit out corsairs, but he stated that the United States might, if it wished, give France permission to fit out corsairs. Judge Wilson specifically said that "it remains in our *Option* whether we will or will not *grant* it to *France*." Because the government clearly had not exercised its option and granted permission, Wilson instructed the grand jury that private citizens were not free to participate in fitting out corsairs.[41]

Wilson's charge on the issue of permission was not a slip of the pen. In an earlier grand jury charge, Chief Justice Jay made the same distinction between right and permission. He stated that levying soldiers in a country is a sovereign right and "no foreign power can lawfully exercise it without Permission." To be sure, Jay and Wilson believed that as a general matter international law required neutral countries to treat belligerents with impartiality. Thus it could be argued that because Article 22 barred the British from fitting out privateers, the rule of impartiality required a similar bar against French corsairs. But when William Loughton Smith made this precise argument the next year regarding the sale of prizes, James Madison successfully argued that the French treaties authorized the United States to permit the sale of prizes.[42]

If the Supreme Court agreed with Madison's analysis, their advice regarding questions eleven and thirteen would have been that the government may, if it wishes, grant France the right to fit out corsairs in American ports. The Court, however, would not have given the president advice on whether permission should or should not be granted. Hamilton understood this, and on a closely related question, he advised Washington that the courts "are not competent to the decision. The whole is an affair between the Governments of the parties concerned . . . to be settled by reasons of state, not

40. Questions Proposed to Be Submitted, July 18, 1793, *Documentary History of the Supreme Court,* 6:747–50 (app.).

41. James Wilson's charge to the Grand Jury of a Special Session of the Circuit Court for the District of Pennsylvania, July 22, 1793, *Documentary History of the Supreme Court,* 2:420–21.

42. John Jay's Charge to the Grand Jury of the Circuit Court for the District of Virginia, May 22, 1793, *Documentary History of the Supreme Court,* 2:387; chapter 9, this volume.

rules of law." To use Hamilton's words, a decision to grant France permission to fit out corsairs would turn on "reasons of state, not rules of law."[43]

A Supreme Court advisory opinion that the government could, if it wished, grant special privileges to France was worse than useless if the president wished the Court's assistance in combating Genet's threatened appeal to the people. Genet's position was that the people wanted to help republican France in its struggle against the combined royalty of Europe. A formal Supreme Court advisory opinion that the government could help France if it wished would be a public relations disaster and actually help Genet.

Given Hamilton's position of strength within the cabinet and his previously announced disinclination to submit neutrality questions to the Court, Hamilton almost surely argued in private to Chief Justice Jay and other justices against the need for an advisory opinion. There remained Genet's threatened appeal to the people, but Hamilton and Jay had a plan to hoist Genet on his own petard. They would publicize the threat as a personal attack on George Washington, which it was, and have the people choose between a French upstart and the man who was first in war, first in peace, and first of the hearts of his countrymen.[44]

43. Alexander Hamilton to George Washington, May 15, 1793, *Papers of Alexander Hamilton,* 14:459.
44. See chapter 9, this volume.

CHAPTER 8

A Naval Duel

> Citizen BOMPARD will wait on
> Capt. COURTENAY . . . at the Hook.
> *Jean-Baptiste François Bompard*
>
> The Gaul had the best of the fight, tis agreed
> The Briton—the best of the race.
> *Anonymous poem*

While the justices were considering the cabinet's questions, Bompard and his crew achieved a stunning victory against the Royal Navy. On the morning of Monday, July 29, *L'Embuscade* was in New York Harbor for some minor repairs. Bompard, probably anticipating a leisurely day, could not possibly have anticipated that in the next three days, a challenge to a duel would lead to a desperate frigate action that would be discussed in President Washington's cabinet meetings and celebrated throughout America in toasts, poems, and songs.[1]

After breakfast he may have turned with a frown to the bane of every captain's existence: paperwork. As he slowly plowed through the accumulated lists, returns, balances, tabulations, and reports, the watch on deck saw a small launch rowing toward *L'Embuscade*. Eventually word reached Bompard that the launch bore an important message from Hauterive, the French consul. A British frigate, the *Boston,* was cruising off Sandy Hook and masquerading as a French ship.

As soon as Bompard heard the message, he knew he had been tricked. He had learned over the weekend that a strange cruiser had appeared off the coast and that the stranger was the frigate *Concorde,* newly arrived from France via Cap Français in the West Indies. Bompard and Consul Hauterive had been delighted by this news of reinforcements and had sent a message out to the *"Concorde"* suggesting that she sail toward Rhode Island to catch a British pirate who was plundering Frenchmen without a letter of marque. Bompard had sent the message in a barge with Lieutenant Whittemore, the Bostonian he had hired in Charleston, and nine other members of *L'Embuscade*'s crew. Undoubtedly the *Boston* had taken the barge and crew, but the ruse hardly could have been a complete surprise. Ships in the eighteenth century frequently flew their enemy's flags in the hope of obtaining some advantage. Indeed, just three months earlier, *L'Embuscade* had flown

---

1. This chapter is drawn from Casto, "Rights of Man."

the British flag before capturing the British merchantman *Grange*. This was an accepted *ruse de guerre* as long as the ship showed her true colors before opening fire.[2]

However irritating the likely capture of Lieutenant Whittemore must have been, the most astonishing news from Consul Hauterive was that the *Boston*'s captain had openly challenged Bompard to a ship-to-ship duel. By chance, the two captains actually knew each other. Some say that Bompard had been taken prisoner by the British captain during the American Revolution, but Bompard's surviving personnel records do not indicate that he was taken prisoner. It is more likely that the two met during peacetime when Bompard sailed on packets as an auxiliary officer or lowly lieutenant, and the Englishman, who was five years his junior, was already an august captain. The misery of those lean peacetime years surely rushed back coupled with an opportunity for revenge against an enemy who epitomized the system of influence that had kept Bompard down for so many years. He resolved to accept the challenge.[3]

The English captain was George William Augustus Courtenay, a rising star in the Royal Navy clearly destined for promotion to admiral at an early age. In 1781, at the age of twenty, Courtenay became a lieutenant and almost immediately received a plum assignment to an admiral's staff. Courtenay had what Bompard lacked: influence. Although Courtenay technically was not a nobleman, his uncle was the second Earl of Bute, his first cousin had served as chief minister of Britain, and another cousin, who was a dear friend, was in Parliament.[4]

For all this influence, Courtenay never viewed his commission as a sinecure. He had entered the Royal Navy when he was fourteen years old, and in a number of battles he proved himself to be a capable and aggressive leader. Promotion to acting lieutenant came in 1780, and he almost immediately became Admiral Rodney's flag lieutenant in the West Indies. In 1782, he distinguished himself in Rodney's victory over the French at the Saintes. Courtenay's cousin later wrote, "When Rodney's genius forc'd the gallic line, / In victory's van he saw you early shine." Rodney was so impressed that,

---

2. Alexander Maurice Hauterive to J. B. F. Bompard, July 29, 1793, Bompard's Personnel File, SHM; Casto, "Rights of Man," 266; see chapter 4, this volume; Timothy Wilson, *Flags at Sea* (London: Her Majesty's Stationary Office, 1986), 109.

3. Casto, "Rights of Man," 266–67.

4. Egerton Brydges, *Collin's Peerage of England* (London: Rivington Otridge & Son, 1812), 2:574–75; George W. A. Courtenay's Lieutenant's Passing Certificate, PRO:ADM 6/89. The cousin in Parliament was John Courtenay.

on the spot, he promoted Courtenay, then twenty-one, to the rank of captain and temporarily gave him the *Anson,* a ship of the line whose captain had been killed in the victory. Such early promotions were unusual but happened on occasion. Horatio Nelson was promoted captain when he was twenty, and August Keppel was nineteen when he became a captain.[5]

Because Courtenay's utter lack of seniority did not warrant command of such a large ship, Rodney almost immediately transferred him to the command of the small, twenty-four-gun frigate *Eurydice.* A few days later, Rodney sent Courtenay back to England with duplicate copies of the despatches announcing the great victory. Courtenay made the most of his new command. Shortly after returning to European waters, he fought a successful battle in which he took a French fourteen-gun brig. When peace came in 1783, his influence kept him from having to serve at half-pay without a ship. He sailed to the East Indies to convey the news that the Treaty of Paris had concluded the Revolutionary War. While in India, he married Frances Ogle, the daughter of a British general.[6]

Although influence can jump a twenty-one year old to the rank of captain, promotion to admiral was another matter altogether. Throughout the eighteenth century, promotion to flag rank in the Royal Navy was based solely upon seniority. In 1793, when war resumed with France and Citizen Bompard sailed *L'Embuscade* to the New World, Courtenay was not quite half way up the captain's list, with 219 captains ahead of him. Nevertheless, he had reason to hope for a somewhat accelerated promotion to admiral. In the late 1780s, the Admiralty began obliquely recognizing merit by forcing unfit senior captains to retire, and in 1787 these forced retirements were in effect approved when Parliament rejected a challenge to the new system. In addition, with war being newly declared, England hungered for victories. Earlier in the summer Capt. Edward Pellew, who fought the first successful frigate action of the war, was knighted the day he set foot back in England. In 1793, Captain Courtenay was an aggressive thirty-year-old officer who knew that the newly declared war would offer similar opportunities for himself.[7]

---

5. John Courtenay, *Elegy to the Memory of George W. A. Courtenay, Esq.* (London: Henry Baldwin, 1793; private 2nd ed., post-1816); *Gentleman's Magazine* (London), Sept. 1793, 862 (obituary); Casto, "Rights of Man," 267.

6. Casto, "Rights of Man," 267.

7. William Laird Clowes, *The Royal Navy* (London: Samson Law Marston, 1898), 3:343–47, 4:476–77; David Steel, ed., *Steel's Original and Correct List of the Royal Navy* (London: D. Steel, May 1793).

After ten years of peace, Courtenay was ready for action. As Bompard rampaged up the Eastern Seaboard, Britain's minister to the United States sent letters to the Royal Navy in Canada, detailing *L'Embuscade*'s exploits and providing a full description of her armament. The minister's cries for help eventually reached the Newfoundland station, where, by lucky coincidence, Courtenay was the senior officer. His frigate, the *Boston,* was older and about two-thirds the strength of *L'Embuscade* in terms of size and number of crew, but the unlike the French frigate, the *Boston* was not undergunned. In addition to the standard thirty-two long guns of her class, she mounted six twelve-pounder cannonades, which made the two frigates' broadsides virtually equal.[8]

Courtenay recognized a golden opportunity when he saw one. Like Captain Wentworth in Jane Austen's novel *Persuasion,* Courtenay hoped to have "the good luck . . . to fall in with the very French frigate I wanted." The capture of *L'Embuscade* would net Courtenay and his crew a tremendous amount of prize money—almost certainly over ten thousand pounds. In addition, a victory would distinguish Courtenay as a top officer who merited the navy's choicest assignments. Finally, given Courtenay's family connections, a victory undoubtedly would have brought him a knighthood and probably a baronetcy.[9]

The *Boston* immediately set sail, and on the way south, Courtenay's last stop in Canada was Halifax, where he stopped to hire a pilot familiar with American waters and probably to replenish munitions. Halifax was a wealthy port with an immense stock of military stores. Its inhabitants generally believed the port was "so ill protected that two vessels of war, and one thousand men . . . might destroy it all." In fact, just a few months earlier, false rumors of an approaching French frigate had thrown everyone into a panic. When the *Boston* arrived off the port's entrance, Courtenay "made a signal for a pilot with a gun" and "exercised [the] Great and small guns." The cannonade immediately sparked a panic. People mistook the *Boston* for a French frigate—probably *L'Embuscade*. Alarms were signaled, and militiamen stumbled out of their houses, farms, and places of business.[10]

---

8. George Hammond to Officer Commending at Halifax, Apr. 27, May 17, 1793, PRO:ADM (photostat in DLC); William James, *A Naval History of Great Britain* (London: Harding, Lepard, 1826), 1:145–46.

9. Richard Hill, *The Prizes of War* (Stroud, Gloucestershire, U.K.: Sutton Publishing, 1998), chap. 17 (quoting Jane Austen).

10. Henry Wansey, *The Journal of an Excursion to the United States of North America in the Summer of 1794* (London: G. & T. Wilkie, 1796), 24; Master's Log of the *Boston,* PRO:ADM 52/2951; *Halifax Gazette,* July 23, 1793.

What a relief when word filtered through town that the menacing frigate was British. When Captain Courtenay announced his plan to sail south and take *L'Embuscade,* an impromptu ball was immediately scheduled. The governor and every prominent person attended, and at the conclusion of the ball, the ladies of the town announced that they would raise a substantial purse to reward the *Boston*'s crew when she returned.[11]

After the ball, Captain Courtenay set sail as soon as wind and tide would permit. On the way south, he did everything possible to prepare for battle. The gunners greased the trucks of the gun carriages and were set to making "swabs & points [and] Wads." Courtenay read and reread the "Articles of War" to his men, and as the *Boston* approached New York, the crew exercised the "Great Guns" each day.[12]

On the way to New York, Courtenay received disturbing intelligence. A French squadron, including two seventy-four-gun ships of the line and several frigates, was in transit from Cap Français in the West Indies to the American Coast. This news, however, did not cause Courtenay to change his plans, and as he continued sailing south, he hit upon a clever idea. If Halifax mistook the *Boston* for a Frenchman, perhaps others would too. He summoned his sailmaker and ordered him to make flags bearing the colors of the new French Republic. Others in the crew set to making tricolor cockades for the quarterdeck crew's hats, and the motto "Liberté et Égalité" was carefully painted on the frigate's stern. When the *Boston* finally arrived off the port of New York, she looked French, and Captain Courtenay had adjusted the duty roster so that all French-speaking officers and men were on deck.[13]

The ruse worked to perfection. Passing ships immediately mistook the *Boston* for the French frigate *Concorde,* known to be in route from the West Indies. Like the *Concorde,* the *Boston* was a "black-sided ship" that bore a long row of gunports not painted in a contrasting color. During the weekend of July 27–28, word of the new "French" frigate filtered into New York, and newspapers actually reported that the newly arrived ship was the *Concorde.*[14]

---

11. *Federal Gazette,* Aug. 9, 1793; *Carlisle (Pa.) Gazette,* Aug. 21, 1793.

12. Master's Log of the *Boston.*

13. *Federal Gazette,* Aug. 9, 1793; O. Troude, *Batailles navales de la France* (Paris: Challamel ainé, 1867), 2:304: *Diary; or, Loudon's Register* (New York), Aug. 6, 1793; *Salem Gazette,* Aug. 6, 1793; Master's Log of the *Boston.*

14. Jacob Whittemore to the Convention of France, Oct. 18, 1793, AECPE, Angleterre, 587:271–73; *Federal Gazette,* July 30, 1793.

The next day, Captain Courtenay continued cruising well outside New York Harbor, and in the midafternoon, the barge, steered by *L'Embuscade*'s Lieutenant Whittemore, provided a little comic relief. The oarsmen had been rowing for about twelve hours first through a "rainy and dark" night and then in bright sunlight. As the crew continued pulling on their oars, Whittemore tried to catch a ride on passing ships out to the "*Concorde,*" but no one would take him. At least two of the passing ships assured him, however, that a French frigate was at the hook. He later related that when he finally reached the *Boston,* "they began to talk French to me, with vous aboarde [*sic*] monsieur." To which he replied, "Oui," and in the next instant, "they had got two guns pointed into me and ready to fire." And so, as Bompard feared, the British took *L'Embuscade*'s barge and crew.[15]

Almost immediately, Captain Courtenay turned his attention to a small schooner within cannon shot. After the *Boston* fired three progressively closer warning shots, the schooner hove to and, upon being boarded, proved to be the eight-gun corsair *Republican.* Until then, the schooner, which had sailed from Cap Français, had passed a moderately successful cruise and had sent at least one prize into New York. For Captain Courtenay, the capture presented an opportunity to communicate with Sir John Temple, the British consul in New York. He placed his most junior lieutenant, John Hayes, who happened to be the consul's nephew, on the *Republican* as a prize master and sent him into port with despatches for Sir John.[16]

Back in New York Harbor, Citizen Bompard knew that there was much work to be done before he could weigh anchor to meet the *Boston.* Moreover, he had only a skeleton crew on board, which complicated the task of preparing the ship for combat. Some time earlier, *L'Embuscade* had suffered damage to her masts in a storm, and he had put into New York for repairs. The crew had worked hard, and the day before Bompard got word of Courtenay's challenge, he had distributed some prize money and given shore leave to virtually the entire crew. So the first order of the day was to recall the crew.[17]

As Bompard gave orders for the recall, he saw more boats pulling toward *L'Embuscade.* News of the coming engagement had already swept through town, and his men were returning of their own accord. Courtenay had sent his challenge into New York via Patrick Dennis, the commander of an

15. Jacob Whittemore to the Convention of France, Oct. 18, 1793.
16. *Federal Gazette,* July 16, 1793; *Carlisle (Pa.) Gazette,* Aug. 7, 1793.
17. J. B. F. Bompard, "Report of the Combat," Bompard's Personnel File, SHM; *Diary; or, Loudon's Register,* Aug. 6, 1793.

American revenue cutter. Immediately after communicating the challenge to Consul Hauterive, Dennis went to the recently built Tontine Coffee House, which was the commercial center of New York. As soon as Dennis got to the Tontine, he told everyone about the challenge and posted a notice on the coffee house bulletin board:

> Last evening came up from Sandy-Hook, the Revenue Cutter, Capt. Dennis, who at 4 P.M. 2 leagues E. by S. from Sandy-Hook, spoke the British frigate *Boston, Capt. Courtenay, who informed Capt. Dennis, he would be very happy to see the Ambuscade.*
>
> The above ship carries 32 guns.

The news flashed through the city.[18]

When Bompard heard about the notice at the Tontine, he sent a messenger over to the coffee house to pin a card immediately below Courtenay's challenge. Bompard's reply was short and sweet:

> Citizen BOMPARD will wait on Capt. COURTENAY tomorrow, agreeably to Invitation; he hopes to find him at the Hook.

The city was agog.[19]

As *L'Embuscade*'s crew turned to their work, New Yorkers gravitated toward the East River wharves and encouraged the crew "with yells of joy and clapping." The crew "appeared in great spirits, and much pleased with the affair, and worked hard in fixing the sails, rigging, &c." While Bompard and his crew busily prepared the ship for action, Consul Hauterive started looking for a pilot to guide the frigate out to sea. The "most extravagant terms were offered" by Hauterive, but to no avail. No pilot wanted to sail on board a frigate that was going into combat. Nor were pilot boats available. One pilot explained that his usual boat "was already engaged to go down to the Hook on a fishing party with a number of merchants." The more probable explanation is that every boat in port was already chartered by sightseers who planned to see the impending battle. At least nine vessels were chartered for this purpose, and one enterprising captain even ran an ad in a local newspaper.[20]

---

18. *Diary; or, Loudon's Register,* Aug. 6, 1793; *Salem Gazette,* Aug. 6, 1793; *United States Chronicle,* Aug. 8, 1793.

19. *United States Chronicle,* Aug. 8, 1793.

20. Edmond Genet to French Minister of Foreign Affairs, Aug. 2, 1793, "French Minsters' Correspondence," 236–37; *Federal Gazette,* July 31, Aug. 3, 1793; *Daily Advertiser,* July 30, Aug. 1, 1793.

In the late afternoon, Lieutenant Hayes, prize master of the *Republican,* sailed into harbor with news of how Captain Courtenay's masquerade had tricked the French. Hayes was a junior officer who had been a lieutenant for only two months.[21] After delivering despatches to his uncle, the British consul, the new lieutenant stepped over to the Tontine for a drink. His intentions were probably innocent, but he became embroiled in a fracas that heightened the city's interest in the coming combat.

As soon as Hayes walked through the coffee house door in his new lieutenant's uniform, someone drew his attention to the posting of Captain Courtenay's challenge and Citizen Bompard's reply. Needless to say, he could not resist proclaiming that he was a king's officer on the *Boston* and that Courtenay would certainly thrash the frog frigate. Hayes's boast delighted "some mercantile persons," who undoubtedly stood him a round of drink. As the evening progressed, Hayes began "vociferating against the Americans as a nation [and] offered to bet a wager of 100 dollars, that the *Boston* would take the Ambuscade frigate." Perhaps someone inelegantly told him to put his money where his mouth was. In any event, Hayes, who was by then drunk on pride, spirits, or both replied that "he would instantly stake the money, provided he was sure it would be *safe* in the country."[22]

In response to Hayes's slur, one Mr. Jessop stepped forward to defend the honor of America and France. Not being schooled in the finer elements of honor, Jessop knocked the tipsy lieutenant to the ground with a haymaker. Hayes struggled to his feet with his hand on his sword and started to say something. But Jessop was not interested in talk and swords. He stepped in close, and again the good lieutenant went to the ground. Then bystanders "seized [Hayes] by the nape of the neck and the waistband of his breeches" and gave him the bum's rush out of the Tontine. They "tossed [him] from the gallery into the street," and when his "mercantile [friends] attempted to be insolent in his behalf, [the friends] were soon hushed by a saving glimpse of the *Liberty Cap.*"[23]

By Tuesday, brags and counterbrags had immersed the city. Everyone eagerly anticipated the coming battle. Francophiles gloried in Jessop's premonitory pounding of Lieutenant Hayes. A local newspaper reported that

---

21. David Syrett and R. L. DiNardo, eds., *The Commissioned Sea Officers of the Royal Navy, 1660–1815* (Aldershut, U.K.: Scolar Press, 1994), 210.

22. *Carlisle (Pa.) Gazette,* Aug. 7, 1793; *Pennsylvania Journal,* Aug. 7, 1793; *Augusta (Ga.) Chronicle,* Sept. 14, 1793.

23. *Carlisle (Pa.) Gazette,* Aug. 7, 1793; Charles William Janson, *The Stranger in America* (London: J. Cundee, 1807), 430–31; Casto, "Rights of Man," 271.

"the great majority [support] our gallant *Gallic* friends [and] many bets are laid on the subject." Another paper reported that "business was almost at a stand." On board *L'Embuscade,* the crew had labored incessantly to prepare the frigate for action, and Bompard was ready to sail. But there was still no pilot, and some in town began to suggest that perhaps the French were not eager to engage the *Boston.* Bompard finally decided to leave without a pilot. He sailed *L'Embuscade* into the upper bay, dropped anchor, and waited for the tide. But contrary winds prevented a Tuesday departure, and the battle would have to await another day.[24]

The contrary winds let up the next day, and *L'Embuscade* sailed through the narrows and began searching for the *Boston*. At about the same time, Captain Courtenay encountered the French squadron from Cap Français and managed to elude it. He and Bompard continued searching for each other until they finally met in the early morning of August 1, the next day. Both ships beat to quarters, but neither captain wished to close. Dawn had yet to arrive, and Bompard could not ignore the possibility that the dimly perceived phantom frigate was actually the *Concorde*. As for Courtenay, he knew that the French squadron that he had eluded earlier might be in the area and decided not to close until he could see how many enemy ships were about. Dawn came at 5:00, and the two ships began to approach each other.[25]

In the coming engagement, Bompard had a real advantage. The wind was behind *L'Embuscade,* blowing in the *Boston*'s general direction, which gave Bompard the weather gage. The French would be assisted by the wind in any maneuvers taken toward the *Boston,* and the *Boston* would be hindered in its maneuvers toward *L'Embuscade*. Captain Courtenay well understood his handicap and set his ship on a course parallel to and somewhat ahead of his adversary. His plan was to "reach" *L'Embuscade*. In effect, he sought to take the weather gage away by making a large U-turn around Bompard. To counter this tactic, Bompard sailed his ship on the same course as the *Boston* and at a slight angle that would prevent Courtenay from reaching him but cause the two frigates to converge.

Bompard's plan worked to perfection, and as the two frigates gradually converged, Courtenay had to think fast. If he let Bompard get too close on a parallel course and Bompard maneuvered his ship effectively, *L'Embuscade*'s

---

24. *Federal Gazette,* July 31, 1793; *Pennsylvania Journal,* Aug. 14, 1793; *New-York Journal,* July 31, 1793; *Maryland Journal and Baltimore Advertiser,* Aug. 6, 1793.

25. The following account of the battle is drawn from Citizen Bompard's action report, Lieutenant Edward's draft action report, the Master's Log of the *Boston,* and several eyewitness accounts. See Casto, "Rights of Man," 280n35, for citations.

opening broadside could be devastating. The problem was inherent in the design of sailing ships. Cannon were mounted along the sides of a warship and could not fire directly forward or aft. If ships were close to each other and on a parallel course, their crews could slug it out and see whose gunnery was superior or luckier. But if a ship could manage a raking maneuver by crossing close ahead of or behind a target ship, the ship could fire an unopposed rolling broadside into the target ship. The comparative advantage of the weather gage greatly enhanced the probability that *L'Embuscade* would be able to rake the *Boston,* and Courtenay saw this well before the opportunity arose. He put the *Boston* about and turned inside *L'Embuscade*'s course so that the two ships wound up sailing directly toward each other on parallel courses. Bompard still had the weather gage, but the closing speed between the ships was at such a rapid pace that a raking maneuver would be more difficult.

As the two frigates converged, Bompard made a private recognition signal to establish whether the *Boston* was a French vessel. Instead of replying with the proper signal, Courtenay struck his French colors, hoisted British colors, and fired the *Boston*'s only cannon that could bear forward. Each crew now waited to give and receive broadsides, and finally the ships met at a distance of about a hundred yards. The *Boston* fired her broadside battery, but *L'Embuscade*'s guns were silent.

During the long period of maneuvering after the ships first sighted each other at daylight, there was ample time to load each cannon with care and precision. Bompard wanted his first broadside to be a devastating raking fire against the enemy's stern. As the two ships converged, he ordered his crew not to fire and instead prepared to put his ship about. His plan was to cross the *Boston*'s stern as soon as she passed by. But all went for naught because *L'Embuscade* missed her stays. As a result, she floundered somewhat into the wind, backed her main and mizzen top sail, and wound up sailing on the same tack as before. Meanwhile, the *Boston* wore ship and came back parallel to *L'Embuscade*. The time for fancy maneuver was over, and the two frigates settled into a pounding match.

For about an hour, the ships blasted away at each other, and each suffered grievous losses. On the *Boston,* the French broadsides struck down key members of the crew. Because Lieutenant Hayes was unable to rejoin the ship, Captain Courtenay had only two commissioned naval officers to assist in managing the battle: Lieutenant Edwards, his first lieutenant, stayed by his side on the quarterdeck, and Lieutenant Kerr supervised the cannon on the main deck. As the battle progressed, grapeshot struck Kerr in the shoulder, and splinters permanently blinded one eye and temporarily blinded the other. Splinters also got to Edwards, who suffered a concussion. At the same time, "a splinter which being driven in horizontal direction thro' the fleshy part of his nose, there lodged, remaining fixed something in the manner of a ship sprit sail yard."[26] After the ship's first and second lieutenants went to the sick bay, Captain Courtenay and a lieutenant of marines were the only officers left on deck.

The loss of these key officers, however, did not diminish the *Boston*'s murderous broadsides. As the pounding match progressed, the British gun crews proved to be more efficient than the French. According to a British report, the *Boston* managed to fire three shots for every two fired by the French, and one of *L'Embuscade*'s officers later conceded that the French fire "was not quick." The hours of gunnery practice imposed by Captain Courtenay paid off. In addition, the *Boston*'s cannon had a new flintlock firing mechanism. After the battle, Lieutenant Edwards reported with satisfaction that the new locks were "of great service, by not having one Gun misfire during the Action."[27]

On board *L'Embuscade,* Bompard did everything he could to counter the *Boston*'s superior rate of fire. To keep the crew's spirits up, he had a sailor sing the great revolutionary songs, and during sporadic moments of silence, the crew was urged on by the "Ca Ira," the "Marseillaise," and other songs. As the British continued their effective fire, Bompard knew he was at a disadvantage and three times attempted to close on the *Boston* and board her. But Captain Courtenay had commanded a king's frigate for over ten years and was an excellent sailor. Each time, he managed to maintain enough distance between the two ships to prevent boarding. After two unsuccessful attempts, Bompard finally got *L'Embuscade* almost close enough to board. A wag later wrote:

> Close as a lover to his mistress dear,
> Close as a pillory to a rascal's ear,
> Close as a miser to a bag of Joes—
> So close hung *Ambuscade* to *Boston*'s nose.[28]

But Courtenay managed to keep a slight distance, and as the ships came close to touching, he pulled a card out of his sleeve: he ordered his gunners to charge their cannons with canisters containing pieces of "old iron, nails,

26. *Dairy; or, Loudon's Register,* Aug. 12, 1793.
27. *Federal Gazette,* Aug. 9, 1793; John Edwards to the Admiralty, Aug. 1793, PRO:ADM 1/2863.
28. *Daily Advertiser,* Aug. 19, 1793.

broken knives, broken pots, and broken bottles." When *L'Embuscade* hung close to *Boston*'s nose, the British fired at point-blank range. Bompard saw entire swaths of rigging and sails dissolve before his eyes. He still had the weather gage, but the *Boston*'s devastating broadside virtually destroyed his ability to maneuver. A spectator reported that *L'Embuscade* "appeared to be in much confusion." Her fire slackened, and Bompard saw the specter of defeat.[29]

But before Captain Courtenay could take advantage of his crippled opponent, chance and the French gun crews' stubborn determination reversed the tide of victory. Either at this point or perhaps earlier, Bompard threw tradition to the wind. He believed his presence on the quarterdeck had "more of a ceremonious parade in it, than real utility." He knew that all was lost if *L'Embuscade*'s gunnery did not improve, so he left the quarterdeck to devote himself personally to "the management of his main deck great guns." Driven on by the words of the "Marseillaise" and the hands-on encouragement of their captain, the French gun crews redoubled their efforts and extracted a murderous dividend from their enemy. The French cannonade shot away the *Boston*'s main top mast, and its huge sail fell to the deck and covered most of the guns on one side of the ship. Even worse, one of *L'Embuscade*'s cannonballs struck the *Boston*'s quarterdeck and found Captain Courtenay and his lieutenant of marines. An anonymous poet later wrote,

> One random shot from fate's sure bow,
> Lays Boston's mighty monarch low.

The two men died instantly.[30]

At about the same time, the wind shifted almost imperceptibly. *L'Embuscade* still had good steerage, and her sailing master briefly turned the frigate slightly toward the wind, which caused the ship to slow down. The *Boston* moved ahead, and using the remaining steerage, *L'Embuscade* managed to creep across the *Boston*'s stern.

The next minute would determine the battle. There was time for only one broadside, and every shot must count. Under Bompard's direct and personal supervision on the main deck, the gun crews prepared to fire. As the *Boston*'s stern eased slowly into view at close range, the gunner of *L'Embuscade*'s forward most cannon blew the slow match on his linstock and touched it to the gun's vent. The priming charge caught fire, and the gun carriage leapt backward as the gun cast its twelve-pound ball, or perhaps a

29. *Federal Gazette,* Aug. 2, 9, 1793.
30. *Carlisle (Pa.) Gazette,* Aug. 21, 1793; *Hartford Courant,* Jan. 6, 1794.

wreath of scrap metal, at the enemy. There were twelve more guns on the main deck, and *L'Embuscade* delivered a slow, rolling—almost rhythmic—broadside of destruction.

The battle was over. Bompard had won. The final broadside had wasted everything connected to the *Boston*'s mizzenmast, and a sailing ship cannot effectively maneuver without the mizzenmast and sails in its rear. The broadside had "cut the spars, sails and rigging of the *Boston* in such a manner that they had very little command of their ship." The destruction was too much for the British sailors. They had seen every officer cut down, and without leadership, they briefly panicked. A number of gun crews fled their guns and huddled in the forward part of the ship, away from *L'Embuscade*'s devastating fire. The *Boston* could not maneuver, a fallen sail and mast had disabled one whole side of her gundeck, the crew had abandoned their stations, and not a single commissioned officer remained on deck. All *L'Embuscade* had to do was limp along side the *Boston* and board her.[31]

But the same wind that had been Bompard's ally all morning snatched away complete victory. The mangled sails and masts in the *Boston*'s rear prevented her from doing anything but sail with the wind. In an instant, the breeze caught the undamaged sails on the *Boston*'s foremast and without direction by any human hand spun her before the wind and wafted her gently along. Poor Bompard watched in disbelief as the vessel sailed slowly but inexorably away. He immediately attempted to wear ship and give pursuit, but his rigging and sails would not allow it. The French crew leaped to the masts to jury rig the frigate, and *L'Embuscade* was off and running in about fifteen minutes. As both ships raced before the wind, Lieutenant Edwards staggered to the quarterdeck sporting the gruesome splinter through his nose and wearing a shirt with a dark brown mantle of dried blood. He later explained that he was "in so weak a state as to be obliged to support myself for some time by the breast work Barricade on the Qr Deck."[32] Given the state of his ship and his knowledge that a French squadron was somewhere in the area, he concluded that flight was his only viable option.

Unfortunately for Bompard, the *Boston* had a head start and was able to crowd on more canvas. The British broadsides had shot through *L'Embuscade*'s mainmast, impaired the foremast, and severed the mainstay, which supported and steadied the main mast. Still Bompard persevered in the chase. He had been to sea since he was fifteen, and he knew that a mishap

---

31. *Federal Gazette,* Aug. 6, 1793; Clowes, *Royal Navy,* 4:478; *Gentleman's Magazine,* Sept. 1793, 862.

32. John Edwards to the Admiralty, Aug. 1793.

aboard the *Boston* might bring her once more under his guns. As the pursuit continued, axmen cut away the railing on *L'Embuscade*'s bow and gunners shifted cannon forward to serve as makeshift bow chasers in the hopes that a fortunate shot might disable the fleeing British frigate. Bompard continued the chase for two hours, but the pursuit was to no avail, and the *Boston* escaped. With regret, Bompard turned his ship back toward New York.

The arrival of the French squadron from Cap Français preceded *L'Embuscade*'s return to New York. Two ships of the line and fourteen other vessels dropped anchor off the Battery, and thousands flocked to the tip of Manhattan. The squadron and the Battery fired salutes to each other and "three cheers [came] from the amazing concourse attending." Then word swept through town that *L'Embuscade* could be seen coming from the narrows. The crowd swelled to "nearly ten thousand persons," according to one newspaper—to four thousand according to a careful lawyer. Then the victorious frigate sailed gracefully into view, "under a full suit of canvass with a light breeze." The crowd of "people assembled were at a loss how to express their joy, having heard of the gallant behavior of Citizen Bompard . . . and his crew." As *L'Embuscade* came closer, she shattered the silence with a triumphant artillery salute. Immediately everyone "answered as if each had the lungs of Stentor." Spontaneous cheers burst forth, and "continued shouts and huzzas were vociferated." As *L'Embuscade* sailed slowly by toward anchorage in the East River, Bompard and his crew returned the cheers.[33]

Word of the engagement quickly swept throughout the United States, and countless poems, songs, and toasts celebrated the victory. A few days after the battle, "a number of citizens met at the house of citizen Richardet [in Philadelphia] to celebrate the victory," and after dinner the celebrants drank numerous toasts. The first was to "the patriotic band of heroes who composed the crew of the L'Ambuscade." The party concluded with a vow of Franco-American solidarity. Everyone raised their tankards and pledged, "The republic of America & France: may their emulation only tend to a love of each other!" In Boston, the toast of the day was "Success to the *Embuscade*." In far off Charleston, South Carolina, the celebrations were much the same. A "large company of reputable citizens assembled" for an evening of "great festivity," and after dinner the first of countless toasts was to "Citizen

---

33. *Federal Gazette,* Aug. 5, 6, 1793; James Kent to Moss Kent Jr., Aug. 3, 1793, James Kent Papers, DLC; Walter Livingston to Henry Walter Livingston, Robert Livingston Papers, NHi.

Bompard and his heroic crew: may liberty always have such gallant defenders." Immediately there followed "3 cheers."[34]

The British implicitly agreed that *L'Embuscade* had won the day and tried to explain the outcome as turning upon a significant disparity in the raw size of the two frigates' crews. In addition, a week or so after the battle, word began to circulate that the powerful French squadron came upon the battling frigates and forced the *Boston* to retire.[35] The disparity of crews might have been significant if *L'Embuscade* had managed to board the *Boston*, but she did not. The notion that the French squadron forced the *Boston* to withdraw should be dismissed as a post hoc fabrication. Neither Lieutenant Edwards's action report, Citizen Bompard's action report, the master's log of the *Boston*, nor any other early eyewitness account of the battle mentions an intervention by the French squadron.

Today, some two hundred years later, the elation of the pro-French Americans and the implicit concession of the British seems unwarranted. Two frigates of roughly comparable strength inflicted serious damage on each other. Neither ship was completely victorious, and after repairs both ships returned to active duty. In strictly military terms, the engagement clearly was a draw. Yet virtually all Americans, including those who leaned toward Britain, saw the battle as a French victory.

The reason for this parallax between eighteenth- and twentieth-century views of the battle lies in the fundamental nature of *L'Embuscade*'s mission to America. The political impact of Bompard's depredations was far more significant than his success as a commerce raider. As Edward Livingston explained, *L'Embuscade*'s exploits revived the "spirit of seventy-six."[36] Bompard took prizes and effectively fought off the *Boston,* but the main impact of his mission was to provide reassurance to the majority of Americans who wanted to support the cause of revolutionary France.

In the United States, the battle was a major political victory for revolutionary France, and American reaction was unkind to Captain Courtenay. Although he had bravely given his life in service to his country, Americans who sought to bolster commercial relations with Great Britain were quick to revile the fallen captain. When word of the battle reached Thomas Jefferson, he was in a cabinet meeting and could not resist rubbing Henry Knox's

---

34. *Federal Gazette,* Aug. 7, 1793; *Daily Advertiser,* Aug. 9, 1793 (Boston); *Boston Gazette,* Oct. 7, 1793 (Charleston).

35. See, for example, William Windham to Captain Lukin, Mar. 22, 1794, in William Windham, *The Windham Papers* (London: Herbert Jenkins, 1913), 1:210–12.

36. See chapter 4, this volume.

and Alexander Hamilton's noses in the French victory. With gloating satisfaction, he noted that "both shewed the most unequivocal mortification." Knox immediately "broke out into the most unqualified abuse of Capt. Courtenay," and Hamilton, "with less fury, but with deepest vexation, loaded [Courtenay] with censures." In retrospect, this invective comes across as churlish, Monday-morning quarterbacking. The only thing that can be said in their defense is that perhaps they did not know that Courtenay had given his life for his country.[37]

Pro-French Americans were equally quick to launch unseemly ad hominem attacks. Newspaper articles variously attacked Captain Courtenay as "arrogant," a "Bragadocio," an "envenomed ruffian," and even a "gasconading poltroon." He was full of "British bombast," and a man given "to bluster and threaten." His conduct was "a striking example of the bullying, sanguinary disposition of the British nation" and was "an indelible stain upon their boasted national character." Citizen Bompard, however, refused to participate in this riot of invective. He gave "due credit to the valour and intrepidity of his antagonist [and spoke] only of the victory, as one obtained over a respectable foe."[38]

The reason for the overblown American reaction to the battle lay in the belief that the Royal Navy was superior to any navy in the world and certainly superior to the navy of a country such as France, which was newly founded on republican principles. Shortly before *L'Embuscade* put the *Boston* to flight, an American consul in Europe reported, "By Sea the Republic makes but a despicable figure, and I think it good policy that it does not attempt much in that line." Back in America, a newspaper noted the "old English prejudice, 'that an Englishman is a match for three Frenchmen,'" and Senator Pierce Butler of South Carolina wrote the same thing in a private letter. Another paper noted that some believed that "an English frigate was an over match for any frigate of more than equal force." In the wagering frenzy preceding the battle, those "who believed in the invincibility of the tars of Old England had given large odds that the Ambuscade would be taken." This assumption of British superiority galled Americans, who saw France as following the trail blazed in the American Revolutionary War. The French, like the Americans, had rejected monarchy in favor of

---

37. Notes of a Cabinet Meeting, Aug. 3, 1793, *Papers of Thomas Jefferson,* 26:607–8.
38. *Federal Gazette,* Aug. 5, 6, 7, 1793; *Diary; or, Loudon's Register,* Aug. 3, 1793; *National Gazette,* Aug. 3, 1793; *Carlisle (Pa.) Gazette,* Aug. 14, 21, 1793. For Bompard, see *United States Chronicle,* Aug. 22, 1793.

republicanism, but Americans could not help but believe that the king's Royal Navy was superior to a republican navy.[39]

Citizen Bompard's steadfast conduct put the lie to this galling belief in the Royal Navy's superiority. Newspapers triumphantly proclaimed that the victory was "a compleat refutation of the old superstition" of English superiority. Bompard came to America "armed for the defense of the rights of man" and by force of arms proved that a crew of citizen-sailors could defeat a king's ship of comparable strength. Americans delighted in this proof. A writer from New York crowed, "The cool and systematic bravery of the Frenchman has carried all before it." Senator Butler and others saw Bompard's triumph as a clear refutation of the myth of British superiority. A writer in New York who relished the *Boston*'s flight from battle explained that "the Frenchman won the BATTLE, the Briton won the Race." A poet in Philadelphia proclaimed, "The Gaul had the best of the fight, tis agreed / The Briton—the best of the race." In Philadelphia, citizens drank to *L'Embuscade*'s "patriotic band of heroes" and then lifted their glasses again to the toast: "May British bombast ever meet the fate of Capt. Courtney, when opposed to the sons of freedom."[40]

39. Nathaniel Cutting to Thomas Jefferson, June 8, 1793, *Papers of Thomas Jefferson,* 26:229; *Boston Gazette,* Oct. 7, 1793; *Federal Gazette,* Aug. 5, 1793; *Augusta (Ga.) Chronicle,* June 8, 1793 ("French navy . . . must be ultimately deficient"); Pierce Butler to Edward Rutledge, Aug. 9, 1793, Pierce Butler Letterbook, 1:133–34, PHi; Henry Remsen to Thomas Jefferson, Aug. 1, 1793, *Papers of Thomas Jefferson,* 26:600; Isaac Q. Leake, *Memoir of the Life and Times of General John Lamb* (Albany, N.Y.: J. Munsell, 1850), 342.

40. Pierce Butler to Edmond Rutledge, Aug. 9, 1793; Henry Remsen to Thomas Jefferson, Aug. 1, 1793; "Letter from New York," *National Gazette,* Aug. 7, 1793; *Carlisle (Pa.) Gazette,* Aug. 21, 1793; *Federal Gazette,* Aug. 7, 1793; *National Gazette,* Aug. 24, 1793; *Dunlap's American Daily Advertiser,* Aug. 5, 1793.

CHAPTER 9

The Fall

> Mr. Genet . . . said that he would appeal to the people from certain decisions of the President.
> *John Jay and Rufus King*
>
> The P[resident] is an overmatch for all the efforts Republicanism can make.
> *James Madison*

L'Embuscade's victory marked the high tide of American enthusiasm for the French Revolution. While the nation was celebrating Citizen Bompard and his crew, steps were under way to discredit Citizen Genet. A song written after Bompard's heroic victory unwittingly prophesied the public relations catastrophe that shortly engulfed the French cause. Most of the song's twenty-five stanzas are devoted to "*gallant* BOMPARD" and his crew, who fought "like lions . . . for *freedom* [and] in *Equality's Cause*." The song also called for a toast to "Citizen GENET" but urged Americans to raise their glasses only when Genet "treats with respect the MAN whom the PEOPLE adore." Nothing was left to inference. The man whom Genet must respect was "GEORGE WASHINGTON . . . who saved *Columbia*'s brave *Land*."[1]

Chief Justice Jay Enters the Fray

The problem was that Genet's threat to appeal George Washington's decisions to the people was anything but respectful. Certainly the president was personally infuriated by the threat. Thomas Jefferson complained to a close friend that at an August 1 cabinet, "Hamilton pressed eagerly [the] appeal to the people." In his private notes, Jefferson complained that "Hamilton made a jury speech of ¾ of an hour as inflammatory and declamatory as if he had been talking to a jury." At that meeting, the cabinet decided to demand that France recall Genet. Jefferson hoped the French would agree and wrote James Madison in cypher that Genet "*will sink the republican* interest if they [the French] do not *abandon him*."[2]

In addition to pressing the issue of Genet's threatened appeal during cabinet deliberations, Hamilton and his friends saw to it that the matter was

---

1. "An Excellent new PATRIOTIC SONG," broadside (Boston, 1793).
2. Notes of Cabinet Meeting on Edmond Charles Genet, Aug. 1, 1793, *Papers of Thomas Jefferson,* 26:598; Thomas Jefferson to James Madison, Aug. 3, 1793 (emphasized words in cypher), *Papers of Thomas Jefferson,* 26:606; Sheridan, "Recall of Edmond Charles Genet."

brought to the public's attention. Almost as soon as Genet uttered the threat, rumors began circulating in private. In mid-July, Aaron Burr, who was pro-French, wrote a friend in New York:

> We have a rumor here, (very grateful to the Tories,) that Genet has come to an open Rupture with the President—That he has publicly threatened to appeal to the people, that as preparatory to this step he goes about Visiting Mechanics, and the lower orders of people, leaving Cards at their houses when they are not at home! &c. &ca.

In mid-July, Hamilton wrote an anonymous newspaper essay alluding to the threat and charging that Genet was beginning the appeal. A few weeks later, someone in New York with the pen name Junius garbled the rumor by claiming that Genet had threatened to appeal a judicial judgment to the people.[3]

These rumors and anonymous newspaper articles could be easily dismissed as lacking credibility. As one observer noted, the truth of the rumors "had been rendered problematical by the positive denial of the Minister's Partisans." In August, however, Chief Justice Jay and Senator Rufus King dramatically raised the political stakes. Less than a week after the Supreme Court formally refused to help the president with an advisory opinion, Jay and King placed a brief notice in a New York newspaper:

> Messrs. Printers:
> Certain late publications render it proper for us to authorize you to inform the public, that a report having reached this City from Philadelphia that Mr. Genet, the French Minister, said that he would appeal to the people from certain decisions of the President; we are asked on our return to that place, whether he had made such a declaration; we answered that he had,—and we also mentioned it to others, authorising them to say that we had so informed them.
> John Jay.
> Rufus King.

This simple notice was political dynamite. A clear public statement signed by high placed and respected government officials could neither be ignored nor

---

3. Aaron Burr to John Nicholson, July 16, 1793, *Political Correspondence and Public Papers of Aaron Burr*, ed. Mary-Jo Kline (Princeton, N.J.: Princeton University Press, 1983), 1:156; Jacobin No. 1, July 31, 1793, *Papers of Alexander Hamilton,* 15:145; "Junius," *Daily Advertiser,* Aug. 7, 1793.

casually given the lie. Federalists bragged to each other that the statement "has made a solid impression upon most reflecting minds [and that] Genet & his party are crumbling fast into dust."[4]

The Federalists coupled the public airing of Genet's insult to the president with a nationwide public relations campaign to support the president and his policies. In town meetings throughout America, concerned citizens passed resolutions supporting the Proclamation of Neutrality. Many of the resolutions also condemned attempts by unnamed foreign diplomats to bypass the executive branch and attempt to speak directly to the people. Beginning in late July, more than thirty resolutions were passed in support of the president's neutrality policy. In Virginia, James Madison and James Monroe attempted to mount a counter-offensive, but in the end even the resolutions they personally drafted mildly condemned Genet's threatened appeal as a personal transgression that should not be attributed to the new French Republic.[5]

Jay and King's formal notice created serious problems for Genet. He had in fact threatened an appeal, and if Jefferson's July 10 memorandum to the president became public knowledge, the truthfulness of Jay and King's notice would be virtually impossible to deny. As soon as Genet learned of the notice, he dashed off an intemperate letter to the president that slyly dodged the basic accusation. He insisted that Washington was "sacrificing [French] interests to those of our enemies" and that the executive branch's "conduct did not appear to correspond with the views of the people of America." As for the accusation, he demanded "an explicit declaration [from the president] that I have never intimated to you an intention of appealing to the people." By couching his answer in terms of direct conversations with the president, Genet avoided the fact that his threats had been made to others and not directly to the president.[6]

Jefferson tersely responded that "diplomatic characters [were not] to have any direct correspondence" with the president but should communicate with the secretary of state. In any event, Jefferson informed Genet that the president would not "bear evidence against [the] declaration." In response,

---

4. L. Cadwalader to Rufus King, Aug. 25, 1793, *Life and Correspondence of Rufus King,* 1:495; Messrs. Printers, Aug. 12, 1793, *Life and Correspondence of Rufus King,* 1:459; Robert Troup to James Duane, Aug. 14, 1793, James Duane Papers, NHi.

5. See Harry Ammon, "The Genet Mission and the Development of American Political Parties," *Journal of American History* 52 (Mar. 1966): 725–41.

6. Edmond Genet to George Washington, Aug. 13, 1793, *Papers of Thomas Jefferson,* 26:677–78, and *Columbian Gazetteer,* Aug. 22, 1793 (English translation).

Genet released his letter to the press, and it was reprinted throughout the country. In effect, Genet was prosecuting his appeal to the people.[7]

As the scandal continued to percolate through the nation, Genet decided to publish another letter justifying his conduct and attacking Jay and King. Governor Moultrie of South Carolina had asked him if he had indeed threatened to appeal an the people. In October, Genet responded and immediately sent copies of Moultrie's letter and his response to the press. Although the two letters have the air of a staged colloquy, Moultrie's inquiry was sincere and Genet's secretary told the French consul in Charleston to assure Moultrie that the reports of the threat were false. He insisted that Jay and King, whom he described as "the authors of the falsehoods," were part of a "dark and deep intrigue." Genet refused to sink to their level because, he declared, "I too much despise [the authors] to produce proofs against the absurdity of their accusations." He informed the public that he would submit the issue to Congress.[8]

Careful readers of Genet's latest publication noted that it did not contain "any direct Denyal" that he had made the threat. Once more Genet, by releasing his letter to the press, seemed to be prosecuting his appeal to the people. In the October letter, he could not resist charging that "the conduct of certain officers of the Federal Government . . . appeared to me both destructive of liberty, and favorable to our enemies." He tried, however, to deflect the explosive charge that he was attacking President Washington. Genet was "grief [stricken] at seeing General Washington, that celebrated hero of liberty, accessible to men whose schemes could only darken his glory." Just a few days later, Genet published another letter attacking the administration.[9]

Genet's public dispute with Jay and King was a hopeless battle that he could not win. Alexandre Hauterive, the French consul in New York, thought that the whole affair was ridiculous. He wrote in his diary, "The war of gazettes is always lethal to the persons in power who lower themselves in

---

7. Thomas Jefferson to Edmond Genet, Aug. 16, 1793, *Papers of Thomas Jefferson,* 26:684; *Papers of Thomas Jefferson,* 26:678.

8. William Moultrie to Edmond Genet, Sept. 5, 1793, *Connecticut Courant,* Nov. 4, 1793; Edmond Genet to William Moultrie, Oct. 15, 1793, *Connecticut Courant,* Nov. 4, 1793; Charles François Bournonville to Michel Mangourit, Sept. 25, 1793, Mangourit Papers, MB.

9. Hugh Williamson to Alexander Hamilton, Oct. 24, 1793, *Papers of Alexander Hamilton,* 15:377; Edmond Genet to William Moultrie, Oct. 15, 1793, *Federal Gazette,* Oct. 24, 1793; Ammon, *Genet Mission,* 142–43.

this arena in which it is ridiculous to win and shameful to lose." No matter how capable Genet might be, he was only one man. In Hauterive's eyes, Genet was "all alone against a multitude of enemies who ally themselves under the same name, who write in their own language, who, because of their numbers, can try all tones of voice, and who finally find the most impressive one."[10]

Hauterive's insight also applied to Jay and King, who were the first to enter the arena where "it is ridiculous to win and shameful to lose." If they thought the supporters of France would accept their poisonous notice as a simple act of public service, they were mistaken. Throughout the fall numerous newspaper articles attacked Jay and King. "A Citizen" in New York almost immediately charged that the two men were "officious and activated by improper motives." Another writer rhymed,

> Tho' *Jay, that great judge,* and the *Senator* King,
> To join in their clamors, their evidence bring;
> Yet freemen will see how vain their attempt,
> And treat it as freemen with sovereign contempt.

In Virginia, "Uniform Federalist" charged that Jay's and King's "operating *motive* must have been, a preference of Britain, to France, of British, to French political principles."[11]

Mutiny in the West Indies Squadron

Along with the developing public relations catastrophe for the French cause came a military catastrophe. The arrival of the French West Indies squadron and the defeat of the *Boston* gave the French what seemed to be overwhelming naval superiority in North America. In addition to *L'Embuscade,* which had to be repaired, the French had two ships of the line, three large frigates, one small frigate, and six smaller vessels mounting ten to eighteen guns each. These ships were manned by a combined complement of 2,807 men augmented by 345 soldiers.[12]

---

10. Hauterive, "Journal," entry of Nov. 5. For Hauterive, see Francis S. Childs, "The Hauterive Journal," *New-York Historical Society Quarterly* 23 (1949): 69–86.

11. "A Citizen," *Federal Gazette,* Aug. 15, 1793 (reprinted from *New York Journal*); *National Gazette,* Sept. 28, 1793 (from a Norfolk paper); Jay, *Most Humble Servants,* 148 (quoting the *Virginia Gazette*). For additional attacks, see *Federal Gazette,* Aug. 19, 1793; *Dunlap's American Daily Advertiser,* Aug. 21, 1793; *National Gazette,* Aug. 23, 24, Sept. 4, 7, 21, 1793; *Boston Gazette,* Dec. 16, 1793.

12. Report about the Vessels of the French Republic, Oct. 1, 1793, AECPE, États-Unis, vol. 39; Vessels of the French Republic, Oct. 7, 1793, AECPE, États-Unis, vol. 39.

But ships without effective crews are worthless. The tentative mutiny back in France at the very beginning of *L'Embuscade*'s mission to America had been anything but auspicious. If Bompard had encountered the *Boston* as he was beating across the Bay of Biscay, *L'Embuscade* probably would have been taken. But on the long voyage across the Atlantic and during the initial three months of the campaign in America, the crew of *L'Embuscade* came together as an effective fighting force. When the ship encountered the *Boston,* the crew doggedly kept to their guns during the hour-long pounding match. Bompard and his crew refused to quit and in the end prevailed.

If the entire French squadron had possessed *L'Embuscade*'s esprit de corps, the French would have had a formidable force. But the squadron's morale was more like that of *L'Embuscade* back in Rochefort. From the beginnings of the French Revolution, mutiny was rampant in the French navy. *L'Embuscade*'s full-scale 1791 mutiny in the West Indies and the minor 1793 flare-up in Rochefort were not unusual. By 1793, the revolutionary idea of popular sovereignty was ingrained in the fleet, and there were major mutinies throughout the navy.[13]

Although the West Indies Squadron's initial appearance in New York was impressive, the squadron was rife with dissension. Service in the West Indies had been disastrous for morale. In the colony of Santo Domingo (present-day Haiti), black revolutionaries destroyed the port of Cap Français and slaughtered many of its inhabitants. The white residents fled the island in a hodgepodge flotilla of merchant vessels escorted by the squadron. When they got to New York, there was an orgy of discontent and recrimination in which the squadron's leaders and various factions among the islanders blamed each other for the disaster. Each of these factions made conflicting appeals to the squadron's crews. As the ships swung at their anchors, dissension, intrigue, and uncertainty eroded morale.[14]

While the once-powerful West Indies Squadron was rotting in New York Harbor, Genet was developing grandiose plans for naval assaults on Canada, Florida, and Louisiana. Throughout the fall, he carefully crafted his master plan but never consulted with the squadron. In fact, the "plan was concealed from the [squadron's] leaders." On November 2, he presented his grand strategy as a fait accompli. Bompard and two or three other senior officers came to his room, where they saw "a map laid on a carpet." Genet briskly told them that he would commit the entire squadron to a winter assault on the tiny fishing islands of Saint Pierre and Miquelon in the

---

13. Cormack, *Revolution and Political Conflict in the French Navy.*
14. See Ammon, *Genet Mission,* 111–26; DeConde, *Entangling Alliance,* 271–74.

Gulf of Saint Lawrence. Then Genet proudly explained that, having secured the "good bases, they could rush to the South," apparently to attack Spanish bases in Florida.[15]

Consul Hauterive sneered at the plan as "a house of cards." He sarcastically confided to his journal that at the meeting, Genet did little more than issue a peremptory fiat: "Here is Saint Pierre, here is Miquelon, one comes in the harbor this way, one comes in using the wind current. Go, leave, uphold your patriotic honor, you brave Republicans!" The officers were appalled by Genet's naïve fantasy.[16]

We do not know for certain what Bompard actually thought of Genet's plan, but Hauterive speculated about Bompard's reaction. Bompard understood the dangers of taking the squadron northward through winter storms and realized there would be no safe harbor "to weather a gust [because] northwards of Boston, everything is English." In any event, why risk the entire squadron to a stormy debacle just to take two small fishing islands? Hauterive believed that Bompard would have asked, "Is the glory of taking with the squadron a post that has been taken with a frigate and a sloop worth this danger?"[17]

In addition to winter storms, Genet failed to consider the squadron's low morale. Hauterive, who was on the scene, believed that Genet's plan could not be attained "with a squadron inveterate in the disobedience of the chief staff, itself rooted in the jealousy of the aristocracy [and] on the edge of the animosity with its leaders." Nor could the squadron possibly have had any confidence in or respect for Genet. *L'Embuscade*'s crew had seen him in action for almost a year and knew him for a naval dilettante. They also had seen him voluntarily surrender valuable prizes in Charleston and Philadelphia.[18]

For the squadron's crews, Genet's fool's errand to Canada was the last straw. Hauterive's conjectures about Bompard were accurate. The squadron refused to follow Genet's orders. When it left New York, it sailed not for Canada but for France. Bompard, who had had enough of Genet, apparently was one of the mutiny's leaders. An anonymous informant told Genet that Bompard believed that the ships were not in a sufficient state of repair to weather a winter expedition and that the expedition was of no value to France. He was also furious about the treatment of French prizes. At Genet's

15. Hauterive, "Journal," entry of Nov. 4, 1793.
16. Ibid., entries of Nov. 3, 4, 1793.
17. Ibid.
18. Ibid., entry of Nov. 3, 1793. See chapter 4, this book.

orders, the *Success* and *Wilhelm* in Charleston and the *Grange* in Philadelphia had been returned to their owners, and another *L'Embuscade* prize, the *Catherine,* had been attached by the federal court in New York.[19]

When Bompard arrived in France, he gave the French government "the most unfavorable reports... about the conduct of Citizen Genet." Although Bompard was one of the best fighting captains in the French Navy, his subsequent career was disappointing. He was never promoted to admiral. In 1798, he was taken prisoner after a heroic fight in which his ship of the line battled three British ships of the line for three and a half hours. When he got back to France, Napoleon was in the process of converting the Republic to the Empire, which Bompard, who remained a committed republican for his entire life, opposed. He finally left the navy, never to serve again. He must have been appalled when the monarchy was restored after Napoleon's downfall. He publicly supported the overthrow of the ultra royalists in the July revolution of 1830. Four years later, France finally recognized his service to the Republic and made him a commander of the legion of honor. In 1841, Bompard died in his hometown of Bagnol.[20]

The Appeal to the People

In the wake of the French squadron's mutiny and departure for France, Genet fired another salvo in his war with Jay and King. In mid-November, he wrote Attorney General Randolph a letter finally stating that Jay's and King's publication was "utterly and totally false" and "a public insult to my nation and to myself." A few months earlier, an anonymous newspaper writer had charged that if a similar notice had been posted against the British ambassador, "the printers would have been prosecuted for a libel, and we should have seen the *Federal* judges as unanimous against them as they were in the case of poor Henfield." Genet now insisted that the government bring a criminal prosecution against the two men for the "outrages" they had committed against France and its ambassador. He wrote Jefferson an angry letter the same day, protesting the president's failure to comply with his August 13 demand that the president explicitly declare that Genet had never threatened an appeal. The administration's response to his August 13 demand "being as indecisive as the silence of [Jay and King]

---

19. Ammon, *Genet Mission,* 125; extract of an unidentified correspondent to Edmond Genet, Oct. 16, 1793, Genet Papers, DLC, discussed in *Papers of Thomas Jefferson,* 27:387n.

20. Lequino and Laignelot to Minister of Foreign Affairs, Brumaire 26, Year 2, Ministry of Foreign Affairs Archives, Paris, France; Casto, "Rights of Man," 55.

was profound, a judicial inquiry alone remains for me to confound those who have traduced me."[21]

The attorney general could not ignore Genet's formal request, and Randolph agreed to discuss the matter with him. When Genet immediately sent copies of these letters to the press, the affair began to snowball. Jay and King could not ignore public charges that they were criminals, and at the end of the month they published a detailed account of the circumstances surrounding the threat. Along with this elaboration came a public certification by Hamilton and Knox stating that they were the source of Jay's and King's knowledge and that the information about Genet's threat was "communicated to us by Mr. Jefferson."[22]

At this point, Alexander Dallas, to whom Genet had uttered the threat back in July, jumped into the mud bath and splattered everyone by publishing his own recollection of his conversation with Genet. At the end of a lengthy discussion of his July meeting with Genet, Dallas stated that "Mr. Genet never did, in his conversation with me, declare 'that he would appeal from the President to the People.'" Dallas was aware of Jefferson's July 10 memorandum to the president and implicitly dealt with the memorandum by suggesting the possibility that the rumors about Genet's threatened appeal may have originated in an innocent mistake. Even the "most attentive hearer [e.g., Jefferson] may sometimes misconceive the ideas of the person who addresses him." But Dallas did not let Hamilton, Knox, Jay, and King—who were his political enemies—off the hook. He suggested that as a matter of "common courtesy, as well as common sense," they should have consulted him before publishing their hearsay accounts of the rumor.[23]

Dallas's account put Jefferson in the hot seat because Jefferson had clearly stated in his July 10 memorandum that Genet had threatened an appeal to the people. In early September, moreover, Jefferson had assured James Madison that he would "see much said and gainsaid about G's threat to appeal to the people. I can assure you it is a fact." At the same time, Jefferson had no

---

21. Edmond Genet to Edmund Randolph, Nov. 14, 1793, *Connecticut Courant,* Dec. 2, 1793; Edmond Genet to Thomas Jefferson, Nov. 14, 1793, *Papers of Thomas Jefferson,* 27:367, and *Connecticut Courant,* Dec. 2, 1793 (translation); "An Anti Gallican Federalist," *Dunlap's American Daily Advertiser,* Aug. 21, 1793.

22. "To the Public," Dec. 2, 1793, *Life and Correspondence of Rufus King,* 1:458–61; statement by Alexander Hamilton and Henry Knox on Edmond Genet's "Appeal to the People," Nov. 29, 1793, *Papers of Alexander Hamilton,* 15:418–19.

23. Mr. A. J. Dallas' Statement to the Public, Dec. 17, 1793, *Life and Correspondence of Rufus King,* 1:464–69.

desire to help Jay and King out of their difficulty. He reluctantly prepared a cover letter, which would be used to release his July 10 memorandum to the public, but he never released either the cover letter or the July 10 memorandum.[24]

The new publications by Hamilton, Knox, Jay, and King elicited a second demand from Genet that the government prosecute his accusers for criminal libel. The dispute simply would not go away, and President Washington reluctantly decided that the attorney general should render a formal decision on Genet's request for a prosecution. As a matter of international law, the United Stated had an obligation to protect accredited diplomats such as Genet from harm. Acting on the president's instructions, Jefferson advised Randolph that Jay's and King's allegedly "libelous publications" were against "a public character peculiarly entitled to the protection of the laws." "On the other hand," Jefferson continued, "our citizens ought not to be vexed with groundless prosecutions."[25]

After considering the matter, Randolph refused to prosecute, explaining, "I do not hold myself bound, nor do I conceive that I ought, to proceed against any man in opposition to my decided judgment." He did not, however, completely foreclose the possibility of a criminal prosecution. In a concluding sentence, he advised Genet that "any other gentleman of the profession, who may approve and advise the attempt, will be at no loss to point out a mode which does not require my intervention."[26]

At first glance, there might be a tendency to believe that the fix was in—that there was to be a formal exchange of correspondence officially answering Genet's request in terms of measured neutrality but subject to a clear private understanding that the chief justice and Senator King were not to be prosecuted. Other evidence indicates, however, that there was no such private understanding. When Jay and King learned of the neutral referral to the attorney general and his suggestion of a private prosecution, they wrote an angry letter to President Washington. Although all copies of this letter were subsequently destroyed, King wrote in a private memorandum that

---

24. Thomas Jefferson to James Madison, Sept. 1, 1793, *Papers of Thomas Jefferson,* 27:7; Prepared Public Statement on Edmond Genet, Dec. 16, 1793, *Papers of Thomas Jefferson,* 27:529–32.

25. Edmond Genet to Edmund Randolph, Dec. 16, 1793, and Thomas Jefferson to Edmund Randolph, Dec. 18, 1793, both in *Papers of Thomas Jefferson,* 27:527–28, 587. See Ammon, *Genet Mission,* 152.

26. Edmund Randolph to Edmond Genet, Dec. 18, 1793, *Federal Gazette,* Dec. 24, 1793.

Randolph and Jefferson were "treated with much severity in it" and that the letter included a "charge of injustice" against President Washington.[27]

As for Genet, he took Randolph's advice and immediately consulted Peter Du Ponceau and Joseph Thomas, two Philadelphia lawyers who were sympathetic to France. Du Ponceau, and indeed Genet, had strenuously argued during the summer that absent an act of Congress Gideon Henfield could not be prosecuted for violating the law of nations, but the federal judges emphatically rejected their claim. Now the shoe was on the other foot, and Du Ponceau must have relished the irony. There was no act of Congress making libel a crime, but a libel against a foreign diplomat was contrary to the law of nations. Du Ponceau opined that he was "decidedly of opinion that [Jay and King] have committed an offense not only against the local law of this Country, but against the Law of Nations, for which they may be indicted and punished." He was undecided where "the prosecution ought to be instituted" but was inclined to think that "the Supreme Court has original jurisdiction."[28]

Surviving Supreme Court records give no indication that the planned criminal prosecution was formally commenced, but the case could have been filed there. Du Ponceau noted in his opinion that the Constitution constitutes the Supreme Court itself, as a trial court in "all cases affecting ambassadors." Today the notion of a private person commencing a criminal prosecution is bizarre, and some have thought that Randolph and Du Ponceau had a civil action in mind. Two hundred years ago, however, there was a well-established common-law mode of prosecution called an "appeal" that authorized private persons to institute and prosecute criminal actions. Just four years later, a newspaper editor was convicted for libeling the British consul general, and a contemporary newspaper reported that the consul himself prosecuted the case.[29]

With the opinion letter from Du Ponceau in hand, Genet wrote his fiancée that he was determined that Jay and King "will not get away with

---

27. Rufus King, Memorandum, Feb. 1794, *Life and Correspondence of Rufus King,* 1:476–80.

28. Peter Du Ponceau and Joseph Thomas to Edmond Genet, Dec. 23, 1793, Genet Papers, DLC.

29. Peter Du Ponceau and Joseph Thomas to Edmond Genet, Dec. 23, 1793 (citing U.S. Constitution, art. 3, sec. 2), Genet Papers, DLC; Casto, *Supreme Court,* 139; *United States v. Greenleaf,* unreported (C.C.D.N.Y. 1797), discussed in *State Gazette of North Carolina,* May 3, 1797. For the belief that Randolph and Du Ponceau envisioned a civil action, see Ammon, *Genet Mission,* 152.

this." He continued, "I will file for myself at the supreme court and will obtain justice if it is still held in the United States." At the same time, Genet arranged for Brockholst Livingston, a New York lawyer, to have witnesses brought from New York to Philadelphia, which was then the nation's capital, for proceedings in the Supreme Court. The course of events, however, rapidly overtook and foreclosed Genet's plan. In February 1794, less than two months after Genet's lawyers began planning the prosecution, Jean Fauchet arrived in Philadelphia with orders from the French government to replace Genet and ship him home. Genet believed that he was to "be executed aboard [the homeward bound] convoy or at Brest." When President Washington magnanimously refused to permit this deadly repatriation, Fauchet determined to attempt a settlement of Genet's embarrassing prosecution. Fauchet rightly understood that he had a certain amount of leverage in the settlement negotiations. When the two men met, he reminded Genet that under French law, Genet's mother and sisters were subject to execution if he persisted in embarrassing the French government with his planned prosecution. And so the affair was concluded.[30]

After agreeing to drop the planned prosecution, Citizen Genet retired from public life. He had met and fallen in love with Cornelia Clinton, the daughter of New York's governor, and in the fall of 1793, he had the corsair *Petite Democrate* renamed *Cornelia*. Edmond and Cornelia married in November 1794, and Genet spent the rest of his life as a gentleman farmer in New York. He never returned to France, and he died on his farm in 1834.[31]

Congress

In early December, Congress finally came into session. At the very outset of the crisis, President Washington had asked the cabinet whether he should call a special early session, and as the crisis progressed, newspapers also called for a special session. Within the cabinet, Jefferson favored an early session, but the other cabinet officers disagreed. Jefferson undoubtedly was influenced by the frequency with which he lost cabinet votes, and he believed that Congress was more likely to adopt pro-French policies. A special session, however, was never called.

---

30. Edmond Genet to Cornelia Clinton, Dec. 24, 1793, and Brockholst Livingston to Edmond Genet, Dec. 27, 1793, both in Genet Papers, DLC; "Correspondence of the French Ministers," 279 note a; Edmond Genet to Thomas Jefferson, July 4, 1797, in Minnigerode, *Genet,* 413–27 (app.); Edmond Genet, "To the Editor of the Herald," n.d., Edmond Genet Papers, DLC.

31. Ammon, *Genet Mission,* 125, 171–79; Minnigerode, *Genet,* 361–412.

From almost the beginning, there was a consensus within the cabinet that a special session of Congress was not legally required to deal with the Neutrality Crisis. Jefferson was initially inclined to believe that Congress's war powers included an exclusive power to determine that the United States would remain neutral, and his friend James Madison agreed. But Jefferson abandoned this position early in the crisis. As the months passed, he continued to believe that a special session should be called to deal with the crisis, but his reasons were prudential rather than constitutional. In April, the cabinet decided that a special session was not necessary, and in May James Monroe wrote Jefferson that a special session might be convened to amend legislation that restricted the shipping of American goods in foreign ships, but Monroe wrote, "I can perceive no other cause at present which can make the meeting of Congress necessary." If, however, a special session was to be called, Monroe wanted to know as soon as possible "as it will regulate me in my family and law concerns." A few months later Alexander Hamilton estimated that at least a month's advanced warning would be necessary for a special session. Apparently Jefferson agreed that a special session was not necessary to deal with the Neutrality Crisis, but he nevertheless thought "it more probable than otherwise that Congress will be convened before the constitutional day [in December]." Under the Constitution, only Congress may declare war, and Jefferson believed that the United States would soon be at war. But the enemy would be neither France nor Great Britain. Instead, Jefferson believed that the country would soon go to war against the Creek Nation.[32]

In 1792 and early 1793, the Creek Indians, with the encouragement of Spain, began raiding into Georgia. President Washington and the cabinet met in late May and decided to call up a force of two hundred infantry and cavalry to defend the Georgia frontier against the raids. They hoped this relatively small defensive force would suffice, but the cabinet believed that if "the whole nation of the Creeks [mounted] a serious invasion," the matter would have to "be referred to the provisions of the Constitution." The cabinet apparently thought that in the event of a serious invasion, a congressional declaration of war would be a constitutional necessity. Less than a week later, Jefferson wrote Madison, "The invasion of the Creeks is what will most likely occasion its [Congress's] convocation." At the same time,

---

32. James Monroe to Thomas Jefferson, May 28, 1793; Thomas Jefferson to James Madison, June 2, 1793; and Thomas Jefferson to James Monroe, June 4, 1793, all in *Papers of Thomas Jefferson,* 26:136, 168, 190; Alexander Hamilton to George Washington, Aug. 5, 1793, *Papers of Alexander Hamilton,* 15:195.

newspapers were reporting that "a general indian war, on the western frontiers of the southern states seems inevitable." Fortunately, skillful diplomacy averted the expected war.[33]

Jefferson also thought that the Neutrality Crisis warranted, but did not require, a special session. In a letter to the American ambassador in Paris, he emphasized the likelihood of war against the Indians but also thought that "our affairs ... with the belligerent powers of Europe may occasion the Convocation of Congress." At the same time, a notice in the press stated, "The crisis of affairs, it is generally thought, will demand a session of Congress." Given the voting patterns in the cabinet, Jefferson undoubtedly assumed that Congress would be a stronger supporter of pro-French policies. Finally, in mid-July, shortly after learning of Genet's threatened appeal, the president began thinking once more about a special session. First he asked the cabinet "to reflect" on the matter, and then, on August 4, he formally asked the cabinet for their opinions on whether an early session of Congress should be called.[34]

In seeking the cabinet's advice, the president mentioned a variety of factors. He was worried by the recent verdict in *Henfield's Case* and knew that the decision reached the day before to request Genet's recall would be controversial. In addition, there was "the situation of Indian affairs and the *general* complexion of public matters." When the cabinet met in the president's absence, the vote was three to one against calling an early session. Only Jefferson thought such a session was advisable. Although the president favored calling Congress, he acquiesced in the cabinet's vote.[35]

As the time for Congress to be convened drew nigh, President Washington gathered his cabinet to plan for the opening of the new legislative session. A host of complex and frequently interrelated matters needed to be considered. There were issues with Great Britain related to the northwest frontier and attacks on American shipping, issues with Spain regarding

33. Cabinet Opinion on the Creek Indians and Georgia, May 29, 1793, *Papers of Thomas Jefferson,* 26:138–39; Thomas Jefferson to James Madison, June 2, 1793, *Papers of Thomas Jefferson,* 26:168; *Carlisle (Pa.) Gazette,* June 5, 1793; Daniel Smith, "James Seagrave and the Mission to Tuckaubatchee, 1793," *Georgia Historical Quarterly* 44 (1960): 47–55; "Introductory Note," *Papers of Alexander Hamilton,* 14:490–94.

34. Thomas Jefferson to Gouverneur Morris, June 13, 1793, *Papers of Thomas Jefferson,* 26:275; *Federal Gazette,* June 17, 1793; Notes on Cabinet Meeting on Edmond Charles Genet, July 23, 1793, *Papers of Thomas Jefferson,* 26:555; George Washington to the Cabinet, Aug. 3, 1793, *Papers of Thomas Jefferson,* 26:611.

35. George Washington to the Cabinet, Aug. 3, 1793, *Papers of Thomas Jefferson,* 26:611; Notes of Cabinet Decision, Aug. 6, 1793, *Papers of Thomas Jefferson,* 26:627.

the navigation of the Mississippi River, the possibility of war with Indian nations, the need to enhance the nation's military preparedness, and a host of fiscal matters. The president also sought the cabinet's advice on proposals for neutrality legislation and how to treat the Proclamation of Neutrality in his formal address at the opening of Congress.[36]

On November 18, the cabinet met at the president's house for dinner and revisited the proclamation. Randolph suggested that the president should tell Congress that the proclamation was merely an expression of the president's personal opinion. "Hamilton did not like it" and proposed that the controversy could be avoided if the president used neutral terms that did not address the proclamation's legal effect. Yet Hamilton could not resist restating his belief that the president had authority to make a proclamation "that foreign nations consider . . . as a declaration of neutrality future as well as present." Under this analysis, the proclamation placed the country in a formal state of neutrality until action was taken to alter that status. He also reiterated his understanding that "the declaration would not legally bind Congress."[37]

Jefferson immediately challenged Hamilton and "opposed the right of the Presdt. to declare anything future on the qu. shall there or shall there not be war?" He reminded everyone that back in April he had insisted that under the Constitution, the executive is "incompetent" to decide this question. Although Jefferson believed that the president was not competent to declare neutrality, he made a significant concession. Hamilton had always argued that the president had constitutional authority to maintain the status quo of peace until Congress could decide whether there should be war, and now Jefferson agreed. In his notes, Jefferson wrote, "I admitted the Presdt. having received the nation at the close of Congr. in a state of peace, was bound to preserve them in that state till Congr. should meet again, and might proclaim any thing which went no further."[38]

Jefferson explained that his doubts about the president's constitutional authority had to do with the Treaties of Alliance and of Amity, especially Article 11's guarantee. He believed that "H's construction of the effect of the

---

36. See Washington Memorandum of Matters to be Communicated to Congress, Nov. 1793, in Fitzpatrick, *Writings of George Washington,* 33:160–61; Hamilton's Outline for George Washington's Fifth Annual Address to Congress, *Papers of Alexander Hamilton,* 15:425–30; Jefferson's Materials for the President's Address to Congress, Nov. 22, 1793, *Papers of Thomas Jefferson,* 27:421–24.

37. Notes of Cabinet Meetings, Nov. 18, 1793, *Papers of Thomas Jefferson,* 27:394–400.

38. Ibid., 400.

proclm. would have been a determination of the question of the *guarantee*." Randolph supported Jefferson on this point.[39]

The president, who had remained silent throughout this vigorous debate, then "declared he never had an idea that he could bind Congress against declaring war, or that any thing contained in his proclmn. could look beyond the first day of their meeting, his main view was to keep our people in peace." He asked Hamilton to "prepare a paragraph on this subject for the speech" to Congress. The president and cabinet "were [then] called to dinner."[40]

Three days later the group reconvened, and Hamilton was loaded for bear. He "entered pretty fully into all the argumentation of Pacificus," insisting that the proclamation declared the nations's "neutrality, and that the casus federis on [Article 11's] guarantee did not exist." He restated that the proclamation neither amended nor annulled the article. Rather, it declared that "there existed no circumstances to oblige the U.S. to enter into the war on account of the guarantee." In other words, Article 11, by its own terms and settled principles of international law, did not require the United States to go to war.[41]

At this point, the meeting—at least Jefferson's notes of the meeting—degenerated into a bewildering and abstruse dispute about the nature of the treaty power under the Constitution. We only have Jefferson's notes, and his notes are jumbled. The dispute began innocently enough with Hamilton again reiterating his firm understanding that "Congress might notwithstanding [*sic*] declare war notwithstanding these declarations of the Presidt." Congress's power to overturn a presidential action was a key component to Hamilton's theory of concurrent powers. Then by way of analogy, Hamilton said, "In like manner they may declare war in the face of a treaty, and in direct infraction of it." Then the locomotive jumped the tracks.[42]

Either Jefferson or Randolph may have objected that because Congress, which included both the House and the Senate, has the exclusive power to declare war, a treaty of neutrality, which would require the approval of the president and the Senate but not the House, would be unconstitutional. Hamilton could not resist this bait. He replied that the president and the Senate "might make a treaty of neutrality, which should take from Congress the right to declare war in that particular case." He viewed the treaty power as plenary: "under the form of a treaty," the president and the Senate "might

39. Ibid.
40. Ibid.
41. Notes of Cabinet Meeting, Nov. 21, 1793, *Papers of Thomas Jefferson*, 27:411–12.
42. Ibid.

exercise any powers whatever, even those exclusively given by the constn. to the H. of representatives."[43]

At first glance Jefferson's notes of Hamilton's analysis seem hopelessly inconsistent. In the space of three sentences, Jefferson records Hamilton as saying that Congress "might declare war in the face of a treaty, and in direct infraction of it" and that "the Presidt. and Senate . . . might make a treaty of neutrality, which should take from Congress the right to declare war in that particular case." These two statements seem to be flat contradictions of each other, and Jefferson's notes do not suggest a resolution to that contradiction.[44]

The most likely explanation is that Hamilton meant to address two different issues. Today treaties are understood to perform dual functions. A treaty between the United States and a foreign country is akin to a contract between the countries and gives the countries rights against each other under international law. At the same time, the Constitution's supremacy clause ordains that treaties of the United States are also binding domestic law within the United States. In recognition of the dual nature of treaties, there is a well-established doctrine of constitutional law that Congress is free to override a treaty by statute or, in Hamilton's words, may act "in direct infraction of" a treaty. In such a case, the legislation overriding the treaty supplants the treaty and becomes binding domestic law. But a unilateral act of Congress cannot change the United States' obligations to other nations under international law because under international law no nation is allowed to rescind treaties by unilateral action. To use Hamilton's words, under international law but not domestic law, "a treaty of neutrality . . . should take from Congress the right to declare war in that particular case." Under this well-established dual analysis, an act of Congress that is "in direct infraction" of a treaty simultaneously creates binding domestic law and places the United States in breach of its treaty obligations under international law.[45]

The duality of international law under the supremacy clause is a supple and sophisticated concept, but no one has ever doubted the suppleness and sophistication of Hamilton's mind. Certainly Jefferson's notes are consistent with this analysis, and we know that Hamilton understood that Congress, if

43. Ibid.
44. Ibid.
45. Ibid. For unilateral congressional abrogations of treaties, see Glennon, *Constitutional Diplomacy,* chap. 6; Henkin, *Foreign Affairs and the Constitution,* 195–96, 209–14.

it wished, could enact legislation contrary to a treaty of the United States. Three years later, in the context of the dispute over whether the Jay Treaty should be implemented, he advised President Washington that Congress could enact legislation that would unilaterally "pronounce the cases of non-operation & nullity of a treaty." Of course, the treaty would continue to be binding under international law, and the congressional action would subject the nation to remedies available under international law to nations aggrieved by a breach.[46]

Most of the argument among Hamilton, Jefferson, and Randolph involved the scope of the treaty power under the Constitution. Hamilton's position followed his general inclination to construe the federal government's powers as broadly as possible. He believed that Congress and the president have extensive powers under the "necessary and proper" and "executive Power" clauses. Similarly, he insisted that the president and the Senate, who are the treaty makers under the Constitution, may "exercise any powers whatever, even those exclusively given by the constn. to the H. of representatives."[47]

Eventually the discussion ground to a halt, and the president said that when he agreed to the Proclamation of Neutrality, "he had had but one object, the keeping our people quiet till Congress should meet." In his message to Congress, he was not inclined to elaborate upon the numerous legal issues implicated by the proclamation. "To declare he did not mean a declaration of neutrality in the technical sense of the phrase," for example, "might perhaps be crying *peccavi* [confessing guilt] before he was charged."[48]

When Washington sent his message to Congress two weeks later, he adopted Hamilton's advice to be noncommittal about the legal effect, but he used language drafted by Randolph. After briefly noting the outbreak of war in Europe and the consequent dangers to the United States, he simply stated:

> It seemed, therefore, to be my duty to admonish our citizens of the consequences of a contraband trade, and of hostile acts to any of the parties, and to obtain, by a declaration of the existing legal state of things, an easier admission of our right to the immunities belonging to our situation.

46. Enclosure to letter to George Washington, Mar. 29, 1796, *Papers of Alexander Hamilton*, 20:99.
47. See chapter 5, this volume; Notes of Cabinet Meeting, Nov. 21, 1793, *Papers of Thomas Jefferson*, 27:411–12.
48. Notes of Cabinet Meeting, Nov. 21, 1793, *Papers of Thomas Jefferson*, 27:412.

The president also asked Congress to overrule *Findlay v. The William* and to clarify the confusion caused by Gideon Henfield's acquittal. He requested legislation making violations of neutrality a statutory crime and conferring subject matter jurisdiction on the federal courts to grant restitution of illegally captured prizes.[49]

Finally, the president asked Congress to help him to obtain judicial advisory opinions. Throughout the crisis, the British minister had constantly petitioned the executive branch for the administrative restitution of prizes taken within United States territorial waters. Although this executive procedure had worked well in the case of the *Grange*, in subsequent cases the opposing sides vigorously contested crucial facts. For example in the case of the *William*, Jefferson wrote that "the testimony as to the place of seizure varies from 2 to 5 miles from the sea-shore." The French insisted that the capture was beyond the three-mile limit, and the British argued to the contrary. Courts routinely deal with disputed facts like this, but the cabinet is ill equipped to do so. To assist in making these difficult factual determinations, the president asked that he "be authorized by law to have facts ascertained by the Courts, when, for his own information, he shall request it."[50]

The president's proposed legislation was quickly overshadowed by a serious war scare with Great Britain. Americans had a general belief that the British were encouraging and supporting Indian attacks on frontier settlements in the Northwest. In addition, the British as part of their war effort against France pursued policies that were openly hostile to American maritime commerce. By early 1794, two major assaults on American shipping created a crisis in which war with Great Britain seemed likely.[51]

The initial assault came in the Mediterranean. Until 1793, Portugal had been more or less continuously at war with the Barbary powers, and the Portuguese navy had kept the Barbary pirates at bay. But in the fall of 1793, Great Britain lent its good offices and outright financial support to a negotiated truce that would free up Portuguese naval units to fight the French. Freed from the Portuguese blockade, the pirates immediately poured into the Mediterranean and Atlantic. About twenty Americans vessels were

---

49. *Annals of the Congress of the United States*, 11.

50. Draft by Thomas Jefferson, Nov. 8, 1793, *Papers of Thomas Jefferson* 27:331n10; Thomas, *American Neutrality in 1793*, 113–17 (discussing difficulties of Executive fact finding); *Annals of the Congress of the United States*, 11. The idea of referring factual issues to the courts raised serious constitutional issues. See Casto, *Supreme Court*, 175–78.

51. See generally Jerald A. Combs, *The Jay Treaty: Political Battleground of the Founding Fathers* (Berkeley and Los Angeles: University of California Press, 1970).

seized and their American crews made captive. Many Americans believed that the British has procured the truce between Portugal and the Barbary powers specifically to encourage the ensuing onslaught on American commerce, and supporters of France saw the episode as a chance to enact sanctions against Britain. A calculating Thomas Jefferson wrote, "The letting loose the Algerines on us, which has been contrived by England, has produced peculiar irritation. I think Congress will indemnify themselves by high duties on all articles of British importation. If this should produce war, tho' not wished for, it seems not to be feared."[52]

The Barbary depredations were serious enough, but neither Jefferson nor any other American knew about a secret British plan to mount a major assault on American maritime commerce in the Caribbean. In 1793, the British decided upon a campaign to conquer the French West Indies. As part of this plan, a secret order in council was issued in the late fall of 1793 authorizing the seizure of neutral ships trading with these French islands. American merchantmen had no forewarning of this secret order, and while Jefferson was writing about the Algerine depredations, the British pounced. More than 250 American vessels were captured by British cruisers, and half of the seized vessels were quickly condemned by obliging British Admiralty courts.[53]

These Caribbean attacks, following closely Britain's apparently devious manipulation of the Barbary pirates, strained American patience. In Congress, a small group of influential senators who usually favored neutrality policies that benefited the British met privately and agreed that "war might and probably would be the consequence of these aggressions of England." They advised the president to prepare for war and at the same time send a special envoy to England to negotiate a special solution to the crisis. The president chose Chief Justice Jay, and the Senate approved.[54]

In the midst of these and other issues, a strong Senate committee of staunch Federalists began work on the neutrality legislation that the president requested at the opening of the session. Caleb Strong, a Federalist from Massachusetts, chaired the committee. He was ably supported by Oliver Ellsworth, the de facto Senate majority leader, and Rufus King. Strong conferred with former Attorney General Randolph, who had become secretary of state, and Randolph roughed out a draft bill in January. Strong's committee reported a

---

52. See generally Ritcheson, *Aftermath of Revolution,* 294–96, 298; Thomas Jefferson to Martha Randolph, Dec. 22, 1793, *Papers of Thomas Jefferson,* 27:609.

53. See Ritcheson, *Aftermath of Revolution,* 299–305.

54. Rufus King, Notes, Mar. 10–Apr. 21, 1794, *Life and Correspondence of Rufus King,* 1:517–23; Combs, *Jay Treaty.*

bill to the Senate floor in February, but after initial debate, the senators referred the bill back to committee for amendment. An amended bill came on for consideration in March.[55]

Randolph's draft bill essentially codified the principles that he had supported as attorney general. The first part of his draft created statutory criminal sanctions against Americans who violated U.S. neutrality or otherwise violated a treaty of the United States or the law of nations. Randolph's draft also overruled the *Findlay* case by giving the federal courts jurisdiction over prize restitution cases if the plaintiff was a United States citizen, a citizen of a neutral power, or if the prize was captured in United States waters.[56]

Randolph's proposal was not particularly controversial, but Senator Strong's committee added two provisions that sparked a determined effort to kill the bill. The seventh section of Strong's bill would have changed the status quo to France's detriment. By 1794, many of the French corsairs operating along the coast had been lawfully fitted out in France or the West Indies, and they were free to sell their prizes and cargoes in American ports. Section 7 would have changed this state of affairs and outlawed the sale of any prizes and cargoes, whether they be British or French, in American ports. This restriction meant nothing to the British because they preferred to sell their prizes in British ports in the Caribbean. In any event, Article 22 of the Treaty of Commerce and Amity barred enemies of France from selling their prizes in American ports. In contrast, the new provision would be disastrous for French corsairs who had no conveniently available French ports to sell their prizes. As soon as the Senate took up Senator Strong's amended bill for discussion, opponents moved to strike Section 7.[57]

After the debate, the Senate was as evenly divided as possible, and the vote to strike Section 7 was a twelve-to-twelve tie. Vice President Adams used his constitutional authority to cast a tie-breaking vote in favor of the ban on the sale of prizes. The next day, opponents attempted to strike the eighth section of the bill, which authorized the president in certain circumstances to use military force to enforce rules regulating privateers. Again the motion to strike was defeated by the narrowest of margins. Vice President Adams cast a tie-breaking vote. The entire bill at last passed the Senate, but only after the vice president cast yet another tie-breaking vote.[58]

55. *Annals of the Congress of the United States,* 23, 42, 43, 49, 67–68; Edmund Randolph's Draft Bill, Jan. 1794, Stephen C. Strong Collection, MNF.

56. Edmond Randolph's draft bill, Jan. 1794.

57. *Annals of the Congress of the United States,* 66; Treaty of Amity, art. 22; Miller, *Treaties and Other International Acts,* 2:19–20.

58. *Annals of the Congress of the United States,* 66–68.

After such a close vote in the Senate, the bill's chances in the House were slim because, to quote the British consul general, the pro-French/anti-British coalition in the House was "avowedly predominant." As soon as the bill came over from the Senate, it was scheduled for immediate consideration by the House, but on the appointed day, it was not brought up for discussion. The leaders assured the bill's supporters that it would be taken up before the end of the session, but the actual plan was to kill it through inaction. For two months nothing was heard of the measure.[59]

Things changed in May, when President Washington concluded that one of Genet's schemes, an invasion of the Spanish colony of Louisiana, might actually come to pass. True to his instructions, Genet had attempted to "deliver our brothers in Louisiana from the tyrannical yoke of Spain" by asking George Rogers Clark to raise an army of Kentuckians to attack Louisiana. Clark has done heroic work in the West during the Revolutionary War, and the idea of his raising and leading an army of Kentuckians against Louisiana was plausible. Most westerners understood the need to open the Mississippi all the way to New Orleans.[60]

On May 20, the president sent a formal message to Congress warning of potential attacks by Americans on Louisiana and Florida. The president supported his warning with copies of extensive correspondence detailing the affair. He warned that the "means already deposited in the different departments of government, are shown by experience [e.g., *Henfield's Case*], not to be adequate to these high exigencies." He concluded by recommending the enactment of neutrality legislation.[61]

About a week and a half after the president's special message, one of the bill's supporters in the House moved to consider the erstwhile moribund measure. The bill's reappearance on the floor caught James Madison by surprise, and he continued the delay tactics. Madison and others argued that "it was too late in the session to discuss a subject of such magnitude." Fisher Ames of Massachusetts rose in response and asked, "Had we forgotten the disgraceful annals of last year?" Ames reminded the House of the president's

---

59. Phineas Bond to Lord Grenville, Apr. 17, 1794 (first letter), "Letters of Phineas Bond," *Annual Report of the American Historical Association, 1897,* 549. See *Annals of the Congress of the United States,* 743–45.

60. See chapter 2, this volume; Ammon, *Genet Mission,* 161–69; DeConde, *Entangling Alliance,* 237–40.

61. *Annals of the Congress of the United States,* 710. For the supporting correspondence, see *National State Papers of the United States, 1789–1817,* ed. Eileen Carzo (Wilmington, Del.: Michael Glazier, 1985), 22:257–80.

special message and warned that failure to enact the bill might cause the nation to "be driven into war by the licentious behavior of some individuals." Others warned of "ten, or perhaps twenty, American privateers being prepared to sail against British commerce." If the bill were not enacted, Chief Justice Jay's peace mission would be jeopardized.[62]

When the opponents responded that they "saw no harm in letting the bill lie," the supporters complained that there had been an agreement that the bill would be considered before the end of the session. One of Madison's allies then pretended that there never had been a formal deal and that "he had never heard anything of it more than a whisper between gentlemen in their seats." At this point, the "House [became] impatient for the question" and voted forty-nine to thirty-two to take up the bill.[63]

Although Madison and his allies could not prevent the House from considering the bill, they still had a working majority, and they mounted a successful attack on the provision outlawing the sale of prizes and cargoes. Under the Treaty of Commerce and Amity, enemies of France were forbidden to sell prizes and cargoes, and supporters of the bill explained in great elaboration that the bill would simply extend a similar prohibition to France. Madison emphatically condemned this plea for symmetry. He insisted that under settled principles of international law, a "neutral nation might treat belligerent nations unequally, where it was a consequence of a stipulation prior to the war, and having no particular reference to it." To illustrate, he pointed to the extreme example of a neutral country providing direct military assistance to a belligerent. "It was laid down expressly," he said, "by all the best writers, that to furnish a military force to one of the parties, in pursuance of such a stipulation, without a like aid to the other, was no breach of neutrality." He also noted that the president had decided that the French should be allowed to sell their prizes. For Congress now to decide otherwise would be "impolitic and extraordinary, as it could not fail to give extreme disgust to the French Republic." The opponents carried the day on the sale of prizes, and the motion to strike passed. Nevertheless, there was extreme reluctance to ignore the president's insistence that the legislation was necessary. Madison told Jefferson, "The influence of the Ex. on events, the use made of them, and the public confidence in the P. are an overmatch

---

62. James Madison to Thomas Jefferson, May 25, 1793, *Papers of Thomas Jefferson*, 28:84; *Annals of the Congress of the United States*, 743–44 (remarks of Madison, Ames, and Wadsworth).

63. *Annals of the Congress of the United States*, 743–45.

for all the efforts Republicanism can make." The Senate bill, minus the provision on the sale of prizes, passed the House.[64]

The House passed the bill on June 2, less than a week before the end of the session. Ordinarily there would be negotiations between the House and the Senate over their differences and perhaps even a joint committee of conference. But given the House leadership's opposition, there was no time for negotiations, and the Senate accepted the House decision to delete the sale of prize provision. The British minister reported home that "the Senate in order to preserve the rest, was under the necessity of consenting to the omission of this particular clause."[65]

Madison's partial victory was a disappointment to the British minister, who had viewed the bar against the sale of prizes as the legislation's "principal provision." After word got out that the bar was deleted from the legislation, Hammond glumly reported "the sales of prizes brought into the United States have been revived by agents appointed by the Minister or Consuls of France." Presumably, the sales of the vessels themselves were accomplished with either no decrees of condemnation or clandestine decrees, and the sales were at steeply discounted prices. Although Madison and his allies prevailed in Congress on the issue of selling prizes, the battle was not over. When Chief Justice Jay arrived back from his peace negotiations in England, he brought a treaty that, among other things, forbade the sale in America of prizes taken from Britain. Madison and his allies still controlled the House of Representatives, but the Constitution excludes the House from the treaty-making process. The Senate, which had a Federalist majority, approved the treaty, including the provision against selling prizes, by a narrow margin, and it became law.[66]

A Historical Conclusion

In retrospect, the most puzzling aspect of the Neutrality Crisis is the extent to which the contending factions represented by Jefferson and Hamilton agreed with each other. The crisis engendered intense anger and fierce

---

64. *Annals of the Congress of the United States,* 743–57; James Madison to Thomas Jefferson, May 25, 1793, *Papers of Thomas Jefferson,* 28:84 (discussing the president's influence on passage of neutrality legislation).

65. *Annals of the Congress of the United States,* 757; George Hammond to Lord Grenville, June 9, 1794, PRO:FO 5/5, DLC (transcript).

66. George Hammond to Lord Grenville, Apr. 15, 1794, PRO:FO 5/4, DLC (transcript); George Hammond to Lord Grenville, June 27, 1794, PRO:FO 5/5, DLC (transcript); Jay Treaty, art. 24, in Miller, *Treaties and Other International Acts* 2:245; Casto, *Supreme Court,* 115–17; Combs, *Jay Treaty.*

polemics, but from the outset, Washington, Jefferson, Madison, Monroe, Randolph, Hamilton, and Knox agreed that the country had to remain neutral. Nor was there any dispute over the most significant aspects of the evolving neutrality policy. They specifically agreed that French corsairs should not be outfitted in American ports, that Americans should not serve on the corsairs, and that the French Consular Courts were illegal affronts to American sovereignty.

To be frank, most of the points of actual disagreement, save the continuing validity of the Treaties of Alliance and of Amity, seem trivial. Jefferson thought that transferring French cannon from one ship to another in an American harbor was permissible, but Hamilton disagreed. Hamilton prevailed. Similarly, Hamilton wanted the first few captures by illegally outfitted corsairs returned to the British, and Jefferson disagreed. Jefferson prevailed.

Ironically, the contending factions' intense anger and fierce polemics may have been stimulated by the general recognition that the country had to remain neutral. Jefferson can be seen as an ideal type for sophisticated Americans who viewed the national interest as best served by a pro-French policy. His heart clearly lay with the new French Republic, but he understood the political necessity of neutrality. When he confided to Madison, "I fear that a fair neutrality will prove a disagreeable pill to our friends, tho' necessary to keep us out of the calamities of a war," he was projecting his own feelings on his "friends."[67] His bitterness and discontent with neutrality coupled with his distrust of Hamilton was a recipe for anger. The bitterness and distrust fed on and exacerbated each other.

Within the cabinet, Jefferson thought that he was fighting a losing battle, but he won the political war in the first weeks of the crisis when the president decided that the French treaties would be treated as remaining in effect. He also won a significant skirmish in the *Little Sarah* affair. He surely was right that an exchange of fire between the *Little Sarah / Petite Democrat* and a battery at Mud Island with its "bloody consequences" would have been an unmitigated disaster.[68] His action significantly helped to avoid this potential catastrophe.

The crisis could be analyzed as a kind of political horse race to determine who had the greatest influence upon President Washington. Viewed in this perspective, Madison and Jay must be scratched from the racing card because they were seldom or never in the capital to confer with the president. Jay, who was riding circuit and not in the capital until mid-July, and Madison

67. See chapter 3, this volume.
68. See chapter 7, this volume.

did not return until the December session of Congress. Jefferson wrote Madison in August that the president was "extremely anxious to know your sentiments on the proclamation." Jefferson, however, fobbed off the president by telling him that Madison was "absorbed in farming." There is no record of any correspondence between Washington and Jay and Madison during the first three months of the crisis.[69]

Once Madison and Jay are scratched, the contest becomes a match race between Jefferson and Hamilton, and some of Jefferson's latter-day partisans contend that he won the race.[70] Ultimately, however, the horse race analysis is not helpful. First, it ignores the grim geopolitical helplessness of the United States that dictated a policy of neutrality without regard to individual leaders' desires. Second, it ignores the obvious fact that all the cabinet members, save possibly Secretary of War Knox, played an influential role. Throughout the crisis, Washington carefully listened to Jefferson's, Hamilton's, and Knox's advice. Does it really matter who, if anyone, came in first?

If the focus is shifted from influence on the president to constitutional theory, constitutional law, and constitutional history, Alexander Hamilton clearly was the most significant participant in the Neutrality Crisis. Jefferson's contributions in this regard were modest. In the beginning, he advanced the interesting notion that a declaration of neutrality is comparable to a declaration of war and therefore beyond the president's constitutional power. But he never elaborated upon his idea and almost immediately abandoned it. James Madison is one of the true giants of constitutional history, but his contributions during the crisis to our understanding of the Constitution were comparatively modest. His Helvidius essays are largely devoted to abstruse and meandering attacks on strawmen. Only a few passages, such as his powerful analysis of war powers, have enduring value. In contrast, Hamilton's elaboration of the president's executive power provided President Washington with a firm basis for issuing the Proclamation of Neutrality, and his Pacificus No. 1 is as powerful today as it was two centuries ago.

69. Thomas Jefferson to James Madison, Aug. 11, 1793, *Papers of Thomas Jefferson,* 26:653.
70. Malone, *Jefferson and the Ordeal of Liberty,* xv–xvi.

CHAPTER 10

Lessons from the Founders

At a fundamental constitutional level, the Neutrality Crisis of 1793 provides insights that are as pertinent today as they were in 1793. The strengths and weaknesses of the executive branch in conducting foreign policy were as clear in 1793 as they are in the twenty-first century. By far the most valuable insights from the crisis come from Alexander Hamilton's Pacificus No. 1. He elaborated a comprehensive constitutional theory that explains the president's extensive foreign affairs powers and explains the Constitution's primary check against presidential error. In contrast to the executive branch, the judicial and legislative branches of the federal government were largely ineffectual and unhelpful in dealing with the crisis. They simply failed to act, and the reasons for their relative ineffectiveness are as relevant today as they were some two hundred years ago.

The Judicial Branch

Throughout the Neutrality Crisis, individual federal judges played an active role in supporting the president's policies. After all, Washington had selected every single member of the judiciary. Although the justices rejected a request for a formal advisory opinion, the most plausible explanation for their rejection is that they really did not believe that an advisory opinion was necessary. In contrast, at the very outset of the crisis, Chief Justice Jay willingly advised Hamilton on neutrality issues. As the crisis developed, Jay and Justice Wilson crafted detailed grand jury charges carefully tailored to justify and support the president's declaration of neutrality. Then, in criminal prosecutions against Gideon Henfield in Philadelphia and Joseph Rivers in Savannah, the judges emphatically rejected various legal theories that impeded the enforcement of neutrality. Nevertheless, the high-profile cases that came before the federal courts contributed nothing to and probably impeded the president's policies. In civil cases, the judges refused to review the legitimacy of the French corsairs' depredations. Criminal prosecutions yielded disastrously ambiguous acquittals.

Notwithstanding the federal judges' individual support for the president, the judicial branch was noticeably unsuccessful in rendering formal judicial judgments that could provide timely advice and support to the president. The problem lies in the nature of the judicial function. The judiciary's predominant function has always been to adjudicate cases, and the federal judges adjudicated a number of high-profile cases in 1793. *Findlay v. The William* and *Henfield's Case* epitomize the kind of traditional litigation that provides the courts with a vehicle for participating in foreign affairs crises. At the same time, *Findlay* and *Henfield* illustrate some of the reasons the federal judiciary never has and never will be a reliable participant in the resolution of foreign affairs crises. The federal courts' relatively modest role in the arena of foreign policy is well known. "Overall," Louis Henkin has observed, "the contribution of the courts to foreign policy and their impact on foreign relations are significant but not large. The Supreme Court in particular intervenes only infrequently and its foreign affairs cases are few and haphazard." Even when the Supreme Court intervenes, it has in recent times shown a pronounced tendency to defer to the executive branch rather than exercise independent judgment.[1]

Today observers typically explain the courts' modest role by pointing to a panoply of principles and prudential considerations that hinder the judiciary's ability to address issues of law related to foreign policy. Most of these limitations are corollaries to the fundamental constitutional rule that the judicial power of the United States extends only to cases and controversies. Thus the federal courts may not render advisory opinions, a plaintiff must have standing, and a case must be ripe but must not be moot. These corollaries are not limited to disputes implicating foreign policy issues but are often raised in that context.[2]

In addition, a bundle of considerations loosely labeled the "political question doctrine" frequently influences courts to subordinate their judgment to the political branches. In a leading case, the Supreme Court explained, "Not only does resolution of [foreign relations] issues frequently turn on standards that defy judicial application, or involve the exercise of discretion demonstrably committed to the executive or legislative; but much such questions uniquely demand single-voices statements of the Government's views." Finally, the lower federal courts in the District of Columbia have relied upon their equitable discretion to deny judicial remedies to members of Congress in foreign affairs and other cases.[3]

Although a nascent vision of the political question doctrine played a role in *Findlay v. The William,* the 1793 litigation's enduring value is to illustrate

1. Henkin, *Foreign Affairs and the Constitution,* 147–48; Koh, *National Security Constitution,* 134–49; Stephen Dycus, Arthur L. Berney, William C. Banks, and Peter Raven-Hansen, *National Security Law,* 2nd ed. (Boston: Little, Brown, 1997), 135; Glennon, *Constitutional Diplomacy,* 111–13, 313–25.

2. See Casto, "Foreign Affairs Crises," 237–38.

3. Ibid., 238; *Baker v. Carr,* 369 U.S. 186, 211 (1962).

structural limitations inherent in the Constitution's case or controversy requirement. These structural limitations operate as a general inhibition to the courts' ability to provide clear and timely advice in all cases, but the problem is especially significant in the context of rapidly developing events such as foreign affairs crises. This is not to say that the federal courts never provide clear and timely advice in cases affecting foreign policy. They obviously do on occasion. The case or controversy requirement impedes rather than bars courts from deciding legal issues related to foreign policy, and courts are therefore an unreliable source of advice. These problems usually are analyzed in terms of corollaries to the fundamental requirement of a case or controversy, but the very nature of the judicial process is at least as serious an impediment to the courts' ability to render useful advice. This structural problem is not simply a function of the orderly and usually ponderous pace of the judicial process. Rather, the deficiency lies in a divergence between the general needs of the nation at large and the specific interests represented in actual cases and controversies. The experience of the federal courts in 1793 epitomizes the divergence of general needs and specific interests. The lessons from 1793 are particularly compelling because the Federalist judges wanted to support their president.

Findlay and *Henfield* epitomize modern litigation involving a proper case or controversy. Both cases involved an actual underlying dispute to which the parties sought a judicial resolution in the form of a traditional judicial remedy, and the parties were represented by counsel who vigorously and capably explored the pertinent issues. Yet from the government's and the nation's point of view, the judgments in *Findlay* and *Henfield* were disastrously ambiguous.

Findlay was decided at the height of the Neutrality Crisis, and the executive branch dearly wished for advice on such legal issues as how far United States sovereignty extended out to sea, the legality of fitting out French corsairs in American ports, and the legality of the French Consular Courts. George Washington and his cabinet had no desire to act unlawfully, and formal judicial advice on these issues would have provided valuable guidance in charting a course of lawful conduct. Even in respect of issues the cabinet viewed as clearly settled, a judgment might have been useful in responding to the conflicting protests of the French and British ambassadors. In particular, a judicial opinion would have assisted the Washington administration in the court of public opinion. Most Americans firmly supported the cause of revolutionary France. In this heated political crisis, clear decisions from the courts would have provided valuable political support to the government and valuable legal advice to the nation at large. In addition, the availability of a judicial remedy would have channeled countless petitions for relief from the executive to the courts. With these considerations in mind, the government through Secretary Jefferson actually encouraged the filing of suits such as *Findlay*.

Instead of rendering valuable legal advice, District Judge Peters punted. He dismissed the case for lack of subject matter jurisdiction. Only a court of the capturing nation was empowered to decide the fundamental question of prize or no prize, and the precedents for this proposition were too well settled for a trial judge to ignore. Judge Peters clearly wanted to help the government and strongly hinted that the claimants should appeal his decision, but the claimants decided not to appeal. Instead, they sought an executive remedy. Although the Supreme Court eventually rejected the settled precedent Judge Peters felt compelled to follow, the Court's decision did not come until the following year in another case. By that time, the nation was in the throes of a different crisis.[4]

Findlay neatly illustrates a structural problem that inhibits, which is not to say prohibits, the judicial branch from providing useful advice during foreign affairs crises. Almost by definition foreign affairs crises have broad, national implications, but the federal courts' power to speak to the relevant legal issues is hostage to the comparatively narrow interests of the litigants. The Constitution limits the judicial power of the United States to the adjudication of cases or controversies involving actual disputes between specific parties. The limitation therefore entrusts litigation to the particular interests of specific parties who may be relatively uninterested in more general issues. As a result, specific judicial cases may be resolved without regard to pertinent overarching legal issues of nationwide concern.

Findlay was fundamentally about who was lawfully entitled to the *William*. The French captors had her, and the British claimants wanted her back. On the merits, the fundamental issue of lawful possession turned upon the important national issues of territoriality and fitting out corsairs and also implicated the Consular Courts' legitimacy. The captors would have been pleased with favorable rulings on these important issues, but what they really wanted was to retain possession of the *William*. Because they already had a decree of condemnation from the French Consular Court, their attorneys correctly perceived that a preliminary challenge to the federal courts' subject matter jurisdiction would serve their clients' immediate interests. The captors probably would have preferred a favorable ruling on the more important issues, but in litigation a procedural dismissal of the plaintiff's

4. See chapter 6, this volume.

case almost always counts as a win for the defendant. Judge Peters's decision left the status quo in place, and under the status quo, the French had the *William*. Even if the captors had had an inkling that Judge Peters would rule in their favor on the important issues, their narrow interest in being able to keep and sell the *William* virtually dictated that they challenge the court's subject matter jurisdiction.[5]

The British claimants in *Findlay* were like the captors. For both sides, the major issues of territoriality, fitting out privateers, and Consular Courts were secondary. The claimants, like the captors, wanted the *William*. Judge Peters practically begged the claimants to appeal his decision, but they were more interested in regaining their property than in having a court decide important legal issues. They made an economic calculation that they were more likely to regain their property through diplomatic channels than through further litigation and thus opted not to appeal. They might have simultaneously pursued remedies from both the executive and judicial branches, but perhaps they thought that the president would have stayed his decision pending the outcome of a judicial appeal.[6]

The criminal prosecution against Gideon Henfield illustrates other structural problems inherent in the judicial process. Unlike in *Findlay,* the government's interests in *Henfield* were not entirely hostage to the narrow interests of private parties. The government was the plaintiff in *Henfield,* and its interests were directly represented by the U.S. attorney and the attorney general. *Henfield* was indicted specifically to create a test case on the lawfulness of U.S. citizens joining the crews of French corsairs to fight against the British. The government's attorneys carefully structured the litigation to present this precise issue to the court, but again the case or controversy limitation prevented a clear judicial resolution of the question.

Cases or controversies always arise in the context of specific, sui generis facts, but usually the specific facts of a case are not significant. For example, assuming all other facts remained constant in *Henfield,* it would not have mattered if the *Citoyen Genet* had fitted out in Savannah, Georgia, and Henfield

---

5. There is a rule that federal judges must raise issues of subject matter jurisdiction on their own motion—that parties may not waive subject matter jurisdiction. See Charles Wright, *The Law of Federal Courts,* 5th ed. (St. Paul, Minn.: West Publishing, 1994), 27–31. This cherished bit of federal courts arcania, however, is one of the mysteries of Article III jurisprudence under the Constitution. In contrast, the jurisdictional limitation of prize or no prize came from customary Admiralty law and therefore may have been waivable.

6. In another case, the cabinet delayed executive consideration of a capture pending the outcome of litigation. See chapter 4, this volume.

had joined its crew there rather than in Charleston. Sometimes, however, unique facts become crucial to the ultimate outcome of litigation. *Henfield* is a good example of a case that may have turned upon sui generis facts. The government sought to establish a number of legal propositions of general application throughout the nation. In particular, the U.S. attorney argued that Americans who joined a French corsair's crew acted unlawfully, that notwithstanding the absence of an applicable criminal statute, their unlawful conduct was subject to criminal penalties, and that Henfield's expatriation defense was invalid. Each of these three propositions of law were crucial to the effective implementation of the president's Proclamation of Neutrality. But Henfield had another defense, which was unique to his case. He, in fact, had no knowledge of the proclamation when he sailed on the *Citoyen Genet*. Once the proclamation became common knowledge, which happened almost immediately, this particular fact pattern could not be repeated.

Henfield was a specific case—a prosecution of a specific individual. Although the government sought to use the prosecution as a test case to establish general principles of law, the court, including the jury, had to focus on the far more narrow issue of whether the specific defendant's actual conduct warranted his conviction. The "leading man among" the jurors told Attorney General Randolph that he voted for an acquittal specifically because Henfield had no knowledge of the president's proclamation. If this narrow and not-to-be-repeated circumstance was the basis of the court's judgement, *Henfield* was a nondecision respecting the important legal issues of nationwide significance.

Henfield also illustrates another problem with the case or controversy limitation. Although judicial cases involve legal pronouncements and create legal precedent, this lawmaking function is secondary to the court's primary responsibility to render a judgment. The court is immediately concerned with who wins or loses a case. At the conclusion of litigation, a judgment is entered and the case is resolved. Sometimes the reasons for the court's judgment will be unclear, but ambiguity or lack of clarity in the ratio decidendi usually does not significantly diminish the value of the judgment to the specific parties before the court.

In *Henfield*, the court entered a judgment of acquittal, but to this day no one knows the basis of the court's decision. Attempts to explain the court's judgment as premised on one legal principle or another[7] are misguided. The judge charged the jury that Americans serving on French corsairs were

---

7. See, for example, Prakash and Ramsey, "Executive Power over Foreign Affairs," 344–45 (also citing other attempts).

violating the law, that their service was subject to criminal sanction notwithstanding the absence of an applicable act of Congress, and that the defense of expatriation was unavailable. If the jury based their acquittal upon Henfield's ignorance of the Proclamation of Neutrality, the verdict does not conflict with the judges' clear and unambiguous charges.[8] But "Archy Simple" in South Carolina believed that the *Henfield* judgment supported the expatriation defense, and the court's decision to recharge the jury on expatriation lends credence to his belief. Others read the judgment as a general refutation of the government's case and of the judge's charges. The upshot was that the government's carefully planned test case produced disastrously ambiguous guidance on legal issues crucial to the preservation of American neutrality.

The structural problems that mired the federal courts in 1793 still exist. Certainly the problem of the disparity between the narrow interests of the parties to litigation and the broader needs of the nation persists. For example, efforts to defend against terrorism originating abroad have raised important legal questions, and the prosecution of John Walker Lindh, an American who fought against the United States in Afghanistan, seemed to provide the judiciary with an early opportunity to answer some of these questions. Lindh's attorneys planned to challenge the admissibility of statements that he made after he was taken prisoner, and the prosecution planned to argue that constitutional protections developed to regulate domestic police investigations do not apply to Americans captured abroad in a theater of war. But as in *Findlay,* a funny thing happened on the way to the Supreme Court. Lindh and the government agreed upon a plea bargain. Both parties had narrow interests that trumped the national interest in determining the constitutional rights of Americans captured overseas during the course of antiterrorist military operations. Lindh obtained a possibly lighter sentence, and the government avoided the possibility of an embarrassing not-guilty verdict on some or all of the counts in the indictment.[9]

The problem of ambiguity that bedeviled attempts to understand the judgment in *Henfield* also persists. Of course, ambiguity pervades any project to frame rules for regulating human conduct. The problem lies in the simple linguistic fact that a word and certainly a sentence may have multiple

8. Similarly the verdict can be explained on other comparatively narrow grounds not in conflict with the judges' charges. See chapter 6, this volume.

9. See Neil Lewis, "Traces of Terror: The Captive," *New York Times,* July 16, 2002, A1; David Johnson, "Traces of Terror: A Plea Suited Both Sides," *New York Times,* July 16, 2002, A1.

meanings. This linguistic ambiguity is pertinent in all analyses of the relationship between general rules and specific conduct. An attorney advising a client, a judge deciding a case, and a legislator framing laws must grapple with this linguistic ambiguity. *Henfield,* however, illustrates a different kind of ambiguity inherent in the judicial process. The problem of linguistic ambiguity arises only after a particular rule is identified, but in *Henfield* the particular rule that dictated the judgment of acquittal was never identified. Was he acquitted because serving on a French corsair was lawful, because Congress had not enacted applicable criminal sanctions, because he had changed his citizenship, or because he joined the *Citoyen Genet* without knowledge of President Washington's Proclamation of Neutrality? No one knew the answer in 1793, and no one will ever know. The problem of ambiguity in *Henfield* was antecedent to the linguistic ambiguity that plagues the search for the meaning of a particular legal rule.

Henfield's antecedent problem of ambiguity cannot be dismissed as a function of the archaic eighteenth-century rule that criminal juries had final authority to determine the applicable legal rules. The ambiguity was caused by the lack of a clear explanation of the basis for the jury's verdict and the court's consequent judgment. No one knew which of the many plausible bases for acquittal was the proper explanation of the court's judgment. The antecedent problem of ambiguity, which *Henfield* illustrates, arises from the fact that the primary purpose of adjudication is to resolve specific cases and not to pronounce or legislate applicable legal rules. In the words of the Constitution, the "judicial Power of the United States . . . shall extend to . . . Cases [and] Controversies." *Henfield* involved a dispute between the United States and Gideon Henfield, and the court served its primary purpose with absolute clarity. Henfield won. No one knew why, but everyone knew that he was acquitted.

Our understanding of the judicial process has radically changed over the last two hundred years since *Henfield* was decided. Juries no longer are empowered to decide the law, and judges are now understood to possess law-making power. But the primary purpose of adjudication has not changed. Courts still decide cases or controversies arising from actual disputes between specific parties. Courts legislate legal rules in the process of adjudicating cases, but there is no absolute need for courts to state clearly the basis for their decision. A court's primary purpose is the same as it was some two hundred years ago: to render a judgment in the case before it. The law-making function is secondary.

Goldwater v. Carter is a modern example of *Henfield*. President Carter had given notice of intent to terminate an important treaty, and Senator

Goldwater asked the judiciary to block the termination. Goldwater's theory was that the president lacked unilateral authority under the Constitution to terminate a treaty. In the Supreme Court, four justices believed that the case should be dismissed because the particular issue of presidential power was a political question. One justice concurred because he viewed the dispute as not yet ripe, and another concurred without explanation. Three other justices disagreed with the Court's disposition.[10]

To this day, the nation lacks clear guidance from the Court on whether the president may unilaterally terminate a treaty.[11] This is not to say, however, that the *Goldwater* Court failed to fulfill its constitutional duties. The Court's role is to decide judicial cases and controversies, and in *Goldwater* it did precisely that. There was nothing ambiguous about the Court's fulfillment of its fundamental obligation. The case clearly and finally terminated in the dismissal of the plaintiff's complaint.

Goldwater and *Findlay* illustrate yet another limitation to the judicial power that has lain in plain sight since the Constitution's inception. The judicial function is usually understood to be the resolution of disputes, but the Constitution is more narrow. Article III limits the judicial power to judicial cases and controversies and does not extend the courts' power to the underlying dispute between parties to litigation. Usually the distinction is inconsequential, but the difference was significant in 1793. In *Findlay*, the Court refused to address the lawfulness of the *William*'s capture but unambiguously dismissed the case. In 1979, the *Goldwater* Court did the same. Neither Court addressed the lawfulness of the defendants' actions, and neither resolved the underlying dispute between the parties. Yet each fulfilled its constitutional duties by unambiguously deciding the judicial case before it.[12]

In 1793, President Washington tried to bypass the pits and snares of the judicial process by asking the Supreme Court justices for an advisory opinion. Although the justices refused his request, they were not unalterably

---

10. 444 U.S. 996 (1979).

11. See Fisher, *Constitutional Conflicts,* 242–45.

12. For an example of an ambiguous decision that did resolve the underlying dispute, see the *Steel Seizure Case,* in which President Truman's nationalization of the steel industry during the Korean War was challenged as unconstitutional. Seven justices wrote opinions, but there was no majority opinion. Notwithstanding the disagreements among the justices, a majority believed that the seizure was unconstitutional. Under these circumstances the decision provides no authoritative guidance for future disputes, but the Court's judgment clearly resolved the underlying dispute between President Truman and the steel industry.

opposed to advising the executive branch. Eighteenth-century British judges advised the Crown, and acting within this established tradition, American justices advised the president and his cabinet before and after the Neutrality Crisis.[13] Nevertheless, the 1793 refusal is at least the first step on the road to today's firm rule against advisory opinions.

The Legislative Branch

The least significant branch of government during the Neutrality Crisis was the legislative. Congress, to use an eminent Victorian's phrase, was the dog that did not bark in the night. From the beginning of the crisis until its end, there was a legislative silence because Congress was not in session. But like the dog that did not bark in the night, Congress's silence provides valuable insights. Under the Constitution, Congress is structurally impeded from dealing effectively with sudden or rapidly evolving crises. To be sure if there is a broad national consensus upon a particular matter, Congress can act swiftly and decisively. When Japan attacked Pearl Harbor, Congress responded immediately with a declaration of war. A common and more serious problem arises when there is significant disagreement within the nation about a foreign policy issue. Perhaps there will be serious disagreement at the outset or perhaps the disagreement will evolve from an initial consensus based upon mistaken assumptions. The Neutrality Crisis epitomizes the former and illustrates the enormous friction that impedes congressional action when the lack of a national consensus is reflected in Congress.

In 1793, Congress was adjourned throughout the Neutrality Crisis and was literally incapable of acting. As the crisis progressed, there were calls within and without the government to convene a special emergency session, but each time the issue was considered within the administration, President Washington decided against a special session. A special factor counseling hesitation in 1793 was the long lead time required for a special session, but two hundred years later, the immense logistical problems confronting the founders no longer exist. Communication is instantaneous, and travel is virtually instantaneous. More significantly, today's legislators are full-time professional politicians. They live in the capital, and some maintain only nominal homes in their residences states. In any event, there is seldom a need for an emergency session of Congress. In 1793, the second session of the second Congress adjourned in early March, and the next session did not

---

13. See chapter 7, this volume.

convene until early December. Congress was out of session for nine months, but today, Congress typically is in session for most of the year.

The enduring lessons from 1793 regarding the legislative branch relate to how Congress acted after its regularly scheduled session commenced.[14] President Washington requested neutrality legislation in one of his initial messages to Congress in early December, but the congressional silence continued for half a year. Congress did not enact a neutrality statute until the next June. The reasons for the six-month delay are inherent in the structure of the Constitution.

It has always been commonplace that the Constitution creates a government of separated powers to assure wise governance, and in the 1794 Congress, separation of powers operated with a vengeance. Congressional action requires the concurrence of two bodies of legislators. Even when legislators want to support their president, it can take time to push legislation through just one of the houses of Congress. In the 1790s, no members of Congress supported George Washington's Federalist administration more staunchly than the Senate committee that drafted the neutrality legislation. Caleb Strong, Oliver Ellsworth, and Rufus King were a dream team for the president. Yet they took two months to draft a bill.

Part of the problem was that the senators had to come up with a bill that they believed would be acceptable to a majority of the Senate. The fact that their initial bill was in effect recommitted to their committee suggests that they were not entirely successful. In addition, although they were the president's firm allies, they were independent of him. At the beginning of the process, Secretary of State Randolph gave Senator Strong a draft bill, but the senators had their own ideas about what was best for the country. Instead of rubber stamping or merely fleshing out Randolph's draft, their bill had significant additional provisions. The passage of the neutrality bill through the Senate illustrates what can happen when the president's supporters have working control. From 1789 to 1796, Ellsworth was the de facto Senate majority leader for the Federalist coalition, and Vice President John Adams was the president of the Senate. The president's supporters, with the assistance of tie-breaking votes by Adams, eventually secured passage of a bill significantly stronger from the one initially proposed by the secretary of state.

The House of Representatives, however, was another matter. House leaders such as James Madison opposed the administration's proposed neutrality

---

14. See chapter 9, this volume.

legislation. In the House, the Senate bill was almost dead on arrival. Rather than voting the measure up or down on the merits, the opposition chose a more subtle strategy to defeat the measure. They scheduled the bill for consideration, but somehow more significant items continuously took precedence. As the session was coming to a close, the opposition bootstrapped their tactics of delay into an argument that the measure was so important that it required extensive consideration that would only be possible in the next Congress. The bill surely would have died a silent death but for the president's intervention. A majority of the representatives could not ignore George Washington's formal request that the House vote on the bill. The procedural tactics of delay failed, but a majority still opposed the bill's ban on the sale of French prizes, which the British minister thought was the bill's "principal provision." The House struck this provision from the bill and then reaped a secondary benefit from the delay tactics. With the session ending in less than a week, there was no time for negotiation between the two chambers. The Senate leaders had to acquiesce in the House's decision.

The neutrality bill's journey through the House illustrates the legislative weapons available to prevent a president from accomplishing legislative objectives. On the merits, the opposition gets two bites from the apple. A bill must pass both the House and the Senate, and the ban on the sale of prizes passed only the Senate. In addition, the controlling coalition—now political party—in each chamber can play a procedural game of hide and seek. If they do not want to have a public disagreement with the president, they can simply use procedural tactics to avoid a vote on the merits. On the other hand, if the president is willing to spend political capital by formally requesting a vote like Washington did in 1794, Congress will usually acquiesce and have an up or down vote.

The Neutrality Crisis's practical lessons on the working of separation of powers are equally relevant to issues that do not involve foreign affairs, but the specific issue of the sale of prizes illustrates an obscure wrinkle in the Constitution that is unique to foreign affairs. In 1794, the ban passed the Senate but not the House. That same year, Chief Justice Jay went to Britain and negotiated a treaty that banned the French from selling prizes. After the Senate approved the treaty, the ban became binding federal law without being considered by the House of Representatives. In more recent times, Congress has occasionally used a reverse version of this constitutional wrinkle. For example, NAFTA is fundamentally an agreement between the United States and foreign nations and therefore might be accomplished by a treaty, which would require a two-thirds rate of the Senate. Because NAFTA probably could not meet this supermajority requirement, it was restructured as legislation that would require only a bare majority vote in each chamber of Congress.[15]

The Neutrality Crisis also suggests some of Congress's inherent political strengths under the Constitution. As a practical matter, Congress is more representative of the nation than either the judiciary, which is not elected, or even the president can be. Congress consists of legislators chosen by different people from different sections of the country. In an extended republic, there will always be significant disagreements within the electorate, and Congress provides a diverse body that will reflect these disagreements. In 1793, juries refused to convict Americans such as Gideon Henfield, who violated the president's neutrality policy. After Congress passed the Neutrality Act, government prosecutors were able to obtain criminal verdicts against individuals who violated neutrality. These convictions suggest, but by no means prove, that a considered act of Congress will receive more credence within the nation at large than a unilateral presidential decision.[16]

The Executive Branch

Unlike Congress, the president is always in session and has the ability to act quickly and decisively when problems arise. The president is a single individual who in theory can assess a situation and make an immediate decision. In 1793, President Washington reached the capital on April 17, and after consulting the cabinet, he approved the Proclamation of Neutrality, which was issued less than a week later on April 22. His quick response to the crisis contrasts sharply with Congress's sporadic efforts the next year to enact neutrality legislation.[17]

The very presidential unity that enables quick and decisive action is also a source of weakness. The president is only one human being and therefore cannot accurately reflect the nation's diverse values and judgments the way Congress can. Washington, the only president in American history who was elected unanimously, is the exception that makes the rule. Nevertheless, in the Neutrality Crisis, he did not reflect the majority of Americans, who desired a foreign policy more supportive of French interests. In recent history, presidents have been elected by a slight majority, a plurality, or even a minority of the popular vote. Presidents take into account the diverse judgments within the nation at large but cannot accurately reflect the nation's rich diversity of opinion the way Congress can. In 1793, President Washington

---

15. Ibid.
16. See chapter 6, this volume.
17. See Koh, *National Security Constitution,* chap. 5.

declared neutrality and authorized the prosecution of Americans such as Gideon Henfield and Joseph Rivers who violated his policy. These prosecutions, however, were out of step with the people, and the verdicts of acquittal can and probably should be viewed as popular rejections of the president's policy.

In addition to illustrating some of the president's strengths and weaknesses in the administration of foreign affairs, the Neutrality Crisis gave Alexander Hamilton an opportunity to bequeath to the nation a simple, elegant, and utterly persuasive explanation of the president's constitutional authority over foreign affairs. In Pacificus No 1, he explained that the Constitution's intendment is found in the opening line of Article II, which vests the president with the "executive Power" of the United States. Hamilton understood that this broad authority would inevitably encroach upon Congress's legislative powers and used the concept of concurrent constitutional authority to explain the problem of executive encroachment.

Unfortunately, the wisdom and truth of Pacificus No. 1 has not always been understood. In one of the most highly regarded opinions ever written by an American judge, Justice Robert Jackson noted in the *Steel Seizure Case* that he was "surprised at the poverty of really useful and unambiguous authority applicable to concrete problems of executive power." The available materials, he continued, are "almost as enigmatic as the dreams Joseph was called upon to interpret for Pharaoh." In the field of presidential authority over foreign affairs, the 1793 newspaper debate between Hamilton and Madison has been the classic example of enigmatic materials, and Justice Jackson had Pacificus and Helvidius specifically in mind.[18]

In the twentieth century, everyone recognized the brilliance of Pacificus and Helvidius, but most were reluctant to assess the relative strengths of the apparently conflicting arguments. In the history of the Republic, few have equaled, and none has surpassed, Hamilton's and Madison's understanding of the Constitution. We are reluctant, therefore, to conclude that either man did not understand the Constitution's allocation of executive and legislative powers. Some dismiss the essays as turning more on partisan politics than constitutional principals. Others ignore them. Justice Jackson resolved the problem by simply noting that a "Hamilton may be matched against a Madison," and "they largely cancel each other." Today most have followed his lead. The essays usually are read as alternative, conflicting expositions of executive

---

18. *Youngstown Sheet & Tube Co. v. Sawyer,* 343 U.S. 579, 634 (1952) (Jackson, J., concurring).

power under the Constitution. Unfortunately, this common perception has obscured some of the most valuable constitutional insights ever written.[19]

The unfortunate history of Pacificus and Helvidius in the twentieth century was shaped by two highly talented and much-admired men. At the beginning of the century, Edward Corwin misread the essays and pronounced them to be a fundamental dispute over the general meaning of the executive power clause. A few decades later, Robert Jackson considered the essays, perhaps under the influence of Corwin's analysis. Jackson's views probably began to form on the eve of the nation's entry into World War II, when he was the attorney general. In any event, when he was a Supreme Court justice about a decade later, he pronounced that Hamilton and Madison "largely cancel each other." In the second half of the century, what were students of the subject to do when the most respected scholar of the presidency and a highly regarded Supreme Court justice—with special expertise on the interplay between the Constitution and foreign affairs—had so spoken?[20]

Reading the Pacificus and Helvidius essays is a rite of passage for students of foreign affairs and the Constitution. First comes Hamilton's luminous essay and then the dark pit of Helvidius. Madison had valuable learning to impart, but his essays are lengthy, meandering, disjointed, tedious, and at times hypertechnical. The work is almost impossible to organize into a cohesive system. Helvidius is truly enigmatic. This daunting problem of interpretation probably has contributed to a tendency to accept Corwin's and Jackson's pronouncements on faith.

The net result has been a scholarship at war with itself. A good example is found in Louis Henkin's enormously valuable book, *Foreign Affairs and the U.S. Constitution*. Everyone recognizes the empirical fact that in the two centuries since Pacificus and Helvidius, the president has routinely exercised a broad executive power over foreign affairs that cannot be justified by reference to the specific powers and duties listed in Article II of the

---

19. Ibid.; William Goldsmith, *The Growth of Presidential Power* (New York: Chelsea House, 1974), 1:404. For numerous additional citations, see Casto, "Pacificus and Helvidius Reconsidered," 2000–2001n3. I first presented my analysis of Pacificus and Helvidius at the annual meeting of the Society for the History of American Foreign Affairs in the summer of 2001. For an excellent and similar analysis of the "executive Power" clause published after my earlier paper but developed independently from my analysis, see Prakash and Ramsey, "Executive Power over Foreign Affairs."

20. Edward Corwin, *The President's Control of Foreign Relations* (Princeton, N.J.: Princeton University Press, 1917), chap. 1; Corwin, *President,* 16–17, 210–11; *Youngstown Sheet & Tube Co. v. Sawyer,* 634.

Constitution. Henkin believes that under Hamilton's theory, the president's accumulation of vast powers "is neither surprising nor improper (and the Constitution ceases to be as strangely inarticulate about foreign affairs as appears)." Then he immediately invokes Helvidius to establish that Hamilton's analysis has been "often challenged [and] has had a mixed reception." Henkin and others expressly rely upon Corwin and Jackson to paint a picture of two centuries of presidential conduct that perhaps is of dubious constitutional validity.[21]

Corwin, Jackson, and Henkin simply misread Helvidius. Madison and Hamilton agreed that the president possessed significant executive powers not specifically enumerated in the Constitution, and they agreed that the executive power clause is the font of the president's general authority. Justice Jackson said of the clause in the *Steel Seizure Case,* "I cannot accept the view that [it] is a grant in bulk of all conceivable executive power but regard it as an allocation to the presidential office of the generic powers thereafter stated." His bald assertion, however, must be read in the context of his opinion. Jackson was not considering whether the clause was a significant grant of power but addressing whether the clause granted the president an exclusive power "beyond the control of Congress" to seize the steel industry. Neither Madison nor Hamilton believed that the clause was a grant of exclusive power, but both agreed the clause was a significant grant of authority. Indeed, a majority of the Supreme Court in *Myers v. United States* so held. When Hamilton and Madison agree upon an analysis of constitutional power, a majority of the Supreme Court has followed that analysis, and a course of presidential conduct spanning two centuries is consistent with that analysis, we may safely limit Jackson's opinion to comparatively rare situations in which there is actually a direct conflict between Congress and the president. Jackson himself so limited his opinion. He specifically stated that "we can sustain the President [in this case] only by holding that [the president's actions are] within his domain and beyond control by Congress."[22]

Restraints upon Executive Action

Justice Jackson was concerned that the executive power clause seems to be "a grant in bulk of all conceivable executive power," that the clause had no readily discernable limits. Madison was concerned with the same problem,

---

21. Henkin, *Foreign Affairs and the Constitution,* 39–40. For the same view, see Koh, *National Security Constitution,* 79–80; Fisher, *Constitutional Conflicts,* 16–17.

22. *Youngstown Sheet & Tube Co. v. Sawyer,* 640–42; *Myers v. United States,* 272 U.S. 52 (1926). See generally Fisher, *Constitutional Conflicts,* chap. 3.

and his Helvidius essays are an extended explanation of two specific limits to the president's executive power. He stated and frequently restated that the Constitution does not give the president power to declare war and does not give the president unilateral power to make treaties. There is no conflict between Helvidius and Pacificus on these two specific issues. Hamilton clearly agreed that these specific constitutional grants of power to Congress and the Senate limit the president's power. Some have assumed that Hamilton was arguing that these specific grants were the only limits upon the president's broad and amorphous executive power, but that clearly is not the case. His position was that the Constitution itself limited executive power by vesting Congress and the Senate with an exclusive power to declare war and consent to treaties and appointments of officers. In addition, Hamilton's theory of concurrent powers, which usually is viewed as an expansion of presidential power, provides a supple and pervasive constitutional process for checking the president's expanded power.[23]

Today everyone agrees that the president and Congress exercise concurrent powers, but some ambivalence persists about the doctrine's theoretical legitimacy. Notwithstanding Hamilton's articulation of the doctrine in Pacificus, some have relied upon Helvidius for the proposition that the founders rejected the idea of concurrent powers under the Constitution. Instead of tracing the idea back to Hamilton, the modern acceptance of concurrent powers usually is based upon longstanding practice and Justice Jackson's *Steel Seizure* opinion.[24]

To the extent that the ambivalence about the theoretical underpinnings of concurrent powers is based upon Helvidius, the ambivalence is unwarranted. To be sure, Madison strenuously opposed an extreme model of concurrent powers that would have barred Congress from overriding a prior presidential decision. Neither Hamilton nor anyone else, however, has ever advocated the extreme model of concurrent powers that Madison rejected. Instead, Hamilton advocated a looser model, and Madison expressly embraced a loose model of concurrent powers that vested the president with authority to take action that inevitably would have a significant political influence upon Congress. In fact, less than a year after writing Helvidius,

23. See Casto, "Pacificus and Helvidius Reconsidered."
24. Henkin, *Foreign Affairs and the Constitution*, 86, 94–95; Glennon, *Constitutional Diplomacy*, 15–16; Koh, *National Security Constitution*, 107–10. For two otherwise excellent treatments of presidential power that ignore Hamilton's theory of concurrent power, see Powell, "Founders and the President's Authority," and Prakash and Ramsey, "Executive Power over Foreign Affairs."

Madison used the loose model to argue successfully that Congress should not override the president's decision on the sale of prizes.[25]

Although Hamilton surely agreed that Madison's loose model of influence was unobjectionable, Pacificus presents a somewhat stronger or intermediate model. According to Hamilton, the president's proclamation was more than a public expression of George Washington's private opinion. The proclamation announced the U.S. government's official position.[26] Until the president changed that position (presumably in response to changed circumstances) or the position was overridden by Congress (as by a declaration of war), the nation's official status of neutrality would continue unchanged. Perhaps Madison would have objected to this intermediate model as unconstitutional, but we will never know. He never addressed it. He confined his remarks to a strong model of concurrent powers that authorized the president to place Congress under a legal obligation to follow the president's antecedent decisions.

Hamilton presciently understood and briefly explained the practical interaction between the president's and Congress's concurrent powers. The Constitution does not obligate Congress to conform to an antecedent presidential decision. Congress "is free to perform its own duties according to its own sense of them." A presidential exercise of concurrent power, however, "may establish an antecedent state of things which ought to weigh in legislative decisions."[27]

Over the last two centuries, the ability to create "an antecedent state of things" has been one of the president's most significant foreign affairs powers. Madison's argument against the bill to ban the sale of prizes is a good example. An amusing instance of the president's ability to influence Congress through the exercise of concurrent powers occurred when Theodore Roosevelt despatched the Great White Fleet on an around-the-world cruise without sufficient funding to complete the cruise. After the fleet was well on its way, the president requested funds to bring the fleet home. The most dramatic example in recent history is President George H. W. Bush's response to Iraq's 1990 invasion of Kuwait. Within a week, he announced, "I pledge here today that the United States will do its part . . . to induce Iraq to withdraw without delay from Kuwait." To fulfill this pledge, he used his concurrent authority as commander-in-chief to dispatch a quarter of a million troops to the Persian Gulf. In theory, Congress could have called for an

---

25. See chapter 5, this volume.
26. Pacificus No. 7, *Papers of Alexander Hamilton*, 15:135.
27. Pacificus No. 1, 15:42.

ignominious return of those forces in 1991, but as a practical matter, the president's unilateral action created enormous political pressure in support of his unilateral decision. To use Hamilton's words, the president "established an antecedent state of things which ought to weigh in the legislative decisions."[28]

Today no one seriously questions the existence of concurrent powers. The more serious constitutional issue arises from the fact that when two branches of government have concurrent authority over the same subject matter, the branches inevitably come into conflict. Moreover, the potential for conflict is enhanced by the breadth of the overlap between Congress's and the president's powers. Hamilton undoubtedly understood the potential overlap to be broad. As a general proposition, he believed that the Constitution's grants of authority to the national government should be construed broadly. As Madison explained, Hamilton advanced "broad and ductile rules of construction." He believed that Congress had a broad legislative authority and that the president had a similarly broad executive authority.[29]

The existence of a broad overlap of concurrent powers necessitates a method for resolving the conflicts between the legislative and the executive. Hamilton understood this problem and decided that Congress's exclusive power to declare war includes a power to override the president's concurrent power to declare neutrality. Because Hamilton's purpose in writing as Pacificus was specifically to defend the Proclamation of Neutrality, he did not elaborate upon conflicts between Congress and the president over matters other than the proclamation.

Although Hamilton did not offer a general framework for resolving foreign affairs conflicts between Congress and the president, a century and a half later, Justice Jackson filled the analytical void. The three-part model he outlined in the *Steel Seizure Case* orients all contemporary analyses of these conflicts. He proposed that presidential actions could be organized into three categories. The first involved presidential action taken "pursuant to an express or implied authorization of Congress." In such a case, lawful executive power

---

28. See Henkin, *Foreign Affairs and the Constitution,* 390n67 (Great White Fleet). For the Persian Gulf War, see Dycus et al., *National Security Law,* 322–28; *Public Papers of the Presidents of the United States: George Bush* (Washington, D.C.: GPO, 1991), 1990:1108 (President Bush's pledge).

29. See James Madison to W. C. Rives, Jan. 10, 1829, *Letters and Other Writings of James Madison* (Philadelphia: Lippincott, 1867), 4:3–5; Clinton Rossiter, *Alexander Hamilton and the Constitution* (New York: Harcourt, Brace, 1964), chap. 6; Pacificus No. 1; Alexander Hamilton, Opinion on the Constitutionality of an Act to Establish a Bank (1791), *Papers of Alexander Hamilton,* 8:97.

"is at its maximum, for it includes all that he possesses in his own right plus all that Congress can delegate." When the president acts pursuant to congressional authority, "the strongest of presumptions and the widest latitude of judicial interpretation would be used to support the lawfulness of the President's actions."[30]

Jackson's second category recognizes the concept of concurrent presidential and congressional authority. If Congress has neither delegated nor denied authority to the president, "he can only rely upon his own independent powers, and there is a zone of twilight in which he and Congress may have concurrent authority, or in which its distribution is uncertain." Jackson confined his discussion of the second category to a single brief paragraph because he believed that the president's action in the *Steel Seizure Case* was contrary to the will of Congress.[31]

The third category involves presidential "measures incompatible with the express or implied will of Congress." In this situation, the president's "power is at its lowest ebb, for then he can rely only upon his own constitutional powers minus any constitutional powers of Congress over the matter." In other words, courts "can sustain exclusive presidential control in such a case only by disabling Congress from acting upon the subject." Jackson devoted most of his opinion to analyzing whether the Constitution vests the president with exclusive power beyond the control of Congress to seize the nation's steel industry. It was in this narrowly focused context of exclusive presidential power that he rejected a broad reading of the executive power clause.[32]

If Jackson's and Hamilton's essays on presidential power are combined, a workable framework of constitutional governance of foreign affairs emerges. Hamilton's understanding that the executive power clause is a general grant of authority, including authority concurrent with Article I's grants to Congress, works a significant expansion of presidential power. The immediate constitutional problem is to determine how that power is to be checked and presidential mistakes are to be corrected. Undoubtedly, the most powerful counterbalance to unwise executive action is the president's practical need to have political support from the nation at large and from important special interest groups. These influences operate generally upon the government and may even induce a presidential self-correction. In addition, the Constitution

---

30. *Youngstown Sheet & Tube Co. v. Sawyer*, 635–37. The model is ably discussed in Henkin, *Foreign Affairs and the Constitution*, 94–96; Koh, *National Security Constitution*, 107–13; and Glennon, *Constitutional Diplomacy*, 8–16.

31. *Youngstown Sheet & Tube Co. v. Sawyer*, 637, 640.

32. Ibid., 640–55.

establishes "auxiliary precautions" against mistakes and abuse. Within the federal government, the judiciary and Congress are expected to act as restraints upon unwise presidential action.

We are accustomed to viewing the courts as a bulwark against undesirable presidential action, but for a long time the federal courts, including the Supreme Court, have notoriously avoided reviewing and overturning presidential actions in the arena of foreign affairs. This practice is an empirical fact and is due in large measure to the lack of judicially manageable standards for judging the lawfulness of presidential actions. In many areas of constitutional law, the courts are willing to flesh out vague standards such as due process or equal protection, but foreign affairs decisions are different. Judges believe that foreign affairs issues should be decided by the [more] political branches of government. The desirability of the judges' deference is debatable, but the fact that they routinely defer is not.[33]

As a practical matter, the courts' reluctance to second guess the president coupled with the firm tradition against advisory opinions has resulted in a significant expansion of presidential power under the Constitution. Although there are good reasons supporting the rule against advisory opinions, the rule has facilitated a significant aggrandizement of executive power over foreign relations. The rule does not diminish the president's need for legal advice. Rather, it excludes the judiciary from the advisory process and effectively places the process entirely within the executive branch. After the justices refused their advice in 1793, the cabinet itself worked out the applicable legal rules. Over the next two hundred years, the attorney general became the president's chief legal adviser, and in the last few years, the advisory function has shifted to the Office of Legal Counsel. As a result, the president does not receive independent legal advice. His legal advisers are literally employees reporting to their boss.[34]

Anyone who has ever advised a client in or out of government knows that advice is always given with an eye toward the client's overall policy or business objectives and that the advice is tailored to facilitate the achievement of the clients' objectives. Respected commentators have noted that "the flavor of politics hangs about the opinions of the Attorney General."[35] To be sure,

33. See Glennon, *Constitutional Diplomacy,* 313–25; Koh, *National Security Constitution,* chap. 6.

34. See Paul Bator et al., *Hart and Wechsler's The Federal Courts and the Federal System,* 3rd ed. (Westbury, N.Y.: Foundation Press, 1988), 71–72.

35. Ibid., 71. *Accord,* Nancy Baker, *Conflicting Loyalties: Law and Politics in the Attorney General's Office, 1789–1990* (Lawrence: University Press of Kansas, 1992).

legal advice must rest upon plausible and reasonable legal analysis, but there usually is room for judgment. A good attorney or adviser always exercises professional judgment—with appropriate provisos and disclaimers—in favor of the client. A legal adviser who does not consistently exercise his or her judgment to facilitate the client's objectives will find his or her position as an adviser in jeopardy. In any event, a good adviser wants to facilitate the client's projects and finds great pleasure in crafting legal analyses that will enable the accomplishment of the client's goals. In practice, this sometimes results in a subtle shift from advising the client as to what is legal to advising the client as to what is arguably legal.[36]

An independent judge providing an advisory opinion is not necessarily committed to tailoring legal advice to further extralegal policy objectives. Alexander Hamilton undoubtedly understood this pragmatic fact of life in 1793, and in the last two hundred years, other examples come to mind. Before the United States entered World War II, for example, President Roosevelt wished to provide fifty obsolete destroyers to the British, and Attorney General Jackson wrote a legal opinion in support of the president's objective. It is inconceivable that President Roosevelt would have preferred an opinion from the independent judiciary to that of his attorney general.[37]

In many situations a legal adviser in the private practice of law is reluctant to adopt extreme or highly questionable legal positions because the advice is subject to independent review by government regulatory agencies or by courts at the behest of private individuals. These practical constraints, however, are seriously attenuated in respect of matters related to foreign affairs. There is no independent regulatory agency, and in practice the courts tend to defer to the executive in matters of foreign policy. The normative desirability of judicial deference is debatable, but the empirical reality of frequent deference is not. In the foreign policy arena, judicial deference to the president is commonplace. This absence of effective judicial review offers further encouragement to advisers who seek to push the legal restrictions on presidential power from what is legal to what is arguably legal.[38]

---

36. This analysis of the shift from legal advice to arguably legal advice is elaborated with examples in Casto, "Executive Advisory Opinions."

37. See Baker, *Conflicting Loyalties,* 78–82; Thomas Franck and Michael Glennon, *Foreign Relations and National Security Law,* 2nd ed. (St. Paul, Minn.: West Publishing, 1993), 449–57.

38. See Casto, "Executive Advisory Opinions." See also Koh, *National Security Constitution,* 117–18.

Hamilton's theory of concurrent constitutional authority implicitly vests Congress with significant power to correct presidential errors. Hamilton undoubtedly intended that the executive power clause be construed broadly, but his theory of concurrent constitutional authority provides a supple and pervasive constitutional process for checking the president's expanded power. Judicial review of presidential action must be made by reference to general rules, but congressional review of the same action can be based upon general and ad hoc political considerations. Moreover, while courts would be loathe to judge the substantive merits or wisdom of a president's foreign policy decision, Congress is elected to make precisely these kinds of judgments.

If Congress enacts a statute outlawing particular presidential action, the problem of judicially manageable standards can be eliminated. For example the federal courts notoriously avoided ruling upon the legality of the Vietnam War until Congress enacted legislation ending American involvement on August 15, 1973. Once the courts had this clear rule for guidance, they had no problem enforcing the statute.[39]

When Congress enacts legislation forbidding a particular course of presidential action, Jackson's third category becomes applicable. A court will enforce the legislation unless the subject matter is committed to the president's exclusive control and is therefore beyond the power of Congress to regulate. As a matter of theory, very few presidential actions are beyond Congress's reach. In any event, as a practical matter, the question of exclusive presidential power will almost never arise because the pertinent legislation inevitably would be based upon negotiations between the president and Congress. Therefore, a presidential challenge to the negotiated legislation would be highly unlikely. An example is the 1983 dispute between the president and Congress regarding the deployment of marines to Lebanon. During negotiations with Congress, the executive branch rejected a twelve-month time limit to the operation because it might unduly impact the 1984 elections, but they accepted an eighteen-month limit. The president claimed that the resulting legislation improperly impinged upon his constitutional authority but nevertheless signed the act and subsequently complied with it.[40]

---

39. Joint Resolution Continuing Appropriations for Fiscal 1974, sec. 108, Pub. L. 93–52, 87 Stat. 130, 134 (1973). See generally Dycus et al., *National Security Law*, 238–89.

40. Multiforce in Lebanon Joint Resolution, Pub. L. No. 98–119, 97 Stat. 805 (1983), discussed in Dycus et al., *National Security Law*, 319–21.

If Congress does not enact corrective legislation, a president's action falls into Jackson's second category, in which there is congressional silence. In the *Steel Seizure Case,* Justice Jackson brushed over this category because he believed that the president had acted contrary to the will of Congress. To Jackson, the second category was "a zone of twilight." He believed that "in this area, any actual test of power is likely to depend on the imperatives of events and contemporary imponderables rather than on abstract theories of law."[41]

In practice, the second category is more significant than Jackson suggested because corrective legislation may be difficult to pass. As the saying goes, "'Tis many a slip twixt the cup and the lip." The 1794 passage of the Neutrality Act demonstrates some of the difficulties when there is significant opposition in either chamber of Congress. In addition, legislation to curb presidential action is likely to be opposed by the president's partisan supporters in Congress. Although organized political parties with party discipline did not exist in 1793, they pervade modern political life. Jackson thoroughly understood the nature of political parties and noted that the president heads his or her political party: "Party loyalties and interests, sometimes more binding than law, extend [the president's] control into [Congress]."[42] These loyalties and interests create a standing corps of presidential supporters in Congress that can be counted on to oppose efforts to curb presidential actions. This enormous political friction is multiplied by Congress's bicameral organization and the Senate's extraconstitutional tradition of filibuster.

Members of the president's party who oppose legislative efforts to overturn presidential decisions will have a wealth of weapons available to them. In 1794, James Madison bitterly complained, "The influence of the Ex. on events, the use made of them, and the public confidence in the P. are an overmatch for all the efforts Republicanism can make." Although no other president in history has come close to equaling George Washington's political stature, modern presidents possess enormous influence. Again Jackson noted, "By his prestige as head of state and his influence upon public opinion [the president] exerts a leverage upon those who are supposed to check and balance his power which often cancels their effectiveness." Finally, the president possesses a constitutional weapon of last resort. He may veto legislation intended to overturn his decisions. Indeed, even a threatened veto may preempt congressional efforts.[43]

41. *Steel Seizure Case,* 637.
42. Ibid., 654.
43. See chapter 9, this volume; *Steel Seizure Case,* 653–54.

In theory, even if Congress is unwilling to overturn a presidential decision, the courts might declare the president's actions unlawful, but the problem of judicial deference to the president persists. Yet judicial deference is not the same thing as judicial abdication. Although the Constitution gives scant guidance regarding the extent of the president's foreign affairs powers, the mantle of foreign affairs cannot cloak all presidential actions. Certainly Alexander Hamilton stated and restated during the Neutrality Crisis that only Congress is constitutionally empowered to "transfer the nation from a state of Peace to a state of War." He reiterated this firm position a few years later on at least two occasions. During the Neutrality Crisis, John Jay, James Wilson, Thomas Jefferson, James Madison, and many other founders affirmatively took this same position. In fact, there is no record of any member of the founding generation even stating that the president may lawfully start a war.[44]

Although the Constitution clearly vests Congress with the exclusive power to transfer the nation from a state of peace to a state of war, that small word, "war," does not provide the courts with very much guidance. Are petty presidential adventures in banana republics such as Grenada, Panama, and Haiti "wars" forbidden by the Constitution or merely dramatic and bloody shows of force within the president's authority?[45] Courts have been reluctant to answer these questions in the absence of supplemental guidance from Congress, and perhaps they are right. If Congress lacks the will to protect its own exclusive power in a close case, why should the courts intervene? On the other hand, military action can be so clearly war making that the theoretically troubling vagueness of the constitutional standard becomes irrelevant. In the Persian Gulf War, a federal district judge signaled to the president that moving a quarter of a million troops to the Middle East as part of a combined allied force of over a half million troops and launching an all-out military attack on one of the region's strongest military powers would infringe upon Congress's exclusive war power. The president took the hint and sought congressional approval.[46]

Except for extreme cases like the Persian Gulf War, the courts may be right to stay clear of disputes regarding unilateral presidential authority

44. See chapter 5, this volume. For an exhaustive elaboration, see Michael Ramsey and John Yoo, "Exchange: War Powers," *University of Chicago Law Review* 69 (2002): 1543–1720.

45. Compare chapter 9, this volume (Creek Indians).

46. *Dellums v. Bush,* 752 F. Supp. 1141 (D.D.C. 1990); Authorization for Use of Military Force against Iraq, Pub. L. No. 102–1, 105 Stat. 3 (1991). But see *Ange v. Bush,* 752 F. Supp. 509 (D.D.C. 1990).

over foreign affairs. In the rough-and-tumble realm of politics, a congressional reluctance to constrain the president may properly be viewed as acquiescence. The case for judicial deference is not as compelling, however, when the constitutional issue shifts from the president's extensive but vague foreign affairs powers to positive constitutional prohibitions designed to protect individuals. Certainly most of the tactics of deference do not work in situations in which these rights come into play. A criminal defendant's defense during the course of a criminal prosecution can not be dismissed as moot, not ripe, not supported by standing, a political question, or involving remedial discretion. Nor are these avoidance devices appropriate in the context of a petition for habeas corpus. In these situations, the courts must enforce the Constitution's guarantees of individual rights.

Of course, the courts' inclination to defer to the president may reappear as a significant consideration in shaping the actual substantive scope of the individual protections under the Constitution. In deciding whether to defer to a prior presidential decision in shaping the scope of constitutional protections, courts should consider the fact that possibly unconstitutional governmental action is almost never directed at members of society who, because of their majority or socioeconomic status, have a significant influence on government. Neither Congress nor the president, therefore, is likely to champion their targets' legitimate interests. Deference to the president in this context entrusts the scope of constitutional rights to attorney / advisers of the president who probably craft their opinions with an eye to what they believe is arguably constitutional rather than what they believe is actually constitutional. Justice Jackson fully understood the difference between a judge and an attorney/adviser. In the *Steel Seizure Case*, attorneys for the president used a formal opinion written by Jackson when he was attorney general to support President Truman's later seizure of the steel industry. Jackson firmly rejected his opinion written a decade earlier: "I do not regard it as a precedent for this, but even if I did, I should not bind present judicial judgment by earlier partisan advocacy."[47]

The grand constitutional lesson of the Neutrality Crisis of 1793 is that in theory, Congress and the president make foreign policy jointly, but in practice, foreign policy is made primarily by the president. As a practical matter, the president possesses important structural advantages over Congress. The president can almost always act first and thereby define the terms of the debate and "establish an antecedent state of things which ought to weigh in the legislative decisions." But to say that the president possesses important

---

47. *Steel Seizure Case*, 647. See Baker, *Conflicting Loyalties*, 31–32.

structural advantages over Congress is not to say that the president's decisions are best for the country.

There must be a constitutional check to presidential mistakes, and Hamilton's theory of concurrent powers provides a constitutional process for rectifying persistent presidential error. Congress has the power if it will exercise it. Justice Jackson understood this difficult political fact, and at the end of his *Steel Seizure* opinion he warned:

> But I have no illusion that any decision by this Court can keep power in the hands of Congress if it is not wise and timely in meeting its problems. A crisis that challenges the president equally, or perhaps primarily, challenges Congress. If not good law, there was worldly wisdom in the maxim attributed to Napoleon that "the tools belong to the man who can use them." We may say that power to legislate for emergencies belongs in the hands of Congress, but only Congress itself can prevent power from slipping through its fingers.[48]

48. *Steel Seizure Case,* 654.

Table of Cases

Ange v. Bush, 752 F. Supp. 509 (D.D.C. 1990), 189
Baker v. Carr, 369 U.S. 186 (1962), 166
Bas v. Tingy, 4 U.S. (4 Dall.) 37 (1800), 72
Castello v. Boutelle, 5 F.Cas. 278 (D.S.C. 1794) (No. 2504), 90, 102
The Catherine, DECREE ON THE ADMIRALTY SIDE OF THE DISTRICT COURT OF NEW YORK (Evans no. 26, 915; 1794) (D.N.Y. Jan. 28, 1794), 90
Del Gol v. Arnold, 3 U.S. (3 Dall.) 333 (1796), 45
Dellums v. Bush, 752 F. Supp. 1141 (D.D.C. 1990), 189
Findlay v. The William, 9 F. Cas. 57 (D. Pa. 1793) (No. 4790), 45, 48, 49, 86–90, 94, 157, 159, 166, 167, 168, 169, 171, 173
The Flad Oyen, 165 Eng. Rep. 124 (Adm. 1799), 40
Folger v. Lecuyer, Boston Centinel, Jan. 4, 1794 (D. Mass. Dec. 6, 1793), 90
Georgia v. Brailsford, 2 U.S. (2 Dall.) 417 (1793), 95
Glass v. The Sloop Betsy, 3 U.S. (3 Dall.) 6 (1794), 90
Goldwater v. Carter, 444 U.S. 996 (1979), 172–73
Henfield's Case, 11 F. Cas. 1099 (C.C.D. Pa. 1793) (No. 6360), 91–97, 99, 160, 166, 167, 169, 170, 171, 172
The Henrick and Maria, 165 Eng. Rep. 529 (Adm. 1799), 38
Little v. Barreme, 6 U.S. (2 Cranch.) 169 (1804), 76, 77
Moxon v. The Fanny, 17 F. Cas. 942 (D. Pa. 1793) (No. 9895), 90
Myers v. United States, 272 U.S. 52 (1926), 180
The Perseverence, 165 Eng. Rep. 302 (Adm. 1799), 40
Soult v. Africaine, 22 F. Cas. 805 (D.S.C. 1804) (No. 13, 179), 35, 36
The Steel Seizure Case, 343 U.S. 579 (1952), 63, 173, 178, 179, 180, 181, 183–84, 188, 190, 191
United States v. Greenleaf, unreported (C.C.D. N.Y. 1797), 149
United States v. Henfield, see Henfield's Case
United States v. Olmstead, unreported (C.C.D. N.C. 1793), 101–02
United States v. Rivers, unreported (C.C.D. Ga. 1793), 100
United States v. Smith, 27 F. Cas. 1192 (C.C. N.Y. 1806) (No. 16, 342), 76
Youngstown Sheet & Tube Co. v. Sawyer. See *The Steel Seizure Case*

Bibliography

American State Papers: Documents, Legislative and Executive of the Congress of the United States. Vol. 1, *Foreign Relations.* Washington, D.C.: Gales and Seaton, 1832.

Ammon, Harry. *The Genet Mission.* New York: Norton, 1973.

———. "The Genet Mission and the Development of American Political Parties." *Journal of American History* 52 (Mar. 1966): 725–41.

Annals of the Congress of the United States. 42 vols. Washington, D.C.: Gales and Seaton, 1834–56.

Blanning, T. C. W. *The Origins of the French Revolutionary Wars.* New York: Longman, 1986.

Bowman, Albert. *The Struggle for Neutrality.* Knoxville: University of Tennessee Press, 1974.

Carroll, John, and Mary Ashworth. *George Washington: First in Peace.* New York: Scribner's, 1957.

Casto, William R. "The Early Supreme Court Justices' Most Significant Opinion." *Ohio Northern University Law Review* 29 (2002): 173–207.

———. "Foreign Affairs Crises and the Constitution's Case or Controversy Limitation: Notes from the Founders." *American Journal of Legal History* 46 (2004): 237–70.

———. "The Origins of Federal Admiralty Jurisdiction in an Age of Privateers, Smugglers, and Pirates." *American Journal of Legal History* 37 (1993): 117–57.

———. "Pacificus and Helvidius Reconsidered." *Northern Kentucky Law Review* 28 (2001): 612–39.

———. *The Supreme Court in the Early Republic.* Columbia: University of South Carolina Press, 1995.

———. "'We Are Armed for the Defense of the Rights of Man': The French Revolution Comes to America." *American Neptune* 61 (2001): 263–80.

Cormack, William S. *Revolution and Political Conflict in the French Navy, 1789–1794.* New York: Cambridge University Press, 1995.

Corwin, Edward. *The President: Office and Powers, 1787–1984.* 5th rev ed. Edited by Randall Bland, Theodore T. Hindson, and Jack W. Peltason. New York: New York University Press, 1984.

The Counter Case of Great Britain as Laid before the Tribunal of Arbitration, Convened at Geneva. Washington, D.C.: GPO, 1872.

DeConde, Alexander. *Entangling Alliance: Politics and Diplomacy under George Washington.* Durham, N.C.: Duke University Press, 1958.

Documentary History of the Supreme Court of the United States, 1789–1800. 4 vols. to date. Vol. 1, edited by Maeva Marcus and James R. Perry; vols. 2–4, edited by Maeva Marcus. New York: Columbia University Press, 1985–92.

Doyle, William. *The Oxford History of the French Revolution.* Oxford: Oxford University Press, 1989.

Dycus, Stephen, Arthur L. Berney, William C. Banks, and Peter Raven-Hansen. *National Security Law.* 2nd ed. Boston: Little, Brown, 1997.

Elkins, Stanley, and Eric McKitrick. *The Age of Federalism.* New York: Oxford University Press, 1993.

Fisher, Louis. *Constitutional Conflicts between Congress and the President.* 4th ed. Lawrence: University Press of Kansas, 1997.

Fitzpatrick, John C., ed. *The Writings of George Washington.* 39 vols. Washington, D.C.: GPO, 1931–44.

Glennon, Michael. *Constitutional Diplomacy.* Princeton, N.J.: Princeton University Press, 1990.

Grenville, William Wyndham. *The Manuscripts of J. B. Fortesque, Esq., Preserved at Dropmore.* London: Her Majesty's Stationary Office, 1927.

Hauterive, Alexander Maurice. "Journal." New-York Historical Society.

Henkin, Louis. *Foreign Affairs and the Constitution.* 2nd ed. Oxford: Oxford University Press, 1996.

Hyneman, Charles S. *The First American Neutrality.* Urbana: University of Illinois, 1934.

Jackson, Melvin. *Privateers in Charleston, 1793–1796.* Washington, D.C.: GPO, 1969.

Jay, Stewart. *Most Humble Servants: The Advisory Role of Early Judges.* New Haven, Conn.: Yale University Press, 1997.

Jenkins, Ernest H. *A History of the French Navy.* London: Macdonald & Jane's, 1973.

King, Charles R., ed. *The Life and Correspondence of Rufus King.* 6 vols. New York: G. P. Putnam's Sons, 1894–1900.

Koh, Harold Hong Ju. *The National Security Constitution: Sharing Power after the Iran-Contra Affair.* New Haven, Conn.: Yale University Press, 1990.

Miller, Hunter, ed. *Treaties and Other International Acts of the United States of America.* 8 vols. Washington, D.C.: GPO, 1931–48.

Minnigerode, Meade. *Jefferson, Friend of France, 1793: The Career of Edmond Charles Genet, Minister Plenipotentiary from the French Republic to the United States, as Revealed by his Private Papers, 1763–1834.* New York: G. P. Putnam's Sons, 1928.

The Papers of James Madison. 17 vols. to date. Vols. 1–7, edited by William T. Hutchinson and William M. E. Rachal; vol. 8, edited by Robert A. Rutland and William M. E. Rachal; and vols. 9–10, edited by Robert A. Rutland. Chicago: University of Chicago Press, 1962–77. Vols. 11–13, edited by Robert A. Rutland and Charles F. Hobson; vol. 14, edited by Robert A. Rutland and Thomas A. Mason; vol. 15, edited by Thomas A. Mason, Robert A. Rutland, and Jeanne K. Sisson; vol. 16, edited by J. C. A. Stagg, Thomas A. Mason, and Jeanne K. Sisson; and vol. 17, edited by David B. Mattern, Jeanne K. Cross, Susan H. Perdue, and John C. Stagg. Charlottesville: University Press of Virginia, 1977–91.

The Papers of John Marshall. 6 vols. to date. Vol. 1, edited by Herbert A. Johnson; vol. 2, edited by Charles T. Cullen and Herbert A. Johnson; vol. 3, edited by William C. Stinchcombe and Charles T. Cullen; vol. 4, edited by Charles T. Cullen;

vol. 5–6, edited by Charles F. Hobson. Chapel Hill: University of North Carolina Press, 1974–90.

The Papers of Thomas Jefferson. 28 vols. to date. Vols. 1–20, edited by Julian P. Boyd; vols. 21–23, edited by Charles T. Cullen; vols. 24–25, edited by John Catanzariti. Princeton, N.J.: Princeton University Press, 1950–92.

Powell, H. Jefferson. "The Founders and the President's Authority over Foreign Affairs." *William and Mary Law Review* 40 (1999): 1471–1537.

Prakash, Saikrishna, and Michael Ramsey. "The Executive Power over Foreign Affairs." *Yale Law Journal* 111 (2001): 231–356.

Sheridan, Eugene. "The Recall of Edmond Charles Genet: A Study in Transatlantic Politics and Diplomacy." *Diplomatic History* 18 (1994): 463–88.

Syrett, Harold C., ed. *The Papers of Alexander Hamilton.* 27 vols. New York: Columbia University Press, 1961–87.

Thomas, Charles Marion. *American Neutrality in 1793: A Study in Cabinet Government.* 1931. Reprint, New York: AMS Press, 1967.

Turner, Frederick Jackson. "Correspondence of the French Ministers to the United States, 1791–1797." Vol. 2, *Annual Report of the American Historical Association, 1903.* Washington, D.C.: GPO, 1903.

Wheeler, Russell. "Extrajudicial Activities of United States Supreme Court Justices: The Constitutional Period, 1790–1809." Ph.D. diss., University of Chicago, 1970.

Index

Adams, John, 61, 76, 159, 175
admiralty jurisdiction. *See* U.S. courts
Aimée Marguerit (corsair). *See L'Aimée Marguerite*
ambassador, distinguished from minister, 3
Ambuscade (frigate). *See L'Embuscade*
Ames, Fisher, 160–61
anonymous essays: An American, 60; Americanus, 94; Anonymous Note (Randolph), 99; Archy Simple, 99, 171; A Citizen, 143; A Democrat, 60; The Examination (Hamilton), 69–70; Federalist No. 51 (Madison), 74; Federalist No. 75 (Hamilton), 71–72, 74; A Freeman, 60; A Friend of Peace, 60, 61, 66; Helvidius (Madison), 67–74, 164, 178, 179, 181–82; Junius, 140; An Old Soldier, 59; Pacificus (Hamilton), 60–66, 75–80, 154, 164, 178, 179, 181–82, 183; A Republican, 74; To the President of the United States, 60; Uniform Federalist, 143; Verior Hac Veritate, 60; Veritas, 59–60, 79; When Foreign Nations Engage in War (Randolph), 67
Anti-George (corsair), 46, 100

Baker, Hilary, 91, 95
Barbary pirates, 157–58
Beckwith, George, 23
Belle (prize), 101
Bompard, Jean-Baptiste François: career before and after 1793, 11–13, 146; duel with *Boston,* 122–38, 139; mutiny, 144–46; prizes, 18, 36–38, 39, 40–41, 103
Boston (frigate), duel with *L'Embuscade,* 122–38
Bradford, William, Jr., 109–10
Brissot de Warville, Jacques Pierre, 7, 8, 15
Burr, Aaron, 140
Bush, George H. W., 182
Butler, Pierce, 137, 138

Canada, 15, 18, 144. *See also* Halifax
Carmichael, William, 20
Castries, Marshall de, 12

Catherine (prize), 90, 146
Catherine II, opinion of Genet, 6, 7
Charleston, S.C., 35–40, 45–48, 135
Citoyen Genet (corsair), 46–49, 50–51, 86, 87, 91, 96
Clark, George Rogers, 160
common law crimes. *See* U.S. courts
Concorde (frigate), 43, 122, 126, 130
consular courts: legality of, 40, 51–52; operation of, 39–40, 49
Cornelia (corsair), 150. *See also Petite Démocrate*
corsair (French for privateer). *See* privateers
Corwin, Edward, 179, 180
Courtenay, George William Augustus, 123–37
Cushing, William, 110, 116, 118

Dallas, Alexander, 104, 105, 147
Davie, William, 102
Deblois, Lewis, 95
Dennis, Patrick, 127–28
Duane, James, 116
Dumouriez, Charles-François, 7, 8
Duponceau, Peter Stephen, 88, 94, 149–50

Edwards, John, 131, 132, 134
Ellsworth, Oliver, 175; advisory opinions of, 115–16; quoted, 15, 158
Eurydice (frigate), 124

Fair Margaret (corsair). *See L'Aimée Marguerite*
Fauchet, Jean, 150
Florida, 15, 18, 144, 160
Four Brothers (prize), 18, 37–39
Four Sisters (prize; also called *Four Brothers*), 37
France, money owed to by U.S., 15–16, 24, 54–55. *See also* Genet, Edmond Charles
French navy, 10, 12–13, 16; squadron from Cap Français, 130, 135, 136, 143–46. *See also* Bompard, Jean-Baptiste François, *L'Embuscade*

Genet, Edme Jacques (Genet's father), 5
Genet, Edmond Charles: appeal to the people, 56–58, 107, 141–43, 146–50; appointment, 9; early life and career, 5–9; initial reception in U.S., 53–54; instructions, 14–17; opinions of, 6, 8; relations with executive branch, 55; relations with Gov. Moultrie, 35; subsequent career, 150; voyage to America, 9–11, 17–18
Gillon, Alexander, 35
Goethe, at Valmy, 7
Grange (prize), 40–41, 50, 55, 86, 146, 157
Great Britain, and 1794 crisis, 157–58. See also Hammond, George
Grenada, 189
Grenville, Lord, 19

Haiti, 189. *See also* Santo Domingo
Halifax, Canada, 125–26
Hamilton, Alexander: attitudes toward France and Britain, 22–23, 24–25; criticized in press, 32–33, 59–60; French treaties, 26–28, 32–33; Henfield's Case, 91, 94, 95, 99; influence on Washington, 163–64; *Pacificus*, 60–66, 75–80, 154; relations with British diplomats, 23; Revolutionary War, 16, 29
Hammond, George: describes American policy, 19–24, 107; protests French actions, 49–51; relationship with Hamilton, 21, 23
Hauterive, Alexander Maurice (French consul in New York), 13, 45, 128, 142–43, 145
Hayes, John, 127, 129, 131
Hector (ship; renamed *Vainquer de Bastille,* then renamed *Port-de-Paix*), 101. See also *Vainquer de Bastille; Port-de-Paix*
Henfield, Gideon, 47–48, 55, 85–86, 146; prosecution against, 91–97, 152, 160, 165, 169–72; Revolutionary War experience, 100; subsequent experience, 100
Henkin, Louis, 166, 179, 180
Hutchinson, Edward, 40

Indian nations, 9, 22, 151–53, 157
Ingersol, Jared, 89, 94

international law: distinguished from law of nations, 3–4; French treaties not binding, 61; revocation and suspension of treaties, 32–33, 66, 154–56; U.S. territorial waters, 50. *See also* U.S. Congress
Invalid Pensioners Act, 116
Iraq, 182–83
Iredell, James, 94, 110, 113, 114, 117

Jackson, Robert H., 178, 180–81, 183–84, 186–88, 190–91
Jay, John, 176; attacks Genet in press, 140–43, 146–150; consults with executive branch, 28, 31, 83–84, 115, 117, 163–64, 165; grand jury charges, 84–85, 112
Jay Treaty, 156, 158, 176
Jefferson, Thomas: attitude toward France and Britain, 22, 24, 25; disdain for Knox, 32; dislike of Hamilton, 32, 33; Henfield's Case, 86, 91–92, 99–100; influence on Washington, 163–64; relations with Genet, 58, 105, 139, 147; U.S. Constitution, 29, 69
Jemappes, battle of, 8, 15
Jessop, Mr., 129
Johannene, Peter, 47
jury. *See* U.S. courts

Keppel, August, 124
Kerr, Alexander Robert, 131–32
King, Rufus, 140–43, 146–50, 158, 175
Knox, Henry, 30, 31, 33, 42, 98, 105, 118, 136–37, 163, 164
Kuwait, 182

L'Aimée Marguerite (corsair), 102
law of nations. *See* international law
Lebanon, 187
Lebrun, Pierre Helene Marie, 8
L'Embuscade (frigate): duel with Boston, 122–38, 143; morale of crew, 9–10, 37, 144, 145–46; prizes, 18, 36–38, 39, 40–41, 43, 103; reception in Charleston, 35; reception in Philadelphia, 41–43; reception in New York, 135; size and armament, 13; voyage to America, 9–11, 35
Lewis, William, 89, 95
Lincoln, Abraham, 73

Lindh, John Walker, 171
Little Democrat (corsair). See *Petite Democrat*
Little Sarah (prize; renamed *Petite Democrat*), 41, 103–7, 163
Livingston, Brockholst, 150
Livingston, Edward, 49, 136
Louis XVI, 9, 56, 106
Louisiana, 15, 18, 144, 160
Lowell, John, 90

Madison, James: correspondence with Jefferson, 29, 33, 51, 59, 64, 67–68, 105, 114, 139, 141, 147; Helvidius essays, 67–79; influence on Washington, 164; opinion of Hamilton, 33, 79–80, 183
Mangourit, Michel, 35
Marshall, John, 62–63, 76, 98
Mifflin, Thomas, 42, 103–4
minister, distinguished from ambassador, 3
Miquelon, 144–45
Monroe, James, 22, 141
Morgan, John, 95
Morning Star (prize), 36–37, 39, 80
Moultrie, William, 35, 46, 142
Mud Island, 105
Murray, William Vans, 61

natural law, 95–96
Nelson, Horatio, 124
Neutrality Act. *See* U.S. Congress
Neutrality Proclamation, 25–34, 55, 60–61, 153–56
New York, N.Y., 122–23, 127–30, 135
Nootka Sound Crisis, 115

Olmstead, Gideon, charges against, 100–102

Panama, 189
Patterson, William, 45, 76
Pellew, Edward, 124
Pendleton, Nathaniel, 100
Persian Gulf War, 189
Peters, Richard, 45, 168; prize cases, 86–90
Petite Democrate (corsair, renamed *Cornelia*), 103–7, 108, 163. See also *Little Sarah*; *Little Democrat;* and *Cornelia*

Port-de-Paix (corsair), 102
Portugal, 157–58
privateers: distrust of, 45; fitting out and operating, 37, 43–44, 46, 103–4; importance of, 18, 43–44; legality of, 46, 52, 55–58
prizes of war, 18; prize courts, 37–39, 44–45, 49; rules regulating, 37; sale of prize ships, 37, 39–40, 80–82, 125, 161–62; sale of prize cargo, 39, 80–81, 161–62
Proclamation of Neutrality. *See* Neutrality Proclamation
Providence (prize; renamed *L'Aimée Marguerite*), 101–2. See also *L'Aimée Marguerite*

Randolph, Edmund, 147–49, 163; anonymous essays, 67, 99; cabinet votes, 32, 118–19, drafts neutrality bill, 158–59, 175; Henfield's case, 91–92, 95; Neutrality Proclamation, 28–29
Rawle, William, 88, 92, 94, 95
Republican (corsair), 46, 127
Rivers, Joseph, prosecution against, 100, 165
Roosevelt, Franklin D., 73, 186
Roosevelt, Theodore, 182

Saint Pierre, 144–45
Sally (prize; also called *Four Brothers*), 37
Sans Culottes (corsair), 46
Santo Domingo, 144
Scott, Sir William (Lord Stowell), 38
Sergeant, Jonathan Dickson, 88
Short, William, 20
Simmons, Jonas, 95
Singleterry, John, 47–48, 86, 94
Sitgreaves, John, 113
Smith, William Loughton, 81
St. Clair, Arthur, 9
Stowell, Lord. *See* Scott, Sir William
Strong, Caleb, 158, 175
Success (prize), 37, 146

Temple, Sir John, 127
Treaty of Alliance (with France), 14; Article 11 of, 17, 20–21, 26, 29, 61, 153–54
Treaty of Amity and Commerce (with France), 14; Article 17 of, 17, 21, 81;

Treaty of Amity and Commerce (*continued*)
    Article 18 of, 17; Article 22 of, 17, 22, 52, 57, 120, 153, 159, 161
Truman, Harry S., 173, 190

United States: assistance received from France, 15–16; money owed to France, 15–16, 24; pro-British attitudes, 22–24 ; pro-French attitudes, 20, 21–22
United States Army, weakness of, 9, 22
United States Navy, non-existant, 9
U.S. Congress: early session considered, 34, 150–52; exclusive war power, 29, 69–74, 77–80, 180, 189–90; Neutrality Act, 80–82, 157, 158–62, 175–76, 188; power to review presidential action, 75, 77, 153–54, 187–91; statutes contrary to international law, 155–56; strengths and weaknesses, 174–76, 190–91
U.S. Constitution: Article II, ß2, 114; concurrent legislative and executive powers, 75–82, 180–91; congressional power, 62; Hamilton's analysis of presidential power, 60–66; Madison's analysis of presidential power, 67–74, 77–79; necessary and proper clause, 62, 183; presidential power, 29, 30, 56–57, 60; president's removal power, 64, 70–71; take care clause, 65–66
U.S. courts: advisory opinions, 107–21, 173–74, 185; common law crimes, 86, 91–102; consulting the Supreme Court, 107–21; deference to executive, 185, 189–90; grand jury charges, 84–85; juries, 95–96, 172; limitations, 165–74; political questions, 89, 120–21, 166–67; restitution of prizes, 86–90;
U.S. president: power to modify treaties, 69–72, 180; power to preserve peace, 30, 65, 75, 153–54; "sole organ," 62–63; strengths and weaknesses, 177–80. *See also* U.S. Constitution

Vainquer de la Bastille (corsair), 101–2
Valmy, battle of, 7, 8, 15
Vans Murray, William. *See* Murray, William Vans

Washington, George: anger towards press, 59, 98; attitudes toward France and Britain, 23; on French treaties, 33; messages to Congress, 152–57, 160; relations with Genet, 54–58, 106–7
Whittemore, Jacob, 47, 122, 127
Wilhelm (prize), 37, 146
Willcocks, William, 106
William (prize), 48–49, 50–51, 80, 85; attempted restitution, 86–90, 101, 157, 159
Wilmington, N.C., 101–2
Wilson, James, 110, 117; grand jury charges, 85, 93–94, 165; Henfield's case, 93–97

Yorktown, battle of, 16